The Self-Organizing School

Next-Generation Comprehensive School Reforms

Alan Bain

Rowman & Littlefield Education
Lanham, Maryland • Toronto • Plymouth, UK
2007

Published in the United States of America
by Rowman & Littlefield Education
A Division of Rowman & Littlefield Publishers, Inc.
A wholly owned subsidary of
The Rowman & Littlefield Publishing Group, Inc.
4501 Forbes Boulevard, Suite 200, Lanham, Maryland 20706
www.rowmaneducation.com

Estover Road
Plymouth PL6 7PY
United Kingdom

British Library Cataloguing in Publication Information Available

Library of Congress Cataloging-in-Publication Data

Bain, Alan, 1957–
  The self-organizing school : next-generation comprehensive school
reforms / Alan Bain.
    p. cm.
  Includes bibliographical references and index.
  ISBN-13: 978-1-57886-601-4 (hardcover : alk. paper)
  ISBN-13: 978-1-57886-602-1 (pbk. : alk. paper)
  ISBN-10: 1-57886-601-4 (hardcover : alk. paper)
  ISBN-10: 1-57886-602-2 (pbk. : alk. paper)
  1. Educational change—United States. 2. School improvement
programs—United States. 3. School management and organization—
United States. 4. Self-organizing systems. I. Title.
LB2822.82.B34 2007
371.2—dc22   2006102515

⊗™ The paper used in this publication meets the minimum requirements of
American National Standard for Information Sciences—Permanence of
Paper for Printed Library Materials, ANSI/NISO Z39.48-1992.
Manufactured in the United States of America.

For
Donna, Andrew, Daniel, and Luke

Contents

Acknowledgments

When a book represents more than a decade of work, there are understandably many people to recognize and thank. First, I would like to express my appreciation to the Brewster Academy Board of Trustees, Grant Wilson, and David Smith for the opportunity to work in collaboration with the school community to try something new and different in secondary education. I would especially like to thank David for his willingness to undertake the many challenging roles necessary to engage in a major process of change and then lead a school that was so different as a result.

The longstanding school leadership—Peter Hess, Kim Ross, Marilyn Shea, Lynne Palmer, Sue LeBlanc, Bob Simoneau, Doug Algate, Shirley Richardson, Bonnie Medico, Pete Caesar, and Bill Lyons—who questioned, challenged, learned, and collaborated to make the big ideas described in this book every day realities.

The wonderful lead teaching faculty and, especially, Bruce Gorrill, Bob Carter (whose technical wizardry is reflected in a number of the tools described in this book), Eladio Moreira, Raylene Davis, Christa Vitzthum, Maria Found, Doug Algate, and, more recently, Doug Kiley and Mary Fallon, who helped to create a different way.

All of the early-career teachers with whom I have worked and, especially, David Harris, John Bishop, Courtney Ulmer, Phil Huss, Peter Clark, Charlie Hossack, and Peter Lassey, from whom I have learned so much.

Bob Richardson, the longest standing faculty member at the school who, after 30 years of service, was one of the first teachers to sign up for the self-organizing school project. Bob, by his actions, showed us all that a commitment to see things differently has nothing to do with age.

I would like to thank Eric Burns and the technology staff who undertake the challenging and relentless job of making the self-organizing school a technological reality. Doug Fallon was a great semi-independent sounding board throughout the change process and contributed some excellent reflections on how people deal with change.

To all the students—they are the reason we do what we do.

To my colleagues in universities and schools internationally who have influenced my thinking on school design and improvement, especially, Josephine Mak and Annisa Chan, whose work in school reform and improvement in Hong Kong is a source of great inspiration, and Clive Dimmock, who introduced me to the area of school leadership and improvement and has helped promote my work from his leadership position in the field.

I would also like to thank Mark Weston and Bernard Percy, who recognized the way in which the self-organizing school was different and who saw the value in the project. They have helped immensely in bringing my work to the attention of others. Many thanks also to Mark for the many conversations about paradigms, borders, and innovation and the thoughtful and incredibly useful feedback on two versions of this manuscript. Thanks, Mark.

A number of my colleagues at Charles Sturt University also provided feedback on the manuscript. Thanks to Julie Lancaster, Lucie Zundans, Bill Green, Zeffie Nicholas, and Robert Parkes. Kal Gulson provided a different perspective on the project and provided enthusiastic feedback both on paper and during mountain bike rides. Thanks, Kal.

Susan Brown worked tirelessly on providing editorial support and feedback on the manuscript, with as much commitment to the message and the product as my own. It is difficult for me to imagine how it would have all come together without her dedication and support. Jill Harris provided wonderful editorial support in the final stages of the manuscript's development, and thanks also to the Faculty of Education at Charles Sturt University for providing support for the final editing process.

Finally, to my wife, Donna, who took time away from her busy career to help me edit and give the kind of honest feedback that every author needs. Thank you.

CHAPTER 1

Introduction

We must either find a way or make one.—Hannibal

Why don't schools exert a greater influence on student learning?

We know from extensive research that successful teachers make a profound contribution to what students know and are able to do, accounting for up to 45% of the variance in student achievement (Brophy, 1986; Hattie, 2003; Rowe, 2003; Scheerens & Creemers, 1989). Yet, when we consider those teachers and their classrooms as a larger organizational unit—the school—we see a much smaller effect. International studies have shown that schools account for only 0%–10% of the variance in student achievement and that those achievement effects diminish as the factors studied move further away from the direct classroom experience of students (Hattie, 2003; Rowe, 2003; Scheerens & Creemers, 1989).

In addition, achievement differences detected among schools are most likely to represent classroom-level, rather than school-level, factors (Rowe, 2003). One explanation for this discrepancy is that classrooms, as the basic unit composing schools, "soak up" most of the effects available to the school as a whole (Rowe, 2003). However, if this were the case, we can expect school-level reforms that focus on systemic improvement in classroom practice to yield effects consistent with those attributed to classrooms and teachers. They do not (Borman, Hewes, Overman, & Brown 2003).

SCALE

In the way that they are designed and managed, schools do not seem to magnify the effect of successful teachers at scale. I use the term *scale* (or *scaling up*) throughout the book to describe how a practice that is implemented in a smaller unit (e.g., a classroom or single school) is translated into the practice of multiple units (e.g., many classrooms or many schools). The term does not denote an idea of a fixed condition in time and space. Rather, *scale* is a dynamic concept that is determined by the context and ever-changing networks within which ideas, innovations, and people function (Nespor, 2004).

Many of the factors known to alter classroom learning — including the type and quality of instruction, the role of feedback, and the deployment of technology — appear highly amenable to school-level influence. This can occur through change in school-level decision making, professional development, the systematic use of technology, the way that communication happens, and the organization of the school to focus on students' needs.

Despite the amenability of these factors to school-level intervention, examples of sustained research-based innovations at scale within and across schools are rare. The contemporary literature on school reform suggests that, despite an enormous and diverse multigenerational effort, it is difficult to exert a sustainable influence on schools and systems (Berends, Nataraj Kirby, Naftel, & McKelvey, 2001; Elmore, 1996; Fullan, 2001; Sarason, 1996; Taylor, 2005; Tyack & Cuban, 1995; Zhang, Shkolnik, & Fashola, 2005).

Moreover, extensive research indicates that substantial teacher and classroom effects are unlikely to exist as part of the routine practice of teachers in most schools (Goodlad, 1984; Lortie, 1975; McLaughlin & Talbert, 2001; Sizer, 1984). As such, students and parents cannot expect those effects as a routine outcome of their educational experience. They are much more an expression of the possibility of better ways to teach and learn than the reality of research-based practice in local schools.

Research has not found its way into the routine practice of schools.

INDIVIDUALIZATION

The consequences of this possibility/practice gap are exacerbated by an increasing expectation that schools become much more responsive to the learning needs of individuals (Cicchinelli, Dean, Galvin, Goodwin, & Parsley, 2006; Walker & Dimmock, 2000). Individualization is deemed essential for effective participation in a global information-based economy, whereas the future of nations is predicated on enfranchising total populations with a differentiated and more adaptive school experience (Suarez Orozco & Baolian Qin Hillard, 2004). This more adaptive experience stands in contrast to the historical role of schools as vehicles of mass enculturation (Carlson, 1975), inclusion (Haring & McCormick, 1990), and workforce preparation (Goldin, 1998). Although schools have been deemed successful in addressing their historical purpose (Weston, 2006), much more is now being asked in terms of the value that they add to the experience and achievement of each student.

To individualize is to employ practices that differentiate the content, process, and product of school learning (Tomlinson, 2001). Differentiation is made possible through the use of individual feedback, cooperation, collaboration, instructional and curricular adaptation, and new technologies (Mastropieri & Scruggs, 2004; Tomlinson, 2001). These are the things that effective teachers do to enhance individual student achievement. They are also the practices that drive the impressive teacher effects described at the beginning of this chapter. As such, the scaling up of research-based professional practice is critical, if schools are to shift from their historical roles as institutions of "mass response" to environments that are genuinely capable of differentiating instruction in response to individual learner needs.

Individualization is dependent on research-based practice at scale.

PARADIGM CRISIS

Given its educational, economic, and social consequences, the long-standing failure to successfully scale up research-based innovation from

classroom to school looms as a paradigm crisis (Kuhn, 1996) in schooling and school reform. Paradigm crises occur when existing theories,
systems, and practices fail to adequately explain or resolve a phenomenon of interest (Kuhn, 1996). In the case of schools, their modest effects
on student achievement implies a limited capacity of the present-day educational paradigm to help its adherents resolve and account for their
core activity—student learning.

Although the term *paradigm crisis* may be evocative of something
radical or transformational, the assumption here is that there can be
nothing more critical than sharing with all children in all schools what
the field knows about better ways to teach and learn. Not to do so is to
deny those children the maximum opportunity for moral, economic,
and social health and well-being, all of which are inextricably connected to the quality of the education that they receive.

> The gap between the possibility of research-based practice and its
> presence in schools represents paradigm crisis and future opportunity.

THE CONTENT AND PROCESS OF REFORM

The history of reform indicates that scaling up research-based practice
requires much more than the design and adoption of new and purport-
edly better ideas. Such a shift requires new theories, systems, and practices (Kuhn, 1996), a new theory structure capable of addressing the
process of scaling up innovative practice as well as its content.

The content of most educational reform efforts invariably has some
connection to theory, particularly in relation to the content of their innovations. However, the practical theory that is necessary to connect
the content with the schools that they seek to affect is frequently overlooked. This is the kind of theory that helps teachers and schools go beyond simply adopting or learning a new teaching approach, curriculum,
or technology. It explains how those innovations can successfully engage with what we know about the people, the process, and the organization of schools.

The purpose of the self-organizing school is to reconcile the content
of a reform with its process. It does so by focusing on a theory and
practice of how to change as a way to understand what to change in

site-based school reform. The emerging body of research on site-based school reform, described in chapter 2, points to a pressing need for theory that adequately accounts for the nature and needs of schools.

This kind of theory and practice work usually emerges on the edges or borders (Aronowitz & Giroux, 1991) of the existing paradigm, in the space between what is and what ultimately may be. It is in this border space that the self-organizing school takes up the question of scaling up school effects. In doing so, it seeks to contribute to the conversation about the role of new theory and practice in school reform by articulating an alternative theory and practice of school design. Such theory and practice may produce new models of reform that go further, last longer, and possess the sophisticated capacity to respect, as well as deeply influence, what teachers and schools do and the results that they produce.

> To be complete, a reform must attend to its content as well as the process of change.

COMPREHENSIVE SCHOOL REFORM

This book is situated within the U.S. comprehensive school reform literature (U.S. Department of Education, 2004). The premise of comprehensive school reform is that a comprehensive schoolwide reform model can be used to deploy innovative practices and processes that influence student learning at scale within and across schools. Comprehensive school reform is a systemic response to the paradigm crisis in schools and school reform, and it focuses on a schoolwide approach to improve student achievement through the implementation of research-based practice.

However, the research on comprehensive school reform implementation to date (described in chapter 2) raises questions about whether reform models are singularly capable of embedding and sustaining effective teaching and learning practice in schools. The self-organizing school contributes a solution to this problem by offering theory, practice, and evidence in support of a comprehensive school reform design and an implementation approach that is complete and thus capable of scaling effective practice to the level of the school.

The goals and challenges of comprehensive school reform also pertain to basic school reform issues that, in large measure, appear to occur from school to school, system to system, and even country to country. Comprehensive school reform can be seen as the large, highly visible tip of the school reform iceberg, as represented by efforts to change schools in many different systems and nations. The challenge of school reform is a global phenomenon where the identified issues and points of breakdown seem to be highly consistent from place to place (Dimmock, 2000). As such, the research, theory, and practice that I describe in this book are also intended for use by international educators engaged in the challenging pursuit of starting or reforming schools.

SELF-ORGANIZATION

The self-organizing school describes the way that six theoretical principles—derived from the field of self-organization and complex adaptive systems (Kauffman, 1995; Prigogene & Stengers, 1984; Waldrop, 1993)—can help schools and comprehensive school reforms scale up to the school level the factors that influence student learning in the classroom.

The principles and practice of self-organization have generated great interest in human systems because they explain how those systems can adapt to their ever-changing circumstances bottom-up, without continual top-down intervention. This happens because self-organizing systems possess design characteristics that allow the agents working within them to pool their collective intelligence, thus transcending their individual capacities. This book is about how to represent those characteristics in the design and operation of schools.

Reformers can use the principles and practices described here to think differently about the parts of a school, to see clear connections among those parts, to understand the design process, and to disperse control for the implementation of a school reform. This includes alternate ways to realize visions of classroom practice, to understand the role of feedback and how to generate it, and to craft roles for technology in a reform process. In doing so, this book provides a big picture, or metaframework, for understanding the way that school reforms can be designed and implemented, as well as examples of how those big-picture ideas actually work in practice.

THE SELF-ORGANIZING SCHOOL PROJECT

The self-organizing school generates theory and methodology from a longitudinal field-based experience, deriving its principles and practices from an 11-year secondary-school reform project. The field-based approach to theory development and implementation is expressed throughout this book in the form of examples of implementation methods, tools and strategy, and the presentation of longitudinal data that support key elements of the theory in practice.

That said, this book is not the story of a school or an account of the efforts of change agents. The self-organizing school seeks to distinguish itself from the many excellent biographical accounts of small- and large-scale efforts to start new schools (e.g., Bensman, 2000; Fink, 2000) or change existing ones (e.g., Berends et al., 2001) by focusing on the principles, practices, and cumulative experience derived from a field-based experience.

Position and Perspective

One of the challenges of the self-organizing school project is to appropriately position it within a work that is focused on the learning that can be derived from the big picture. It is particularly important to ensure that maximum benefit is derived from the practical experience arising from 11 years of work in situ while retaining a focus on the design theory and principles.

To address this challenge, I clarify throughout where examples are drawn directly from the self-organizing school project. Where data are included, I use the text from articles and reports that describe the background context and methodology for gathering the data.

In taking a general approach to the specific case, it becomes possible to focus attention on the challenges associated with site-based school reform that seem to transcend school type, level, and circumstances. These include the need for theorizing about the reform process, intense and focused longitudinal effort undertaken in schools, thinking differently about the role of technology and the professional lives of all teachers, and building cultures of professional practice in all schools. Each is part of the process of making the way forward for site-based reform.

A second important point of clarification pertains to my role in the self-organizing school project. Over the 11 years of the project (1992–2003), I served as an agent of change in capacities that can be broadly characterized in three phases. I have titled those phases with reference to my responsibilities, although they are generally consistent with Fullan's change model (1991) and its stages of initiation, implementation, and continuation.

The first, a hands-on design/pilot phase (1992–1996), included high levels of direct involvement in the areas of project initiation, management, and model design. Examples of this engagement include designing and implementing a process for schoolwide adoption, designing curriculum and software, building teacher role descriptions and a career path, making adjustments to the design of physical infrastructure, searching the literature, and producing position papers related to the practices included in the design.

This work required input from, consultation with, and decision making by the broader community. Community consultation constituted much of the project management dimension of the role. This phase also involved my direct participation in the design and delivery of the professional capacity-building training for a pilot iteration of the design. In Phase 1, I performed design and management tasks that were beyond the day-to-day work of the teachers and leaders actively involved in the running of a secondary school, while trying to create a comprehensive school reform. During this first phase, a model was designed and a pilot process completed that progressed, over 4 years, from one team to full-school implementation.

The second, or transition, phase (1997–2000) was where the effort evolved from being a project to being the school. In this phase, the new model and design became fully integrated with the organizational design of the school and the roles of its agents. Professional development in this phase became the responsibility of the school's teachers; project management became school management; and the evolution of the design became the responsibility of decision-making teams within the school instead of the change agent.

In the transition phase, I became a member of many of those teams with an active (though much less singular and more collaborative) role in the ongoing design and management of what had become the school. The project was characterized by ongoing schoolwide implementation and the completion of a suite of software tools for reflecting the design in practice. The data that support the theory (described in chapter 10) were gathered during the transition phase and were made possible by the existence of the software.

The third, or consultant, phase (2001–2003) was a period where I withdrew from active involvement with the day-to-day operation of the school. My role became one of responder to the expressed needs of the community as it sought to evolve its program. My role at this time was to provide strategic input to management, to design new versions of software in response to needs identified by members of the school community, and to be a critical friend to the school's leaders and faculty. In this phase, I also limited the scope of my involvement with the school's teams. The school and the project in this phase were synonymous. My role was to help with any and all aspects of the design on a consultant basis and in ways that responded to the needs of the school as determined by its decision-making teams.

Bias

Each of the roles and phases described here required high levels of personal engagement and investment and carried the propensity for bias that can occur when an author has such an active and direct role in a change process. Given this knowledge, I have attempted to build the case for the ideas represented throughout this book within the context of those needs expressed in the existing comprehensive school reform literature, reconciling the theory and practice described in the chapters with the circumstances of current practice.

In chapter 10, I describe the results of the project in a similar fashion, connecting them to the extant challenges and existing research and evaluation benchmarks associated with the study of comprehensive school reform. Most of the data were gathered for the ongoing conduct of the school and not for the explicit purpose of "research." I describe this idea in detail in chapters 3 and 8. One benefit of this approach is that the actual data gathering was dispersed to many members of the school community as a result of its application in the day-to-day work of the school.

The initiatives taken to contextualize this work are not offered as solutions to the validity threats; rather, they emphasize that those threats are recognized and acknowledged and have influenced the presentation of the case. Readers will ultimately decide whether the presentation has gone too far or whether it falls within the bounds of acceptability with respect to the veracity of the argument and the legitimacy of the evidence base.

CONTEXT

In the early 1990s, when the self-organizing school project began, many reformers presumed that scalable effects would emerge from large-scale solutions involving many schools. The scaling of site-based school change was being pursued with immense energy, resources, and a strong sense of need and purpose. The Coalition of Essential Schools was a prominent force among many new players on the educational landscape, which included the for-profit Edison Schools project (Coalition of Essential Schools, 2006; Edison Schools, 2005; McQuillan & Muncey, 1994). The $2-billion New American Schools Development Corporation project was in its design-and-demonstration phase in preparation for scaling its models to many schools (Bodilly, 1996).

The self-organizing school project took a different trajectory. It was premised on the simple idea that "small is big" in school reform. In a field struggling to ground its many contested paradigms and theories in practice, new and more complete ways for improving schools are most likely to emerge from efforts that start small and exist on the borders of the existing paradigm. Those efforts are likely to be longitudinal; initially participant driven, as opposed to consultant driven, in terms of change agency; and likely to result in highly detailed accounts of what to do.

The intensity of focus that characterizes such efforts makes it possible to develop and test the "what to do" of school change and link it with the "how to do it" aspects. The latter involves engaging in the time-consuming process of substantiating the many ideas, processes, and practices that compose a reform in an actual school setting over time.

In situ work of this kind requires that a school, the change forces, and the overall process all stay the course of change over a period of years, which frequently exceeds the "burn time" of most funding and the regimes of leadership that sourced those funds (Fullan, 2001). This book describes the design process, the research, and the learning that accumulated by staying the course for more than a decade.

The "small is big" idea that drove the self-organizing school project was informed by the seminal studies of schools and classrooms undertaken in the 1970s and 1980s by prominent researchers such as Cuban (1982); Goodlad (1984); Huberman and Miles (1984); Lortie (1975); Rutter, Maughan, Mortimore, and Ouston (1979); and Sizer (1984). These authors set the baseline for new reform models showing the then-current condition of schools and classrooms with a depth and clarity that were frequently disturbing and that, most important, punctuated the need for change. They also made clear the distinction between what successful schools and classrooms might look like and the enormous challenge of making those successes happen in any school and at scale.

In 1992, the technology (in the broadest sense) that was required to do site-based school reform was in its infancy, informed by the difficulties of past efforts and a vision for redressing those difficulties. Work describing the characteristics of effective schools undertaken in the late 1970s (e.g., Edmonds, 1979), as well as the accumulation of evidence on teacher and classroom effects through meta-analysis (e.g., Fraser, Walberg, Welch, & Hattie, 1987), provided an initial evidence base for what could be done. However, researchers and reformers were much more confident about what was needed than how to do it. Some would say that reform efforts remain in this condition, an assertion well supported by the New American Schools experience (Berends, Bodilly, Nataraj Kirby, & Hamilton, 2002).

Together, the complex culture of schools, the difficulties experienced by past reform efforts, and the well-documented resistance to change suggested that new models and school designs needed to go much further than the rational planning approaches that dominated the reform landscape at the time.

Given these difficult circumstances, it seemed that the kind of responsive, differentiated classroom on which so many reforms hinged would most likely turn out to be a Pandora's Box for schools unless the approach taken was intensely sensitive to the current conditions of schools and the challenges that they presented. Teachers, schools, and administrators were largely unprepared for the kind of sweeping process that would enable the rhetoric of change to be reconciled with the prevailing reality of classrooms and schools, as described by Cuban, Goodlad, Lortie, and Sizer. However, there was a risk that the processes being developed would not be sufficiently complete and robust to actually make a difference and that, if they were, there was a risk that they would overwhelm schools in their implementation, given the absence of a theory and practice for "doing change" and the questionable readiness of schools to engage in such sweeping reforms.

As the decade played out, the experience of contemporary reformers provided new and insightful accounts into how difficult the challenge of comprehensive school reform is, how long it takes any single school to engage in a reform process, and the effort that is required to make anything of substance happen. Deep insight into the long-standing problem of creating school change at scale was provided through the work of the Rand Corporation in evaluating the New American Schools project, the studies of the Comer School implementations in Prince George's County and Chicago (Cook et al., 1999), the implementation of the Coalition of Essential Schools (Muncey & McQuillan, 1996), and the work of many others.

The self-organizing school project was situated within this broader context, emerging over the decade as a small longitudinal site-based initiative that benefited from both the experience of larger efforts and the focus permitted by a smaller scale. What began as a school's effort to address the commonly perceived problems associated with student achievement, faculty morale, and student conduct became, over a relatively short space of time, a process of building a theory-driven, research-based model of school reform.

Much of what is described in the following chapters reflects the experience that arose from the convergence of a school's needs and a unique research-into-practice opportunity created by those needs. The result is a book whose intent is to offer a next-generation perspective on comprehensive school reform by responding to issues that have emerged from existing comprehensive-school-reform implementation research and the actual practice of doing change in a school setting. The self-organizing school is ambitious, given its underpinning belief that the learning derived from one longitudinal comprehensive school reform experience can meaningfully affect a multi-billion-dollar school-reform initiative. To this end, it embodies the "small is big" intent of the original self-organizing school project by reconciling theory, research, and practice in site-based school reform.

SELF-REINFORCEMENT, DESIGN, AND FEEDBACK

In providing background information for this book, I wish to foreshadow three interconnected assumptions that are described in detail in subsequent chapters. In essence, these assumptions represent the thesis of the self-organizing school.

The "small is big" idea described in the previous section signals the immense amount of energy and detailed work required to make site-based school reform complete in terms of content and process. So why does comprehensive school reform need to be so detailed, so complete, given that numbers of existing school reform models anchor their designs in broad principles of change (e.g., Coalition of Essential Schools, 2006; Core Knowledge, 2006)? The self-organizing school assumes that the answer to this question is found in the relationship between the self-reinforcing nature of a comprehensive school reform design and its capacity to generate and use feedback.

Successful dynamic systems have a capacity to learn from and adapt to the feedback that they generate and receive (Gell-Mann, 1994). When they do things that work, they adapt and enhance those things in the system that generate positive feedback. They stop doing things that generate negative feedback. However, such feedback can occur only when there is a degree of predictability between what the system does and what happens as a result.

Such knowledge is elusive in schools. The ambiguity that surrounds the core activity of schooling (teaching and learning) makes it immensely difficult for most schools to receive the kind of feedback that makes a system dynamic. For example, debate abounds regarding what constitutes successful methods for learning and teaching. The uptake of successful innovation is far from uniform, and it does not seem to last in schools. Further, there is immense ambiguity about the nature of the causal relationship between teaching, student aptitude, and achievement history as they relate to student learning. Schools have been unable or reluctant to take a clear stand on what they mean by teaching and learning. This has made it difficult for teachers and schools to get and use feedback about what they do.

Murnane and Cohen (1986) note that successful feedback in schools requires the ability to define and recognize what effective teaching means. When such is unclear, it is difficult to decide what constitutes successful learning and what it should be attributed to. This problem is emphatically illustrated in the literature of teacher appraisal and evaluation, which describes the many pitfalls and challenges associated with generating the feedback necessary for valid and reliable teacher accountability, reward, and recognition (Davis, Ellett, & Annunziata, 2002; Furtwengler, 1995; Murnane & Cohen, 1986; Riner, 1992; Tucker, 1997).

Despite these problems, we know a lot about the predictable contribution of teachers to learning, as reflected in the effects described earlier in this chapter (e.g., Hattie, 2003; Rowe, 2003). Researchers have also modeled the different factors that contribute to learning (e.g., Bloom, 1976; Walberg, 1986). However, as noted, although studies that contribute to those models and effects are frequently conducted in schools, they rarely focus on what is actually happening at scale in those or other schools. They are much more indicative of what could or should be happening than the reality of current practice at scale. In addition, those findings or models cannot be assumed to reflect the outcomes desired by schools in general, nor can they be assumed to represent widely held cultural values about professional practice. As such, these models and effects do not serve as a term of reference for school design. Evidence in support of this theory-into-practice gap is well documented and is described in chapters 2 and 3.

Because the history of reform suggests that it is extremely difficult to find a solution to this problem, the perspective presented here is that schools and comprehensive school reforms need to make one.[1] This means creating a relationship between what the school does and what happens by design. To be self-reinforcing, schools and comprehensive school reforms need to establish, for their beliefs, values, and practice, the kind of design that helps to generate the feedback necessary for the organization to learn all the time.

Self-reinforcement presumes that the essential features of a comprehensive school reform can be woven throughout a design so that those key ideas, processes, and practices are reinforced irrespective of which part of the design is engaged. Examples could be the way that professional development is explicitly connected to teacher recognition, reward, and advancement in a career path or how technology is employed to design and implement the instruction that was the subject and focus of the professional development.

Because the important factors self-repeat in the parts of the design, teachers are supported to build capacity with those key aspects of the innovation all the time. Great value is assigned to this characteristic throughout the book because, in being self-reinforcing, a design creates the conditions for the school to receive feedback about what it does. Feedback generates the capacity to change, grow, evolve, and be self-organizing.

The self-reinforcement and feedback required to make a school or comprehensive school reform adaptive would seem to be an obvious expectation, given its mandate to be comprehensive (U.S. Department of Education, 2004). However, as described in chapter 2, there is a strong case to suggest that such design cohesion and completeness are yet to be realized. Completeness cannot occur by tinkering with parts of a system.

Comprehensive is an all-encompassing term in this regard. To fail to be comprehensive in a comprehensive site-based reform is to design a point of breakdown into a system that compromises the feedback available to that system. Conversely, to be complete and comprehensive is to create the self-reinforcing conditions for feedback, self-organization, and the dynamic adaptation that make complex systems, including schools, successful.

AUDIENCE

The self-organizing school project is intended for educators interested in systemic site-based school reform. The specific target audiences are

- educators contemplating comprehensive school reform who require information to build their own reform model;
- educators who are interested in gaining a deep understanding of comprehensive school reform to evaluate the strengths and weaknesses of existing models;
- educators currently engaged with a comprehensive school reform model who are interested in how to focus their efforts moving forward;
- educators involved in school start-up initiatives, public, charter, or independent;
- educators in the comprehensive school reform field, including model developers, who are seeking insight about their own comprehensive school reform initiatives and those of their competitors; and
- international educators who are interested in the lessons learned from, and the future prospects associated with, a comprehensive site-based school reform program.

Organization

Chapter 2 employs the comprehensive school reform literature to articulate a case for the existence of serious fidelity issues in the areas of comprehensive school reform implementation, evaluation, and design. These issues are linked to the overarching question of school-level effects described in this chapter and are used to identify nine next-generation targets for the design and implementation of comprehensive school reform or any site-based reform. These targets include the need for theory in the development and design of comprehensive school reform.

Chapter 3 describes a theory of the self-organizing school that focuses on the way that a practical theory can be used to address the nine next-generation benchmarks, as well as the comprehensive school reform fidelity issues described in chapter 2. I describe six theoretical principles in the chapter, along with examples of their application in comprehensive school reform.

Chapter 4 applies the six principles using examples of self-organization. These examples represent work from the self-organizing school project and are used to illustrate the theory in practice.

Chapters 5–9 unpack the design principles in detail, including a number of practical examples from the self-organizing school project. This includes the way to embed key elements of a comprehensive school reform systemically and at all levels of a school's organization, the way that a design process can disperse control to the agents in a school, the role of feedback and networks in school design, and the way that technology serves a self-organizing school. These chapters constitute the practical core of the book, showing how the six principles of self-organization are applied.

Chapter 10 describes the results of the self-organizing school project, providing evidence of what happens when the principles of self-organization are applied over time. The chapter highlights connections between the theoretical principles and the next-generation design targets described in chapter 2. The results include longitudinal studies of implementation, achievement effects, the use of technology, and the role of collaboration.

Chapter 11 concludes the self-organizing school and summarizes the preceding chapters, identifying nine big-picture understandings from the book and the project on which it is based. The chapter uses the metaphor of emergence, which is derived from the study of self-organizing and complex systems, to discuss future directions in comprehensive school reform and the role of self-organization in pursuit of next-generation comprehensive school reform design.

Each chapter concludes with a brief description of key understandings, or *takeaways*, that help to punctuate key points and make connections among the ideas presented in the book.

NOTE

1. Derived from quote attributed to Hannibal: "If you cannot find a way, make one."

CHAPTER 2

Next

Round up the usual suspects.—Captain Renault (*Casablanca*, 1942)

This chapter sets the foundation for where comprehensive school reform could (or should) go next, by identifying nine targets for the design and implementation of next-generation comprehensive school reform.

COMPREHENSIVE SCHOOL REFORM AND THE COMPREHENSIVE SCHOOL REFORM DEMONSTRATION PROGRAM

Comprehensive school reform emerged as an important innovation early in the last decade, first catalyzed by the New American Schools project (Berends et al., 2001) and then in 1997 by the Comprehensive School Reform Demonstration Program (U.S. Department of Education, 2002). This latter program is a federally funded initiative that enables schools to build their own site-based comprehensive school reform model or select from a catalog of existing models (e.g., Herman et al., 1999). The program provides funding for schools prepared to address the following criteria:

Proven methods and strategies: For student learning, teaching, and school management that are based on scientifically based research and effective practices and that have been replicated successfully in schools with diverse characteristics.

Comprehensive design: For effective school functioning; for integrating instruction, assessment, classroom management, and professional development; and for aligning these functions into a schoolwide reform plan designed to enable all students to meet challenging state content and performance standards and address needs identified through a school needs assessment.

Professional development: High-quality and continuous teacher staff professional development and training.

Measurable goals: For student performance and benchmarks for meeting those goals.

Support from staff: Support from school faculty administrators and staff.

Parent and community involvement: Meaningful involvement of parents and the local community in planning and implementing school improvement activities.

External assistance: High-quality external support and assistance from a comprehensive school reform entity (which may be a university) with experience in schoolwide reform and improvement.

Evaluation: Plan to evaluate the implementation of the reforms and the student results achieved.

Coordination of resources: Identification of how other available resources (federal, state, local, or private) will help the school coordinate services to support and sustain school reform.

Scientifically based research: To significantly improve the academic achievement of students participating in such programs, as compared with students in schools who have not participated in such programs. This requirement may also be met by strong evidence that such programs will improve the academic achievement of participating students (added in 2001; U.S. Department of Education, 2002).

Since its inception in 1997, more than $1.8 billion has been disseminated for comprehensive school reform to over 6,000 schools in all 50 states in America (U.S. Department of Education, 2004). The addition of $2 billion expended on the foundational New American Schools project (Berends et al., 2002) makes this the most ambitious site-focused school reform effort to date.

PARADIGM CRISIS AND COMPREHENSIVE SCHOOL REFORM

The Comprehensive School Reform Demonstration Program requirements are targeted at the fragmentation of past reform efforts and the
historical difficulties of altering schools in sustainable and scalable
ways (Cicchinelli & Barley, 1999). Comprehensive school reform represents a concerted effort to address the modest effects that schools
seem to have on student achievement, over and above the influence exerted by successful teachers and effective teaching practices.

Through its comprehensive approach and the widespread resources
of the Comprehensive School Reform Demonstration Program, comprehensive school reform holds the promise of scaled-up professional
research-based practice. From this perspective, the movement can be
viewed as a response to the paradigm crisis described in chapter 1,
given that its essential criteria are focused on bringing research-based
practice to scale in public education. However, in being comprehensive
and attempting to alter the many parts that make up a school (e.g., professional development, evaluation, curriculum, evaluation), comprehensive school reform takes on the issues, challenges, and escalating
complexity associated with addressing all of those elements and the
way that they interact.

The goal of comprehensive school reform is to make the many parts
work together as a self-reinforcing whole. However, the history of
school reform indicates that to make this happen, the content of school
change design needs to be reconciled with the process for accomplishing it. As noted in chapter 1, it is this challenging intersection of content and process that has been the Achilles' heel of past efforts. Tyack
and Cuban (1995) describe the following issues as symptoms of this
failure to intersect: the provision of professional development; a lack of
insight about the nature of the classroom milieu; and an inadequate understanding of the time, resources, and effort demanded by reforms.

Given the challenging and problematic history of school reform, the
question is the extent to which comprehensive school reform possesses
the balanced focus on content and process necessary to successfully respond to a paradigm crisis. Can it produce the deep, rigorous, and sustainable school-level effects that have eluded past reforms (Scheerens,
1992) through the widespread implementation of research-based

approaches that differentiate teaching and learning? In practice, this means that reformers need to scale the content of their designs and the implementation process to the school level.

This chapter makes the case that the full understanding and articulation of the content and process of comprehensive school reform that are required to distinguish it from past efforts have not happened to date (Comprehensive School Reform Quality Center, 2006; Policy and Program Studies Service, 2003). Indicators of this problem include frequent examples of incomplete design, a difficulty scaling up within individual schools, modest achievement effects, limited feedback mechanisms, the underutilization of technology, an overreliance on school leadership, and a lack of theory. The overall effect of these difficulties is reflected in a range of sustainability issues within and between schools.

NEXT-GENERATION TARGETS

What follows is a description of nine targets that represent critical areas of need and potential goals for next-generation comprehensive school reform design: educational power, comprehensiveness, emergent feedback, systemic technology, professional lives, school-level design for school-level influence, effective adoption, implementation integrity, and theory.

Educational Power

The concept of educational power means that a research-based comprehensive school reform should be able to bridge the large gap between the school's contribution to achievement and the contribution currently attributed to classrooms and teachers (Hattie, 2003).

The average effect size for Comprehensive School Reform is .15, established in an extensive meta-analysis of its implementation (Borman et al., 2003). This level of effect falls between the benchmark (0.0–0.1) described in the broader literature as the effect size contributed by schools to student achievement (Rowe, 2003) and the minimum threshold for the educational significance of an innovation. The latter is described by McCartney and Rosenthal (2000) and Slavin (2005) as .2.

A recent randomized study by Borman et al. (2005) that focused on the Success for All model (Success for All Foundation, 2006) reported an overall effect size of .22. This study had much better experimental control than those described in Borman et al. (2003). The Success for All model is also reputed to have one of the highest levels of implementation integrity among comprehensive school reforms, although these results fall just marginally above the levels required for an innovation to be deemed educationally significant (.2).

Zhang et al. (2005) studied 649 schools from 21 school districts in 16 states that were implementing eight comprehensive school reform models and reported similar modest findings to Borman et al. (2003). The authors compared schools implementing comprehensive school reform with nonimplementing schools (z scores were used as a standard score metric) and found that comprehensive school reform schools did not experience larger gains in math or reading achievement than that of comparison schools.

According to Borman et al. (2003), nearly 50% of the findings in comprehensive school reform evaluation are derived from one-group pretest–posttest studies conducted by developers. Where developers conducted their own studies, there is an average .16 increase in effect size (Borman et al., 2003).

Overall, these findings indicate that, at present, comprehensive school reform has a less-than-modest influence on student achievement. Stated simply, the effects currently described in the literature are relatively small when measured against the effort, time, and money expended on comprehensive school reform. To be sustainable as a reform movement, this must change. Next-generation models will leverage the educational power of research-based practice in sustainable ways.

> Next-generation comprehensive school reform will demonstrate its educational power by magnifying the effect of successful teachers and classrooms at scale.

Comprehensiveness: Doing Less by Being More

One possible reason for the modest effect of comprehensive school reform is the overall lack of comprehensiveness in its design. Evidence of this contention includes the common failure to provide the professional development required to implement the model day-to-day in classrooms (Bodilly, 1996); a lack of material support for curriculum development and implementation (Datnow, Borman, & Stringfield, 2000); the conceptualization of evaluation as an add-on, as opposed to an emergent function of the implementation process (Chicchinelli & Barley, 1999); the misalignment of system and school policy goals associated with comprehensive school reform (Datnow, 2003b; Franceschini, 2002); the absence of feedback systems (Berends et al., 2001); and incomplete approaches to the systemic use of technology.

Next-generation models will show how professional development is adequately reconciled with what teachers are required to know and do each day. They will also show how technology fits into the picture in ways that do more than add another curricular expectation but actually help teachers do their jobs. Those models will include feedback systems designed to meet the requirements for teacher tenure and promotion portfolios, keep state and student performance records, and meet the evaluative requirements of comprehensive school reform demonstrations and other funding sources. Comprehensive school reforms will show that, in accomplishing this goal, they can make it possible for teachers and schools to do no more than they are currently required to do.

In doing so, they will address the gaps in professional development, curriculum support, feedback, and school-level design that are frequently described as issues or even points of breakdown in comprehensive school reform implementation. Although it is treated separately, the following discussion, relating to the limited use of feedback and technology, provides examples of missing parts in comprehensive school reform design and is an extension of the rationale for the comprehensiveness target described here.

> Next-generation comprehensive school reforms will be practical by being complete.

Emergent Feedback

Feedback mechanisms have been identified as design characteristics that are essential for the successful implementation of comprehensive school reforms, especially if those designs are to be brought to scale in multiple schools (Berends et al., 2002).

Feedback refers to the capacity of a design to monitor and manage its implementation and effects and to work out its successes and problems as they occur. Unfortunately, the design of systems, processes, and methods for giving feedback has been a significant weakness in comprehensive school reform models. Berends et al. (2001) note in the evaluation of the New American Schools project that none of the seven competing models that reached the scale-up phase had complete formative evaluation and feedback measures included in their designs. This issue is not confined to the New American Schools project. None of the evaluations reviewed in support of the ideas described in this chapter identified a capability on the part of the design to produce the kind of emergent feedback that could inform the day-to-day implementation of the design.

Where feedback mechanisms do exist, they most frequently employ self-report-type questionnaires, interviews, or other rating approaches to establish implementation fidelity. However, they do not provide the kind of detailed corroborative objective information (e.g., Faddis et al., 2000; Supovitz & May, 2004; Zhang et al., 2005) that is required to inform just-in-time decision making. Even the most contemporary comprehensive school reform feedback approaches (see, e.g., Yamaguchi, Harmon, Darwin, Graczewski, & Fleischman, 2005) remain heavily reliant on indirect measurement, specifically, the self-report of those involved in establishing an evidence base for comprehensive school reform implementation.

Researchers engaged in evaluating comprehensive school reform describe the problematic way that this reliance on indirect measurement plays out in their work:

> Teachers tend to self-report very highly [on classroom implementation of practice] on any of the surveys and interviews. But when we triangulate against what we saw in observations, we see teacher-centered direct instruction, independent seat-work, [and] lots of worksheets [used]. (Appelbaum & Schwartzbeck, 2002, p. 9)

Even when multiple methodologies are used in more rigorous designs, it remains immensely difficult to establish the depth and scope of implementation from what are relatively attenuated snapshots of the lives of schools. For example, Datnow et al. (2000), in a study of the Core Knowledge design (Core Knowledge, 2006), describe "full school day observations in classrooms in the first year followed by two or three, one-hour observations per teacher in each grade for each subsequent year" (p. 173).

Despite this more intense methodology, the authors could only report the basic existence of the design across the schools. The nature of that existence is not reported in any objective sense. A full-school-day observation and two or three 1-hour follow-up observations per teacher per year represent a significant commitment in four schools, although it is an exceedingly small sample of the total teaching and learning occurring in the school, and, as such, it is insufficient to gain a deep objective understanding of what is going on in a comprehensive school reform, even when it is triangulated with other indirect sources of information.

It is clear from the evaluation and feedback issues described here that the scope of this reform demands a different and more ambitious evaluation and feedback methodology than that which has emerged to date. In making feedback a focus, next-generation comprehensive school reform designers will be able to express the connectivity in their designs in the way that feedback is gathered and shared. Their approaches will focus on what happens day-to-day, making traditional formative and summative evaluation requirements an expression, at any given point in time, of feedback that is happening all the time.

> Next-generation comprehensive school reform designs will use feedback to work out what to do next instead of what happened.

Systemic Technology

Information technology has been positioned at the core of curriculum models associated with comprehensive school reform designs (e.g., Co-nect, 2006) and as a recommended research-based instructional strategy in the comprehensive school reform literature (e.g., Slavin, 2005). However, its role as a tool to address the systemic issues associated with comprehensive school reform remains underdeveloped. This includes the way that information technology can serve the implementation of comprehensive school reform models in gathering, sharing, and delivering feedback; in knowledge and human resource management; and in the design, differentiation, implementation, and management of curriculum and instruction.

In his book *Good to Great: Why Some Companies Make the Leap . . . and Others Don't,* Collins (2001) describes technology as an accelerator of momentum in organizations. He describes the way that businesses take advantage of technology's potential, by understanding their key transactions, goals, processes, and products. In the next generation of comprehensive school reform, technology can be an accelerator if comprehensive school reforms do a more effective job of articulating their core intentions, transactions, and products. Following the lead of other fields, technology can be embedded in the key transactions associated with teaching and learning. It can be used for curriculum design and delivery, accumulating and sharing feedback of all kinds, and managing the overall operation of the school.

Next-generation comprehensive school reform models will embrace technology as a way to embed the day-to-day transactions of their designs in technology tools. These tools will make "doing the design" easier for teachers, students, and administrators. However, these tools can do much more than automate the designs through electronic record keeping or adding technology to the curricular experience of students, teachers, and parents. They will gather, manage, and deploy the knowledge of the organization.

> Next-generation comprehensive school reforms will deploy information technology to create a genuine technology of teaching and learning.

Professional Lives

Comprehensive school reform is intended to have a profound and sustained effect on practice, but to do so, it must deeply and holistically affect the professional lives of teachers and the totality of the school community. Yet, we know that comprehensive school reform implementation is frequently characterized by initial teacher enthusiasm, which ultimately turns into fatigue and disappointment (Little & Bartlett, 2002).

Even the best-implemented designs have produced mixed impacts in this regard (e.g., Datnow & Castellano, 2000; Jones, Gottfredson, & Gottfredson, 1997). Datnow and Castellano report resistance to the Success for All model by significant numbers of teachers, over the 3 years of their investigation. This occurred despite the model's success in improving instruction and student achievement. The results reflected concerns about the teachers' inability to influence the curriculum. Those concerns were expressed in teacher perceptions of repetitiveness and lack of creativity in the curriculum and its implementation.

Issues associated with model acceptance, teacher time, changes in teacher roles, union contracts, remuneration, and system–school policy alignment (Asenio & Johnson, 2001; Datnow, 2003b; Faddis et al., 2000; Franceschini, 2002; Hodge, 2003) all suggest that the curricular innovation associated with comprehensive school reform is not deeply connected to the totality of the professional lives of teachers and the broader professional culture of the school. These problems play out in diminished implementation integrity and in difficulties in sustaining comprehensive school reform over time (Berends et al., 2001; Cook et al., 1999; Datnow, 2003a). Holistic change needs to be expressed in the way that schools and systems align role definition, rewards, recognition, and professional growth with what comprehensive school reform means for the professional practice of the school.

This includes reconciling the demands and opportunities afforded by the model to the way that the school recognizes, rewards, and manages the growth of all members of its community. In next-generation comprehensive school reform, this reconciliation will occur at the design level. This means that it will occur before negotiation and implementation because developers will be able to effectively articulate what their designs mean for the professional life of a school community and its members.

> Next-generation comprehensive school reforms will connect their designs to the totality of the professional lives of teachers.

School-Level Design for School-Level Influence

Currently, there are no objective accounts of the way that any comprehensive school reform designs have altered the totality of school management; collaboration; technology; or the role, reward, and recognition of teachers in a complete and integrated way. None of the models studied in the New American Schools project exerted a major structural influence on the organization and management of schools, despite their reliance on effective leadership and collaboration for successful adoption (Berends et al., 2001).

In addition, Datnow and Castellano (2000) found that the relatively efficacious Success for All model (Success for All Foundation, 2006) did not effect whole-school changes, including heightened collaboration, interest in reform, change in governance, or the relationship between staff and administration. Cook et al. (1999) found similar results in a large-scale study of the Comer School program. Although that model included processes that were indicative of school-level effect, the design was not sufficiently complete for those elements to exert an influence, when compared to comparison schools.

Next-generation comprehensive school reform designs need to demonstrate that they have the design capacity to influence the organization and management of a school in ways that can support and scale its classroom processes. This includes considering the totality of the organizational design, not just the curriculum and change in classroom practice. Next-generation comprehensive school reform models will provide direct, detailed design intervention beyond the classroom, at the school organizational level.

It seems unrealistic to expect sustainable school-level effects if the designs do not successfully address these school-level factors. Comprehensive school reform must genuinely reconcile the reform with teachers' preexisting roles and responsibilities, rather than graft a larger-than-normal set of reform agendas on top of the status quo.

> To produce school-level effects, comprehensive school reform designs must exert school-level influence.

Effective Adoption

Although the comprehensive school reform literature acknowledges and recognizes the complex nature of school cultures (e.g., Rowan, Camburn, & Barnes, 2004), most of the adoption advice and the descriptions of adoption process exist in the form of needs assessment and planning models (Hansel, 2000; LeFloch, Zhang, & Hermann, 2005). The discussion about adoption focuses on what could be seen as a rational decision-making approach, including voting, self-evaluation rubrics, school-level data analysis, lobbying, awareness raising, and leadership influence.

Largely unacknowledged in this discussion is the overwhelming evidence from the literature on school culture that shows the instability in the values and beliefs of teachers about those critical issues that underpin decision making about change and, specifically, the comprehensive school reform adoption process. These issues include the value that teachers place on autonomy, their perceptions of the needs and drivers for organizational change, the way that they perceive the role of research and data in their practice, the meaning of evidence, what constitutes "what works," and the form and function of collaboration (Dimmock, 2000; Goodlad, 1984; Hargreaves, 1995; McLaughlin & Talbert, 2001; Sarason, 1982, 1996).

Possibly, the best example of this phenomenon is that, despite the clear prioritization of evidence in the Comprehensive School Reform Demonstration Program guidelines and in the literature, more broadly, schools and teachers do not tend to value the evidence base of a model as a high priority when making selection decisions (Hansel, 2000).

Appelbaum and Schwartzbeck (2002) indicate that schools are subject to a complex matrix of forces that influence their readiness for comprehensive school reform, the match between their needs and a model, and the determination of what constitutes success. Developers recognize this challenge, noting that building vision and ownership is much more than conducting a vote to elicit initial buy-in:

> There is a difference between buy in—[the] staff's belief that the program is good and can work—and ownership—[the] staff's belief that it's their program and they need to make it work. The former does not automatically lead to the latter and the latter are necessary for the reform to succeed. (Asenio & Johnson, 2001, p. 8)

High levels of buyer's remorse can be expected when adoption decisions exist at the nexus of information sharing, district and principal influence and persuasion, and a vote.

In an analysis of the Memphis Restructuring Initiative, Franceschini (2002)—drawing on the work of Fullan and Miles (1992) and Fullan (2001)—describes the way that comprehensive school reform employs a faulty map of the change process to engage with schools. According to Franceschini, a schism occurs between school and comprehensive school reform when a hyperrationalized process (Fullan, 2001) of implementation steps, based on untested assumptions, meets the complex and frequently nonrational circumstances of schools.

It should come as no surprise that, under these circumstances, school leadership is touted as such an important factor in comprehensive school reform adoption decision making, given the vast gap between the way that reform adoption happens and the prevailing culture of schools. We know that when leaders have to fill such gaps with personal influence and persuasion, the product invariably becomes nonsustainable (Fullan, 2001).

Next-generation models will recognize that developing support for comprehensive school reform is definitely not a series of needs-assessment events predicated on rational assumptions about the values of a school community. They will focus first on helping schools understand themselves as a necessary foundation for building engagement with the reform. Their approach for engaging with teachers, students, school leaders, and parents will show much more clearly what a design means because developers will possess a deeper understanding of the totality of what they have developed.

Next-generation comprehensive school reforms will include more sophisticated processes for mapping and undertaking the journey that a school and model embark on when engaging with the reform process.

> Next-generation comprehensive school reforms will connect the content and implementation of their designs with the systems, people, and processes that they seek to engage and affect.

Implementation Integrity

Limited implementation data and uneven accounts of the implementation of comprehensive school reform make it hard to determine whether such designs really have engaged successfully with schools

(Borman et al., 2003; Desimone, 2002). Developers feel the pressure to hit a "summative home run" to speak definitively to the educational community and their prospective clients. However, it is difficult to attribute student achievement effects to comprehensive school reform models without detailed information about whether, or how well, they are implemented.

For example, in their evaluation of the New American Schools project, Berends et al. (2001) found that after 2 years, only half of the 40 schools examined were implementing at the levels targeted by their design teams. After 5 years, the levels of implementation were deemed to be low in those schools nominated by designers as high implementers. Further, "about 72 percent of the total variance in implementation was within schools and 27 percent between schools" (p. 77), indicating just how difficult it is to establish implementation fidelity in a single school.

Similarly, Zhang et al. (2005) found that implementation did not necessarily deepen over time. This is of concern in relation to the implementation of any schoolwide reform, especially given that the estimated time for reform implementation is up to 10 years (Fullan, 2001).

Cook et al. (1999) found similar results in a large-scale study of the Comer School program. The authors concluded that the model was only partially implemented in participating schools, including those elements related to school culture and governance. Muncey and McQuillan (1996) reported comparable findings in their study of the Coalition of Essential Schools model in five secondary schools. Like Berends et al. (2002), these authors also found variability in implementation within and between schools and questioned what constituted a successful outcome.

In a 3-year study of 13 schools, Datnow (2003b) found that the comprehensive school reforms ceased in 6 of the 13 schools studied and continued with implementation at very low levels in 2 schools. This research emphasized the fact that "few studies have actually examined the sustainability of reforms over long periods of time, in part because most reforms do not last" (p. 4).

There are exceptions to this somewhat pessimistic picture. For example, a study of the Success for All model, by Datnow and Castellano (2000), found that all three participating schools achieved full implementation of the design. This covaried with gains in reading achievement, academic engagement, and the implementation of pedagogies, when compared to comparison schools. This study was distinguished by its 60 classroom observations of different teaching approaches, student attention, and academic engagement. Observational data were then triangulated with interviews and school documents. The design of the evaluation and depth of implementation made it possible for the authors to determine the integrity with which the Success for All model was implemented and to attribute student achievement effects to the design.

Despite these deep and positive findings, most of the comprehensive school reform implementation literature describes an innovative program that has a relatively tenuous influence on schools. Borman et al. (2003) reported that developers rarely provide information on the quality of implementation. For example, Berends et al. (2002) found that the New American Schools developers seemed to have only a limited understanding of the implementation status of their designs as the phases of the project proceeded. Over time the level of connectedness of the designs and design teams diminished to a point where there was little knowledge of what was actually occurring in schools. "In the latter phases of the [New American Schools] project, most [models] did not collect adequate information about their implementing sites to allow for proper support or to even hazard a guess as to implementation levels in schools" (p. 149). Further, according to Faddis et al. (2000), in a study of 40 Midwest schools, implementation is frequently determined in faculty room conversation.

Given that 15 years have passed since the inception of the New American Schools project, as well as 8 years of Comprehensive School Reform Demonstration Program financial support, the fidelity of implementation remains a genuine cause for concern. Next-generation comprehensive school reform efforts will be able to attribute their effects to their designs because they possess a complete evidence base that shows high levels of implementation integrity.

Next-generation comprehensive school reforms will be able to show that what was intended was implemented and sustained with integrity over time.

Theory

Comprehensive school reform has been described as being essentially atheoretical (Desimone, 2002). In one sense, this assertion is not surprising, given the needs and targets described in this chapter, including the record of incomplete content and process described in the research on implementation. However, it is also alarming that such a complex reform could go ahead in the absence of the theory required to instantiate its content and guide its implementation. The latter seems essential for the success of a reform initiative of such scope and complexity.

The success of any innovation or paradigm depends on the success of its theory structure. From the perspective presented here, complete theory makes for complete designs, generating sound connections across the elements of reform models and helping to predict, describe, and resolve implementation process issues. Theory in its broadest sense is necessary if individual models and the comprehensive school reform movement are to attain the level of implementation integrity and adaptive capacity required to scale up research-based practice.

> Next-generation comprehensive school reforms will produce the theory, systems, and practice capable of scaling research-based practice to the level of the school and beyond.

RISK

The many questions about comprehensive school reform implementation, evaluation, and design fidelity described in this chapter show just how difficult it is to gain a foothold in the complex landscape of schools. They also show that having a multifaceted reform solution may actually make the process harder, not easier. Simply getting established seems to be such a big task that many models may not be able to successfully monitor, manage, and evaluate implementation at scale. There is little time and opportunity for reflection and refinement as developers and schools struggle to get a start.

The current reality, which is characterized by incomplete design, rapid scaling, and thin implementation, has implications for the future of comprehensive school reform, including how or whether it will evolve any further. In sum, these reforms in thousands of schools represent a major breakthrough. Although they may not be sufficiently complete or user-friendly to gain widespread acceptance, they are in play and evolving; they represent Version 1 of systemic site-based reform. However, they do not possess the complete articulation of content and process required to replace the existing model of schooling or to account for what can or will be. As such, they do not exert or represent a paradigm-shifting influence and are at risk of passing into the broader history of school reform if they do not continue to adapt and evolve.

The Usual Suspects

Possibly, the best evidence of the risk associated with comprehensive school reform is the similarity in accounts of the difficulties that it has experienced and those faced by past reforms. Issues of time, money, leadership, resources, professional development, and teacher attitude have been identified as points of breakdown in a host of reforms (Sarason, 1996; Tyack & Cuban, 1995). These are the usual suspects that are frequently identified when accounting for the failure of school reform. They appear consistently in generation after generation of the reform literature and when accounting for the difficulties experienced in educational innovations as diverse as inclusion and technology integration.

For example, the need for "more" was the most striking takeaway from the description provided by the 80 staff members from 30 comprehensive school reform models at the 2000 West Ed developers forum—more time for selecting a model; more time for teacher planning and vision building; more flexibility in policy to restructure the schedule and purchase curriculum materials; more accommodation by unions for collaboration; more contact with state representatives; more financial support; more professional development through coaching, thinking, and reflecting; more professional development days; more access to data; more leadership to address all of the areas of insufficiency; and, finally, more model fidelity (Asenio & Johnson, 2001).

Similar findings were reported by Faddis et al. (2001) in a study of the implementation of 26 different comprehensive school reform models.

The schools identified many of the same issues as the developers, including the need for more time for professional development, as well as teacher contract issues, teacher and administrator turnover, and lack of follow-up support.

There is no question about the substance of these resource concerns in comprehensive school reform implementation in particular and educational reform in general. However, they are more than likely not actual solutions. Prior efforts at providing "more" as a solution to educational problems have been shown to be incomplete and inadequate unless accompanied by a sophisticated problem-solving process that yields a deep understanding of an innovation's real needs and problems. Those problems may be temporarily relieved with more resources, but substantive solutions require a detailed explication of the nature of the problem and the way that it interacts with resource needs and issues. This assertion is supported by research on the educational returns from technology, professional development, and teacher salaries (e.g., Berman & McLaughlin, 1976; Cuban, 2001; Hanushek, Kain, & Rivkin, 1999).

Through its holistic approach, the promise of comprehensive school reform is a deeper understanding of what is going on in a school. A design should provide a metaframework for understanding the key transactions in the teaching and learning process and in problem-solving needs and issues. Yet, the comprehensive school reform studies mentioned in this chapter did not probe deeply into the designs in schools to produce sophisticated solutions. The reporting did not drill down that far. The usual suspects were identified but not interrogated. This raises the specter of comprehensive school reform as yet another potentially failed reform, going the way of so many of its historical predecessors in the absence of sound data and sophisticated problem solving.

SLOWING DOWN

Although the horse may have already bolted in the rush to scale, most evidence to date suggests that comprehensive school reforms may have tried to go too far, too fast. For example, the evaluation of the New American Schools project shows that it did not scale successfully

(Berends et al., 2002). This is significant given that this project is arguably the most comprehensive example of comprehensive school reform implementation, involving multiple models in three phases over a decade. The New American Schools finding is supported by the majority of studies cited throughout this chapter. Even in the case of Success for All, a model distinguished by stronger integrity of implementation, one wonders what could be accomplished if the development of the design were given a higher priority than rapid scaling.

Scaling too fast means that energy that could be expended on making models complete is spent maintaining prototypical iterations in an ever-increasing number of schools. Basic sustainability takes precedence over making the designs substantially better. As a result, reforms find themselves in the risky position of overpromising and underdelivering. The relatively modest achievement effects of comprehensive school reform reported to date suggest that a wiser course may have been to take more time on a smaller scale.

VERSION 1?

One way to interpret the difficulties experienced by comprehensive school reform is to recognize that they are symptomatic of any new endeavor. Like that of a new technology, business, or school, all of the developers' energy is consumed by the act of creation and, in the case of comprehensive school reform, gaining a foothold. Yet, schools are clearly attempting to do things differently; from a curricular perspective, new practices are being implemented and professional development is being conducted because of comprehensive school reform.

Unfortunately, developers may have little time and opportunity for reflection and refinement, and as a result, there are many unanswered questions about how well these prototypes actually work. In some cases, the designs may not even display enough cohesion among their prototypical components to be truly called designs. Others show higher levels of classroom implementation integrity and modest achievement effects.

Although this chapter emphasizes the many fidelity issues in comprehensive school reform, the purpose is an optimistic one, designed to focus on a realistic assessment of the current condition as a term of reference for establishing where comprehensive school reform can go next. There is significant interest in next-generation comprehensive school reform that includes the development of new models, the refinement of existing designs, the improvement of the model selection processes, the development of professional development that builds a working knowledge of the reform, the provision of adequate financial support and school and district leadership, and the improvement of the capacity of the models to meet state accountability standards (Datnow 2003a; Slavin, 2005).

In part, these needs place a strong emphasis on external and internal factors associated with models and the environment in which they function. This includes what sponsors and the government need to do to continue to create the conditions required for the growth and development of comprehensive school reform.

This chapter takes an alternative yet complementary focus, one that drills into the realm of model development and the nature and needs associated with a next-generation design process. The goal is to identify how the design and implementation of comprehensive school reform models need to change to address the fidelity issues of the past and present and alter the trajectory of site-based school reform.

Specifically, this involves the identification of the next-generation design features that characterize what a comprehensive school reform model or design needs to do differently to improve the selection process, make professional development connected to a working knowledge of the design, and meet accountability standards.

It is important to acknowledge just how easy it is for the critic to make lists of things that are "wrong" or that need to be done differently. This chapter can readily be subject to such criticism. Instead, its role is to set the scene for the broader purpose of the book, which presents a theory and practice of next-generation comprehensive school reform.

When viewed together, the nine next-generation design targets represent an immense challenge for comprehensive school reform. They require that developers establish a more sophisticated perspective related to all facets of the design process and then translate that knowledge and understanding into better ways of designing and doing the parts of comprehensive school reform. The remaining chapters describe one way to realize those next-generation design targets.

In concluding, I wish to reiterate an assumption described in chapter 1. I note the similarity between the needs and issues associated with comprehensive school reform and all efforts at accomplishing comprehensive site-based school reform. Although this chapter refers most often to the work of comprehensive school reform model developers, the design issues and targets apply equally to school-initiated efforts at model building and those initiatives that are beyond the purview of the Comprehensive School Reform Demonstration Program. Issues of implementation integrity, scope, and connectedness; the role of technology; and the task of building the case for change with faculty members and schools pertain to all reform efforts. Addressing these issues is a challenge for all current and future school reform efforts.

CHAPTER TAKEAWAYS

1. High-fidelity design, implementation, and evaluation are necessary if proposed effects on learning are to be attributed to comprehensive school reform designs.
2. To be a paradigm-shifting influence, comprehensive school reforms must reconcile the content and process of their designs in more sophisticated ways.
3. Overall, the comprehensive school reform literature indicates levels of implementation integrity that are lower than those necessary to attribute achievement effects to their designs.
4. Most designs do not include or deliver the integrated design elements required to exert an influence at the school level.
5. Power in comprehensive school reform is predicated on first scaling, within individual schools, those design elements that have a track record of success in research and practice.
6. Next-generation designs will affect the totality of the professional lives of teachers and the professional culture of schools.
7. Hyperrationalizing the process of comprehensive school reform implementation (Fullan, 2001) sets in place a faulty foundation for engaging with schools. Next-generation comprehensive school

reform designs will focus first on helping schools understand themselves as a necessary foundation for building a meaningful relationship with comprehensive school reform.

8. Emergent feedback is a part of comprehensive school reform design. The high-fidelity evaluation of comprehensive school reform is predicated on each model's capacity to generate and share its own feedback just in time and all the time.

9. Next-generation comprehensive school reforms will employ technology beyond the classroom to gather, manage, share, and create the knowledge of the school and as a practical expression of the way in which the design influences every aspect of day-to-day teaching, learning, and managing.

10. Theory can drive the big-picture thinking and more detailed design required for next-generation comprehensive school reform development.

CHAPTER 3

Theory

There is nothing so practical as a good theory.—Kurt Lewin

The distinguishing feature of comprehensive school reform when compared to past reform efforts is its comprehensive focus and approach. Yet, the recurring accounts of incomplete design, implementation, and evaluation (e.g., Bodilly, 1996; Borman et al., 2003; Franceschini, 2002) indicate that the actual comprehensiveness of comprehensive school reform and its overall effect cannot be assumed and is thus open to reasonable question.

This chapter takes up the role of theory in addressing the problems and next-generation design challenges of comprehensive school reform by proposing a new theoretical approach to site-based reform. The term *theory* is used here to represent something more than ideas and concepts that explain a phenomenon of interest. According to Kuhn (1996), the explanatory value of a theory resides in the interrelationship between its concepts or beliefs and essential practices, instruments and systems. This means that a complete theory is as much about the way things happen as it is about the lofty, big-picture thinking that is usually attributed to the term.

The purpose of the theory described here is to explain how schools can successfully adopt bodies of research-based practice at scale. The explanation links the rationale for research-based practice described in chapter 1 to the need for next-generation design described in chapter 2. In doing so, the chapter explains how the whole of a comprehensive school reform design can be represented in every part of a school, reconciling the content and process of a school reform.

This chapter focuses on the key concepts of the theory and its principles. Chapters 4–9 describe the essential practices, instruments, and systems required to turn the theory into practice.

The theory presented in this chapter can be used in a number of ways. First, developers can consider the principles as a term of reference for reflecting on existing comprehensive school reform models. In doing so, they may consider the extent to which their models currently possess the capacity to meet the next-generation design targets and, ultimately, become self-organizing. Second, school leaders can use the principles as a framework for evaluating the models currently operating in their schools or those that they may be considering for future adoption. Third, educators involved in starting schools or crafting school-developed comprehensive school reforms or other site-based reform initiatives can use the principles as a term of reference or a framework for developing their own designs.

SIX PRINCIPLES OF THE SELF-ORGANIZING SCHOOL

The description of the six theoretical principles that follows represents the application of theory and research in the field of self-organization and complex adaptive systems (Houchin & Maclean, 2005; Kauffman, 1995; Pascale, Millemann, & Gioja, 2000; Prigogene & Stengers, 1984; Waldrop, 1993) to school design.

Self-organization refers to the way that schools or any other systems can be designed for constant dynamic change and adaptation (Scott, 1991) by producing bottom-up solutions to their needs, drivers, and problems. The individual participants in self-organizing systems generate collaborative bottom-up solutions by pooling their collective intelligence, and in doing so, they transcend their individual capacities. Further, they adapt to the demands of their environment and increase the likelihood of thriving. This can take the form of birds organizing into a flock, people organizing into an economy to meet their material needs, the staff of an emergency room making their process for admitting patients efficient, or, possibly, a comprehensive school reform engaging with a school (Merry, 1995; Odell, 1998; Smith & Fried, 1999).

These theories of self-organization have generated great interest in organizations because they explain how systems can come up with new learning, innovations, solutions to problems, and better ways to address their needs without constant top-down intervention (Merry, 1995; Scott, 1991). They also have a particular allure for education (e.g., Davis & Sumara, 2006; Morrison, 2002; O'Day, 2002) as the field struggles to realize the possibility of dispersed control in the loosely coupled (Weick, 1976) and autonomous circumstances of schools as we know them.

Concepts such as distributed leadership (Spillane, 2006), communities of practice (Wenger, McDermott, & Snyder, 2002), and collaboration and school-based management (Dimmock, 1993; Friend & Cook, 2003) all resonate with complexity and self-organization. What are frequently overlooked or missing, however, are the design characteristics and inherent order possessed by systems capable of realizing the potential of such organizational innovations. This order occurs naturally in physical systems, has evolved in biological systems, and is a function of human agency in organizations (Kowalewski, 1990; Krugman, 1996; Prigogene & Stengers, 1984).

The theory described in this chapter presumes that self-organization or any organizational form does not occur naturally in schools. This assertion is based on evidence derived from the multigenerational ethnographic study of schools that includes the work of Elmore (1996), Goodlad (1984), Lortie (1975), McLaughlin and Talbert (2001), and Sizer (1984), referred to in chapter 1. Each of these authors has characterized schools as predominantly autonomous systems focused on individualized engagement, possessing only limited and idiosyncratic cultures of shared professional knowledge and collaborative action.

The cornerstone of the theory of self-organizing schools rests on the view that the principles of self-organization can be applied intentionally to human systems (e.g., Pascale et al., 2000; Scott, 1991) and, in this instance, to the design of schools and comprehensive school reforms. This view departs from the more common application of complexity to education, which shows a preference for the metaphorical value of the theory over its potential as a design tool (e.g., Davis & Sumara, 2006).

The self-organizing school proposes that schools can be designed for bottom-up self-organization just as readily as they can be designed to perpetuate top-down leadership and decision making. The ultimate test of this theory is whether those schools can realize the benefits of research-based practice at scale and, in doing so, evolve away from their designers to an independent and sustainable self-organizing condition. To do so requires a deeply embedded capacity to adapt.

The design process required for self-organization involves the systematic application of the following six principles, which focus on building an adaptive capability within schools: school-level schema, simple rules, embedded design, similarity at scale, emergent feedback, and dispersed control.

School-Level Schema

A self-organizing school has a schema, a commonly held set of professional understandings, beliefs, and actions about teaching and learning.

A schema is a conceptual framework that defines one's interaction with the world (Marshall, 1995). For example, most people have a checkout schema for purchasing groceries. They apply this schema to a previously unknown checkout because of the recurring consistencies in the process from supermarket to supermarket. A checkout schema permits people's brains to deal automatically with the sameness in the process and focus on any more-or-less subtle change related to a particular supermarket. In doing so, people use a big picture, or metaperspective, combined with a specific understanding of regularity in a system to avoid cognitive overload and create the ongoing potential for adaptation.

In a self-organizing system, a common schema helps participants to work together to identify salient features and plan and execute their particular roles within the system (Gell-Mann, 1994). For example, a common schema permits doctors to work together as triage or surgical teams, and it allows firefighters from different municipalities to pool their collective capacities when working on multiple fronts to extinguish a wildfire. The doctors or firefighters may have never worked together before, yet regularities, common rules, protocols—their common schemas—guide each individual within the broader systems in which they work. These regularities extend beyond organizational conditions, beyond the way that the emergency room schedule operates or the firefighters' roster functions. The regularities reflect a common understanding of the practice undertaken by those professionals, who share a schema that makes their system whole and possible to work at scale.

Irrespective of their sophistication or simplicity, self-organizing systems possess enough similarity for agents to work together in meaningful ways. This regularity and consistency does not mean that a system is static. It is in constant receipt of information about itself and its surroundings that determines not only the success of its schema but whether it is instantiated, modified, or ultimately discarded. Change the checkout conditions or the technology of checking out sufficiently, and an altered or new checkout schema would emerge.

Is there a schema for teachers that is analogous to the one enacted by the doctors or the firefighters? Such a schema would require a common set of professional understandings, beliefs, and actions about teaching and learning, held at the level of the school and shared by all agents. The schema would explain the way that concepts such as professional development, organizational support, curriculum and pedagogy, evaluation, and technology come together in an explicit, coherent form to explain teaching and learning and guide practice. It would also represent the professional knowledge derived from research in the field in ways that are commonly understood, practiced, and valued by the school community.

The work of Goodlad (1984), Lortie (1975), McLaughlin and Talbert (2001), and Sizer (1984) suggests that it is unwise to assume the existence of school-level schemas in the majority of school settings. These researchers' studies of schools found little evidence of coherent and common school-level influences on teaching and learning. This finding, across studies and over time, covaries with the modest effects of schools on achievement reported by Rowe (2003). "Teachers in most high schools were left 'on their own' to practice as they chose, in keeping with norms of professional autonomy in American education" (McLaughlin & Talbert, 2001, p. 2.).

Even in those schools in which McLaughlin and Talbert (2001) found evidence of collaboration and student-centered learning, the evidence did not reflect a strong shared language and body of practice.

These studies suggest that any schema for teaching and learning is much more likely to be represented in the many schemata of individual teachers. The predominance of teacher schema over school schema may also explain why numbers of teachers in the same school could reject a comprehensive school reform model, whereas others were wholehearted supporters (e.g., Datnow & Castellano, 2000). Further, the aforementioned studies would indicate that those many schemata are less likely to be informed by research driven models, and are more readily adapted to autonomous practice rather than collaboration.

For example, a school-level schema has as one of it most important features the development of a common language that is necessary for collaboration. In an article entitled "Communities of Practice and Pattern Language," Smethurst (1997) notes,

> every Community of Practice, from physicists to painters to builders, has its own pattern language, its own way of expressing and discussing the unique qualities of its chosen art. This pattern language consists of the terms that the community uses to express itself, to organize its models and practice. (para. 1)

Such "pattern language" also prevents communities from reinventing the wheel as their members work together (Avgeriou, Papasalouros, Retalis, & Skordalakis, 2003).

Pattern language refers to the use of professional language to describe the dimensions of practice. For example, pedagogies such as explicit teaching or cooperative learning are defined by a lexicon that describes their essential features (e.g., guided practice, individual accountability, task structure; Slavin, 1991). These are the features that drive their well-established achievement effects. Cooperative learning is distinguished from group work and explicit teaching from a lecture by the knowledge and application of what these terms represent in practice. When all members of a school community know and apply these terms, they possess the prerequisite knowledge and language to not only share in the use of those practices but also benefit from their achievement effects.

As such, pattern language is not an idiosyncratic invention of a school community. Rather, it represents the way that community captures and uses the educational power of what has gone before, as represented by the accumulated professional knowledge of the field. In a contested field such as education, this knowledge may assume different forms and may be represented by different "dialects" in different schools. However, these knowledge forms and dialects must exist at the level of the school if the community is to work together to solve problems and give feedback and share perspectives in professionally meaningful ways. A pattern language is the product of a schema and a necessary condition for agents in a system to carry out and develop their schema.

When looking into schools more broadly, the multigenerational studies cited previously found limited engagement with the professional knowledge required for the development of a pattern language, beyond the frequently identified 15%–20% of teachers who are consistent innovators and whose work reflects a translation of theory and research into practice (Elmore, 1996). This may explain why Wenger (2006) noted that, despite the successful application of his communities of practice concept in other fields, it is yet to be successfully applied in education.

The most important takeaway here is that the promise of comprehensive school reform is one of schoolwide influence. In practice, this means the presence of research-based practice scaled up to the level of the school. This influence is derived from a process of systemic and comprehensive change across the school and, in fact, across many schools. In an effort to be comprehensive and exert school-level influence, comprehensive school reforms assume regularities in the values, beliefs, and practice of a school as a system.

However, the literature described in the first two chapters of this book indicates that frameworks for school-level influence may not yet be common in schools. A number of factors all point to the modest overall effect of comprehensive school reform and school-level reform (Borman et al., 2003; Rowe, 2003), and all point to a high degree of variability in the uptake of the values, beliefs, and action that define any given comprehensive school reform or site-based reform. These factors include the accounts of difficulties in comprehensive school reform implementation (e.g., Franceschini, 2002), including high within-school variance (Berends et al., 2001), the instability in levels of support within individual schools (Datnow & Castellano, 2000), and the multigenerational accounts of the circumstances of schools on climate and culture (e.g., Goodlad, 1984; Hargreaves, 1995; McLaughlin & Talbert, 2001; Sarason, 1982, 1996). The result is a gap between the assumptions about the comprehensive adoption and influence associated with comprehensive school reform (and many other reforms) and the current condition of schools.

From the perspective of the self-organizing school, this gap represents the absence of and need for a schema that would reconcile the assumptions and content of comprehensive school reform with the condition and processes of schools. A schema is necessary to make a design truly comprehensive. In a self-organizing school, the schema emerges from the application of the five additional principles of self-organization described here. The product is a widely held practical articulation of what it means to be a school.

A school-level schema is necessary for school-level reform.

Simple Rules

Self-organizing schools possess simple rules that drive the form and function of the school.

One of the most fascinating qualities of self-organizing systems is the way in which relatively simple rules can stimulate remarkably complex behavior when they are part of a schema. Seel (1999) describes the way in which five words—*Prevent harm, Survive, Be nice*—govern the judgement exercised by the Phoenix Fire Department in any situation. It is amazing how much complex behavior these simple rules permit, as well as how much adaptation they encourage. Of course, the fire department has a schema for fire fighting that creates the language for firefighters' actions. With this schema in place, the rules become a powerful force for self-organization.

Rules can also be cumbersome and complex. In an article in the *New York Times,* Glanz and Revkin (2003) describe the out-of-date rules governing power transactions on the U.S. electrical grid that were broken or inadequate even though "there were hundreds of pages of detailed specifications covering seemingly every contingency." The result: huge blackouts when the system became overstressed.

The circumstances of many schools are not unlike the overloaded power grid. Too much to do, too few resources, too little time, and too many thinly implemented innovations combine to overburden schools, making it immensely difficult to fulfill the high expectations of the communities that they serve.

Simple rules are about doing less, well, to accomplish more. They require a school to assign value to what it believes about teaching and learning and, in doing so, to spend much less energy on what it cannot support. This focused effort on a manageable set of beliefs and actions permits the schema development that is required for school-level influence and effect.

Simple rules are not intentions or mission statements; they drive the form and function of the school. They represent design cornerstone and catalyst for the day-to-day activation of the schema. For example, if a school establishes simple rules that "learning is cooperative," "decision making is collaborative," or "practice is based on research," these rules can drive the way that student learning happens in classrooms, the position descriptions of teachers, the teachers' career paths, and the way that the school is organized into decision-making teams. In the self-organizing school, these connections are not implicit, with generic reference to research, collaboration, and best practice. They are explicit. Each rule drives a design process that determines the school's schema and what happens in the school community day-to-day.

Simple rules are about doing less, well, to accomplish more.

Embedded Design

Self-organizing schools embed their beliefs, values, and actions about teaching and learning in every part of the organization's design.

If all self-organizing systems possess schemas, how do you get one? How do you go from simple rules to schema? How do the simple rules play out to produce the commonly understood regularity in teacher roles, organizational structures, and the deployment of technology? If a school or comprehensive school reform decides to create a simple rule about cooperation, collaboration, or research-based practice, how do those rules become a cornerstone of the schema and a catalyst for action?

Successful complex systems exhibit self-repeating patterns within their organizational structure (Waldrop, 1993). Embedded design creates these self-repeating patterns by expressing the simple rules in the school's design and by embedding those design features in all others. Embedded design allows the beliefs and ideas of a theory to be connected to its essential systems and practices. The application of this principle is central to the creation of the self-reinforcing conditions described in chapter 1. Embedded design also creates the predictable relationship between learning and teaching that is necessary for feedback to be shared and understood.

For example, a school's simple rule about cooperation may express a broad commitment in the community to cooperative learning. The rule makes it possible to select a research-based approach to cooperative learning for use in the day-to-day activity of classrooms and the school. Articulating cooperative learning in this way means that its research-based characteristics can then be embedded explicitly into other elements of the design, including teachers' position descriptions, technology tools, professional development, and feedback systems. This creates the conditions required to use the educational power of cooperative learning, given that the characteristics that exert a positive effect on student learning self-repeat in the design.

An approach to cooperative learning or any other aspect of a design reiterated in this way can bring practical day-to-day meaning to the rule. Such articulation helps to build the common understanding required for schema development.

When the design of a system incorporates the principle of embedded design as described here, the potential exists for that system to develop a self-reinforcing quality that builds capacity with cooperative learning or any other practice. For example, when the research-based approach to cooperative learning is reiterated in teachers' roles, in their career paths, in the way that feedback is delivered, in the design of software, in the way that teachers are recognized, and in the way that professional development happens, a teacher can build capacity with cooperative learning when engaged with all or any of these aspects of the school's overall design.

Every time feedback is shared, technology tools are used, or a portfolio is built for promotion, capacity with cooperative learning is developed because it is explicitly represented in each element of the design. Under these circumstances, growth becomes the domain of all aspects of a comprehensive school reform and not simply the responsibility of a professional development program, because the content of cooperative learning (or any aspect) is deeply embedded in what happens all of the time.

The application of the principle of embedded design extends beyond explicitly repeating the content of the design (cooperative learning, in this example) in all of the parts of a comprehensive school reform model (e.g., professional development, roles, technology tools). In the self-organizing school, each design element is embedded in all others. For example, a beginning teacher may learn how to design cooperative learning lessons and deliver peer feedback about cooperative learning by employing software tools included in a professional development program. As the teacher moves into the day-to-day life of the school, the professional development program is reinforced whenever the tools are used.

Because these tools articulate the research-based characteristics of cooperative learning, they reinforce the goals of the professional development program, and giving feedback reinforces a teacher's capacity to build cooperative learning lessons using the tools. This happens not only because cooperative learning is threaded throughout the design but because each of the design elements—feedback, technology, and professional development—is embedded in the others. From the perspective of the self-organizing school, this level of design cohesion is necessary to support and realize the educational power of practices such as cooperative learning.

Teachers rapidly become conversant with the pattern language about teaching and learning necessary for self-organization as a result of their self-repeating interaction with a school designed in this way. This creates the conditions for the attainment of threshold levels of implementation integrity necessary to enable the educational power of the design. This assertion, along with the principle of embedded design, is unpacked in detail in chapter 6, whereas evidence in support of these claims is presented in chapter 10.

Embedded design makes it possible to engage with all of a design by engaging with any part.

Similarity at Scale

Self-organizing schools embed their beliefs, values, and actions about teaching and learning at every level of the organization.

Self-organizing systems can be hierarchical and, according to Waldrop (1993), possess organizational levels. Similarity at scale is what happens when the schema is embedded at all levels, making a system similar to itself (Gleick, 1987; Merry, 1995). One can see this phenomenon in the natural world where, under careful examination, the coastline, a fern leaf, a snowflake, the outline of a mountain, and a head of broccoli are all self-similar (Merry, 1995). They exhibit self-repeating patterns at different levels or scales. The similarity-at-scale principle works reciprocally, with embedded design capturing the self-reinforcing design features that emerge at different levels within an organization.

When applied to the self-organizing school, this principle means that the schema is represented similarly in the roles of agents and groups at different levels in the school. The application of this principle is especially relevant to the design target of school-level influence, and it affects how comprehensive school reform can scale up its curriculum innovations to the level of the school. In practice, this principle relates to how a team of students in a class may function in a way similar to that of a team of teachers in charge of a year or grade level, or to the way that the school management team works in a manner that is similar to that of a teaching team.

Similar in this case means the way that agents use comparable methods and tools as they execute their respective roles. For example, students working in collaborative or cooperative classroom learning teams may use a particular collaborative problem-solving approach. The same approach is used in the team meetings of teachers or the school management team. The students use a software tool to record the results of their meetings. The teaching team and the management team use the same tool. When giving feedback, all three groups use the same feedback criteria and mechanisms. They all understand the collaborative process; they use the same tools; and they share the pattern language necessary for giving and receiving feedback.

The implementation literature described in chapter 1 indicates that many comprehensive school reform models lack the broader organizational impact required to support their classroom visions (Berends et al., 2002; Cook et al., 1999). The similarity-at-scale principle offers a way for comprehensive school reform designs to scale up and extend their scope of influence to the school level. This principle is unpacked in detail in chapter 7.

> Similarity at scale represents the way that the schema self-repeats at all levels in the school.

Emergent Feedback

> Self-organizing schools possess feedbacks systems that are used to decide what they need to do next.

According to Pascale et al. (2000), feedback is the way that a complex system talks to itself. In successful complex systems, feedback can be viewed as a network of constant exchange among individuals and groups. It is referenced to the system's schema, which is constantly revised as a function of the feedback exchange. This approach stands in contrast to the more common use of feedback in schools for time-dependent purposes (e.g., grade reporting, external evaluations, probation decisions). Although this type of information is often gathered under the pretext of future decision making, all too often it comprises an account of what happened (Bain & Parkes, 2006a; Frase & Streshly, 1994).

In a school using an emergent feedback approach (Bain, 2005), the mechanisms for sharing feedback are deeply embedded in the design and are required for its ongoing implementation. Giving and receiving feedback in this way is part of what it takes for all members of the school to do their jobs. It permits every individual to successfully fulfill the roles of administrator, teacher, and learner in interconnected ways. Everyone is responsible to everybody else for the success of the system as it pursues its core activity.

In such a system, any focus on individual performance (student, teacher, or administrator) emerges from a natural cycle of communication within the organization, and it happens constantly, not just at critical times when decisions need to be made about accreditation, tenure, and other time-dependent accountability issues. For example, if a school is using a team-based approach to serve its students, then team performance is expressed by how well the teachers and students on that team are growing and learning by implementing the school's schema. If the school's design and schema create the opportunity for all members of the team (teachers and students) to set performance goals and engage in regular sharing about their growth toward those goals, then the participants have embedded the feedback process in the broader purposes of the team and, ultimately, the school. This assumes the existence of the methods and the opportunity to engage in such exchange. The work of individuals is nested in collaborative structures (e.g., team or school) that are similar at different scales. The team's or school's capacity evolves as it revises its goals and mode of operation, based on the exchanges among individual members of the community. Under these circumstances, feedback tells the agents about what they need to do next.

As such, this next-generation feedback approach is not something done to a reform model, a school, a teacher, or a student. Instead, it is part of what it takes to be that reform model, school, teacher, or student. The whole system learns to talk to itself through the constant exchange of feedback among individuals, and an overall benefit accrues to the system as a result (Gell-Mann, 1994; Johnson, 2001; Waldrop, 1993). Feedback in a self-organizing school is the essential prerequisite for the successful self-organizing behavior of agents. Feedback makes it possible for agents to grow in their capacities and for self-organizing systems to produce emergent solutions (Pascale et al., 2000). The application of this principle in comprehensive school reform design can address the limited conceptualization and historical lack of feedback mechanisms in existing comprehensive school reforms. This principle is unpacked in detail in chapter 8.

Emergent feedback makes self-organization possible.

Dispersed Control

> Self-organizing schools employ networks and collaboration to en-
> able the ready flow of feedback to all levels in the organization.

Bottom-up self-organization demands sophisticated collaboration, and
developing a functional collaborative culture is challenging for schools
(Leonard & Leonard, 2001; McLaughlin & Talbert, 2001). One of the
biggest challenges in this regard is building the organizational structures, network, and pathways required for genuine collaboration to occur. Networks make collaboration possible. They disperse control in
self-organizing schools because they permit the ready flow of feedback
to all levels in the school.

All networks have a form, an architecture. The organizational design
of a self-organizing school captures the form of networks in other self-
organizing systems. Relationships in those systems tend to be short
range where information is exchanged by near neighbors (Watts, 2003).
Those relationships are also frequently nonlinear and expressed in
"small worlds" where friends are likely to be the friends of friends.
(Barabasi, 2002). For example, in a self-organizing school, teachers
work together in teaching and learning teams, instead of working alone.
Teams are employed to capture the potential of small-world relationships by making it possible for individual teachers to engage in constant formal and informal professional communication.

Communication is also promoted by a leveled but not overly hierarchical network structure (Stocker, Cornforth, & Bossomaier, 2002).
Networks with a flat design tend to create larger distances between individuals, whereas levels shorten those distances. For example, in a
self-organizing school, the leaders of each teaching and learning team
work together at the management level to pool the collective intelligence of the teams that they represent. In doing so, they build connections that shorten the pathways between teams, their students, and
teachers. The result is a heightened opportunity for members of one
team to communicate with others because the team leaders create common edges or links between the nodes (individuals) on the network.
This means that any innovation developed on one team can be readily
shared with others. The network structure shortens the professional

distance between nodes, and it contains the levels of management and decision making required to support a comprehensive school reform design in the classroom.

These nodes and short edges also help to create clusters where commonality in professional purpose heightens the probability of more related connections (Barabasi, 2002; Newman, 2003). For example, if, over time, some teachers help their students build an understanding of the school's pattern language, it is likely that those students will share that knowledge with their peers, thus enabling more students to build capacity with the pattern language of the school. This sharing may occur formally in the classes those students attend, as well as informally in other venues where they interact with their peers. The effect of this communication is to empower students, thereby creating the conditions required for the bottom-up self-organizing behavior that is characteristic of complex adaptive systems. Chapter 4 describes an example of the way that students build capacity with the schema.

In the self-organizing school, communication is dispersed because the network structure coexists with the pattern language and the shared approach that arises from applying the principles described earlier. Self-organization happens because there is, along with a network design, a schema derived from simple rules, embedded design, emergent feedback, and similarity at scale that disperses control to the agents in the system.

When applied with the other principles described in this chapter, dispersed control represents a way to address limitations in the organizational design of existing comprehensive school reform models. It also allows for the next-generation design target of school-level influence. When applied interactively, the six principles of self-organization articulate and scale up the schema and design, thus creating the potential for next-generation school-level effects. This happens because the school possesses a network of teams that creates the order to disperse control, and it provides the self-consistency that permits the whole to be more than the sum of the parts. Chapter 7 describes in detail the network design employed in the self-organizing school.

Networks generate the organizational form to disperse control.

RECONCILING CONTENT AND PROCESS

When viewed together, the six principles of self-organization described here are a way to reconcile the content and the process of school reform. For example, the simple rules represent a way for a school to identify its essential content. It can identify those curricular and instructional approaches that make sense for its needs and circumstances while establishing the approaches that it will use to implement what it does. This includes identifying the way that collaboration is employed in the school and how feedback is gathered and shared.

The embedded design principle integrates this content information in a single organizational design. This includes the way that roles are defined for individuals and groups, the manner in which technology serves the organization, the form and function of professional development, and the way that feedback is shared. As noted earlier, through the embedded design principle, the content of the design (e.g., cooperative learning or collaboration) is embedded in all of its process parts (e.g., professional development, technology), whereas every one of those process parts is embedded in all others. This is why, in the self-organizing school, traditional professional development vehicles no longer need to be solely responsible for the transmission of new organizational learning and why technology can do so much more than automate grade books and manage enrollment, attendance, and discipline data.

That this principle is critical to the overall theory, issues, and needs of contemporary comprehensive school reform is apparent in the way that it blurs the distinction between content and process in a reform design. The things that teachers and schools need to learn are deeply embedded in those things that teachers and the school need to do. The way of doing things differently comes to be synonymous with what is done differently.

The principles of similarity at scale and dispersed control scale up this reconciliation of content and process to all levels of the school, providing the organizational connectivity (networks of teams) and virtual connection (deeply embedded technology) that are necessary for self-organization to occur. Emergent feedback sustains and evolves the design. The school, from this perspective, is a self-producing living system. As a result of the interaction among the principles described here, the school can make itself (Urry, 2005) because of the self-reinforcing way that those principles constantly interact in support of each other. The parts and the system evolve as a function of their constant adaptation.

Further, the extent to which innovation succeeds or fails in schools can be seen as a function of the capacity of the school to apply the principles of self-organization to make itself. Where the parts of school support each other in self-reinforcing ways, innovation can flourish. Conversely, and as is illustrated in chapter 7, where the school is incomplete in its capacity to self-reinforce, innovation can diminish.

The ultimate value and validity of any theory lie in its application. How can schools be more adaptive? How can a theory inform practice in a meaningful way? How can theory drive the attainment of the next-generation design targets described in chapter 1? Does a school designed in this way evolve away from its developers? This chapter provides an overview of the principles necessary for self-organization.

Subsequent chapters unpack each of the principles described here and show how their application can generate a more complete design that includes the systemic use of technology and feedback. This includes examples of the way that the principles were applied in the self-organizing school project. Longitudinal evidence will illustrate how a school that is designed using these principles can successfully meet the next-generation design targets and exceed previous implementation levels reported in the comprehensive school reform literature. The chapters also show how the application of the principles results in greater school-level influence, educational power, and achievement effects by addressing the professional lives of teachers and by engaging with schools in complete and realistic ways.

CHAPTER TAKEAWAYS

1. The sum of the reform parts in a comprehensive school reform is not enough to produce school effects. Comprehensive school reforms need a coherent school-level identity, a common set of understandings held by all of their agents that reflect what they believe and how they operate—a schema.

2. Simple rules are the cornerstone of a school's schema. They express what a school values, believes, and is prepared to do.

3. Embedded design is the way that simple rules are translated into what members of the school community do every day. The design provides form, methods, and process—the order to give up control. Embedded design creates the self-reinforcing conditions for a comprehensive school reform to build educational power, employ technology, and use feedback.

4. Self-organization is driven by the feedback that emerges from the ongoing activity of the system. It is the way that the system talks to itself (Pascale et al., 2000), reinforcing regularities in the design that work and identifying areas that need to change.

5. For schools to produce school-level effects, they must be able to scale up their classroom designs to the school level, capturing what works at one level and scaling it up to others. Similarity at scale creates the possibility of school-level effects.

6. Networks make dispersed control happen in self-organizing systems. They enable the agents to exchange feedback and evolve the system.

CHAPTER 4

Self-Organization

Knowing is not enough, we must apply. Willing is not enough, we
must do.—Johann Wolfgang von Goethe

Spontaneous adaptation is the essential feature of a self-organizing system. Chapter 3 describes the discrete principles and characteristics that
make self-organization possible. How then do the principles interact to
produce spontaneous self-organizing behavior, and what does self-
organization look like when they are applied in a school? The following are three cases of the way that the work of teachers and students reflects the principles of the theory in action. They occurred between
1999 and 2001, during the transition and consultant phases of the self-
organizing school project.

The first case describes a response to the kind of theory-into-practice
issues that many schools face when teachers adopt new practice. The second case describes the way that one teacher's capacity with the school
schema transformed his students into teachers. The third case also pertains to students and highlights how spontaneous self-organization happens when the theoretical principles described throughout this book are
implemented in practice. In each case, the examples illustrate the presence of a schema and pattern language and the way that spontaneous individual acts of creativity and innovation can scale up in a school. This
capacity to scale applies the knowledge and will of individual innovators
for the benefit of the total school community.

Each example is deconstructed using the theory and its principles as
a framework. Although the cases describe accounts of actual events,

they are not intended as evidence of the implementation or as effects of the theory. They are shared for illustrative purposes. The longitudinal study of the self-organizing school project, its implementation integrity, and its effects are taken up in chapter 10.

CASE 1: SOME DIFFICULTIES WITH COOPERATIVE LEARNING

The first case occurred during the 1999–2000 school year during the transition phase of the self-organizing school project. It relates to difficulties associated with the use of cooperative learning across the school. As the school community became experienced and deliberate in its use of cooperative learning, numbers of teachers began to air concerns associated with the use of the practice in their classes. They indicated that calculating group scores and personal improvement points, as well as grouping and regrouping students, resulted in excessive time management and data management as compared to that of other teaching approaches. Calculating improvement points and grouping and regrouping students are critical research-based features of cooperative learning (Slavin, Farnish, Livingston, Sauer, & Colton, 1994). Around the same time, a number of teachers reported classroom management issues in cooperative learning lessons. They attributed the problem to reduced student engagement during expert group meetings. The teachers reported that students were too frequently off task when sharing research and reading with their peers.

The concerns about engagement and time and data management emerged, in part, from feedback gathered in classroom observations and reflections. They also surfaced in informal conversations with near neighbors and then in formal team meetings. An unfortunate consensus was emerging that characterized cooperative learning as being unwieldy. It was also perceived as adversely affecting students' time on task and inhibiting their progress through the curriculum. The concerns began to cast some doubt about whether cooperative learning really was an effective way to achieve teachers' curricular goals and objectives.

In response to the issues, two teachers from different teaching teams, who understood and experienced the problems with cooperative learning, began to collaborate on the development of a simple database that automatically calculated group and improvement scores (Slavin et al., 1994) and managed the cooperative learning grouping process.[1] The database also provided a mechanism for automating the calculations to represent student groupings and determine group rewards. To build the new tool, the teachers used some templates from an existing database package, with the idea that the database would become a plug-in-type addition to the school's grade and enrollment management software.

One of the teachers also developed a simple self-monitoring tool that students could use to self-manage the quality of their group process. This tool provided students with a simple self-check sheet for monitoring their interaction during the group meeting component of cooperative learning lessons, including checking whether the group members were on task and working together.

Both the database and the self-monitoring tools were initially tested in their developers' classrooms. After refinement, they were disseminated to the members of the grade-level teaching teams on which they served. After successful field testing and some debugging at the team level, both innovations were presented to a management team meeting of the school where other team leaders could see how the tools functioned.

The management team supported the innovations, and a plan was developed for presenting the tools to additional school teams (including the leadership team) to address the logistics associated with scaling up the innovations for use across the school. This included adjusting the school professional development program to provide initial training in the new approaches and outlining a strategy to incorporate the tools into the school's existing suite of software. The school's technology and management teams made these changes, and the innovations were subsequently disseminated to all teachers and teams to use across the school.

Self-Organizing Cooperative Learning?

One can ask, "Why attach the *self-organizing* label to what may seem to be a thoughtful form of problem solving that no doubt occurs in many schools through the acts of creative teachers?" The answer is best understood by unpacking the case as it relates to the six principles of the theory.

Schema

To provide a solution to a problem that functions at scale, that problem or concern first needs to exist at scale. For example, for all teachers to have a problem with improvement points and grouping in cooperative learning, all teachers need to be using improvement points and grouping. This may seem obvious, but such a specific problem arising from the detailed and widespread implementation of any teaching practice is unusual in schools because widespread implementation requires the existence of regularities and certainties in a school's approach that are consistent with a school-level schema.

A prerequisite condition for the development of such a schema is a broad-based capacity to communicate about the problem. This includes being able to exchange information about the research-based characteristics of cooperative learning, the way that expert groups function, group reward, and grading. In the case, an understanding of these characteristics was common not only to the teachers who identified the problem but also to those who solved it and, ultimately, to all of the teachers who applied the solutions. This widespread shared understanding is described in chapter 3 as a precondition for collaborative work in many professions and as one that is indicative of a pattern language and schema. It is also described as an uncommon condition based on the ethnographic study of schools.

In the case of the self-organizing school project, the schema and pattern language about cooperative learning that developed over the course of the design/pilot phase (1993–1996) and into the transition phase (1997–2000) made conversation and exchange of feedback about it possible. By the time the issue described here emerged, the school had been in full implementation of a design (that included cooperative learning) for 2 years. Teachers' knowledge and skill with cooperative learning grew over the period, to a point where the majority of teachers had substantial experience with it. As a result, those teachers were able to articulate the problems described earlier, within the context of the features of cooperative learning (e.g., improvement points and expert groups) and through its pattern language.

Further, by this time the majority of teachers had experienced the school's professional development program and were using technology tools for building cooperative learning lessons. They had progressed in the school's career path to the point where they had a deep participatory knowledge of the design and the role of cooperative learning within it. This ensured that the problem was widely held and that the solutions could expect to have an equally widespread effect.

Simple Rules

Simple rules exist as the cornerstones of a school schema. They drive the articulation of classroom practice. From the perspective of the self-organizing school in this case, the presence of cooperative learning in the project and the school schema reflected how the community valued cooperation. Simple rules about students' active achievement of learning goals, cooperation, and collaboration were established at the beginning of the design/pilot phase in 1992 and drove the use of cooperative learning and other features of the design. By 1996, all of the teachers and teams in the school used cooperative learning. Thus, the capacity to use the pattern language of cooperative learning and the existence of the problem were a product of what the school believed and valued about cooperation in the learning process and how it chose to express that value in practice. Chapter 5 describes how a school can build its simple rules.

Embedded Design

The self-organizing solution for cooperative learning emerged from an interaction of formal and informal feedback, the work of teams, the role of technology, and the roles and trajectories of individual teachers. Teachers and teams working with each of these design elements produced the solutions. From the perspective of the self-organizing school, the capacity to develop and use those solutions reflects how cooperative learning was embedded in each of those parts of a comprehensive school reform.

In the case of the self-organizing school project, all of the teachers engaged by the school had used its feedback tools and technologies, participated in its professional development program, and were operating with position descriptions and a trajectory, all of which expressed a commitment to cooperative learning. Teachers experienced cooperative learning through their lesson design work, through their personal port-folio development, through reflections on team performance, and through participating in the professional development program. As de-scribed in chapter 3, embedded design involves explicitly repeating the content of cooperative learning (or any practice) in all of the parts of a comprehensive school reform model (i.e., professional development, roles, technology tools) and then embedding each design element in all others.

This embedding created the self-reinforcing conditions necessary to first build the knowledge and pattern language that were needed to "have" the problem described in the case and then do something about it. If cooperative learning had been conceptualized as something different—for example, a form of group discussion without its research-supported characteristics—then it is unlikely that the problem would have existed in the form described. The problem was created by using cooperative learning with integrity. Embedded design created the conditions neces-sary to solve it. The manner in which this actually occurred is described in chapter 6.

Emergent Feedback

From the perspective of the self-organizing school, feedback is fun-damental for any bottom-up solution, including that described here for cooperative learning. To be understood and acted on, the problems and the innovations required highly specific, readily available information. In the case, this involved detailed observation of cooperative learning lessons (described in chapters 6 and 8) and the use of team meetings where objective and subjective evidence was shared about the issues that teachers and students were experiencing with cooperative learning. This "all-the-time" emergent feedback helped identify and then solve the problem. The feedback process was also used to field-test the inno-vations in the developers' classrooms and then communicate those findings more broadly across teaching and management teams.

In this way, an organization talks to itself and in doing so creates the conditions for constant change and adaptation. In the absence of this feedback, cooperative learning could have languished in the school, a victim of its unresolved problems. Instead, the solutions helped to evolve the practice and restore its relevance and utility. Feedback created the conditions for development of those solutions. Data to support this contention is shared in chapter 10, whereas the way to build an emergent feedback system is described in chapter 8.

Similarity at Scale

The problem and innovation described in the case emerged bottom-up as an example of applying and doing, rather than just knowing. It was shared initially by individuals, then within those teachers' teams, and ultimately by the school's network of teams at different levels of the school. From the self-organizing school's perspective, the capacity to scale up the problem and the innovation across the network of teams demonstrates the similar way in which all the teams used the school's schema and pattern language. The feedback about the problem scaled up from individuals to teaching teams to school teams, whereas the development of the solution followed the same course. Because the design, simple rules, and pattern language were expressed and understood at many levels, the problem and solution could be expressed at scale.

By the time that the cooperative learning problem emerged, the school had a full complement of teams that conformed to the three-tier network of teams described in chapter 3. Given the growing capacity with the school's pattern language and the use of a common collaborative problem-solving process, that network of teams was well equipped to manage the process of scaling up the innovations. This included expressing those innovations in new professional development requirements, in the school's software, and in teachers' roles and career paths. These solutions created the conditions for the innovations to evolve and become sustainable over time because they were complete for the prevailing conditions. Of course, in a self-organizing system, being complete and sustainable at any given point of time simply lays a foundation for what happens next.

Dispersed Control

In the parlance of networks and the self-organizing school, the existence of teams at scale created the conditions for dispersed control. In the case, innovations crafted by individuals were first disseminated by near neighbors and then through a network of teams that understood the need, the nature of the solution, and the way that it could be applied across the school. Each teacher did not have to invent a solution to a problem in isolation. Further, no one asked or expected the teachers who produced the solutions to undertake the process of scaling up the innovations. They were driven bottom-up and then dispersed by the school's organizational design.

When this kind of broad-based engagement and dispersed control results in repeated acts of self-organization over time, it becomes possible to evolve a schema in ways that may ultimately blur the distinction between a school and a comprehensive school reform. The design and the schema evolve away from the initial work of the developers. The similarity at scale and the dispersed-control principles are explained in detail in chapter 7.

CASE 2: THE EMERGENCE OF STUDENTS AS TEACHERS

The second case of self-organization is derived from a classroom observation conducted in the spring of 2001. The observation was of a Year 10 Spanish-language class focused on teaching grammar concepts.[2] The students were teaching the concepts to one another in collaborative groups. During the lesson, the teacher asked the students to reflect on the effectiveness of their teaching and to share those reflections. They described what they were trying to accomplish, and they expressed their views on the success of their efforts. The nature of the students' remarks indicated that they knew, understood, and could apply the pattern language of explicit teaching and peer tutoring to describe what they were doing. They described their teaching using terms such as *modeling*, *guided*, and *independent practice* as they reflected on their work. After accounting for their teaching, the class group in turn provided the student teacher with feedback, using the same pattern language and applying what they knew about the schema.

After the class, the teacher explained that he was intentionally teaching the students about the school's body of practice and, in this instance, explicit teaching. He was trying to improve the quality of student exchange in cooperative learning and peer-tutoring activity. To do so, he was teaching students to make their contributions to expert teaching groups and individual peers using the same principles of explicit teaching that the school's teachers used when delivering new material. The teacher indicated that students were required to use the same pattern language when they exchanged feedback with their teaching peers. By having students share their reflections about their work using the characteristics of explicit teaching as term of reference, all students began to build knowledge and skill about an approach that underpinned the school's design and schema.

Students as Agents?

This teacher-led initiative was a spontaneous and emergent act that enabled all of the students in the class to begin to teach one another in ways that were much like the approach taken by their teacher and the school. At the time, the school had not promoted the idea that students would become involved with the school's body of practice. The teacher's decision set in place the conditions for a new role for students in the school. The following is an account of the case using the six principles of self-organization.

Simple Rules and Schema

The case illustrates the way in which the teacher's facility with the school schema created the conditions for extending an understanding of it to students. The teacher used the school's pattern language to educate students about the characteristics of research-based approaches to teaching. The students applied that knowledge to become professional teachers as a result.

The students' facility with the body of practice and pattern language can be seen as an extension of the school's simple rules and schema, made possible by the teacher's ability to share those rules and related schema. From the perspective of the self-organizing school, the teacher's self-organized initiative, like that described in the previous case, was made possible because of the preexisting regularities and consistencies in the school's approach to teaching and learning. Most important is the way that the teacher's initiative reflected his facility with the school schema to communicate it to others. The teacher felt sufficiently comfortable to invite students into the domain of professional teaching practice.

Embedded Design

The teacher's spontaneous act became a transforming event that created the initial conditions for students to become active agents in school's total learning process. That self-organizing act, like that described in the previous case, can be seen as a product of the way that roles, trajectory, feedback, and technology are reconciled in the experience of the teacher. However, the current case implies that it is possible to apply the embedded design principle to roles, trajectories, feedback, and technology for students. For example, Figure 4.1 describes what a student role may look like in the self-organizing school, based on applying the embedded design principle in the manner described in chapter 5.

Figure 4.2 describes how a trajectory can be created for students as they grow in their capacity to engage the schema. Chapter 9 describes the kind of technology that can be made available to students in this context. The case illustrates the potential for students to benefit from embedded design and build capacities similar to those of their teachers. In doing so, intelligence is added to the school's teaching and learning capacity as the distinction between the two becomes blurred by student engagement with the schema.

Emergent Feedback

Knowledge of the schema and growing facility with the pattern language makes it possible for students to provide feedback in ways similar to those of their teachers. Students who know about modeling, expert questions, and guided practice can express that understanding in their feedback. In doing so, they can accurately describe strengths and weaknesses in the curriculum, individual lessons, and the delivery of those lessons from a student perspective. This knowledge can also be used to understand and problem-solve learning from a student perspec-

Student in the Self-Organizing School

Responsibilities

Students are expected to partner with the members of the community in the process of learning, sharing, growing, and providing feedback, ensuring that they assume responsibility for their own growth and that of the learning community.

Learning

The student knows and understands the curriculum, his or her current placement, and expected growth—short, medium, and long term.

The student actively manages his or her own growth portfolio and curriculum plan in collaboration with his or her advisor and teacher.

The student deploys the body of practice to support his or her own performance and that of his or her teachers and peers.

The student monitors short-, medium-, and long-term growth using the feedback tools at his or her disposal.

The student actively contributes to the growth of others through excellence in his or her contribution to peer and collaborative learning.

The student has full understanding of and demonstrated capacity with the student learning tools in the school operating system.

The student has a high expectation of self, peers, teachers, and school in support of learning and demonstrates an accurate understanding of roles and responsibilities as learners.

Sharing

The student demonstrates excellence in all aspects of the collaborative process.

The student takes responsibility for assisting each member of the team to make the best possible contribution.

The student uses the team structure and process as a problem-solving and solution-generating opportunity.

The student deals directly and openly with all members of the community.

The student works collaboratively toward the achievement of personal, team, and school goals.

The student delivers on all learning and team responsibilities in a timely fashion.

The student seeks assistance from peers, team leaders, and the administration.

The student manages own computer and network participation in an ethical manner.

The student demonstrates advanced problem-solving skills with respect to computer hardware and software and can apply those skills to student difficulties.

Feedback

The student demonstrates excellence in the use of all feedback tools in the school operating system.

The student provides timely feedback to all peers and teachers.

The student uses feedback to inform progress toward the attainment of personal, team, and school goals.

The student ensures that all agents are maximizing the use of their feedback tools and translates feedback into action by problem solving individually and through teamwork and collaboration.

Growth

The student takes responsibility for own growth.

The student integrates feedback data into portfolio.

The student takes responsibility for the growth of the team and school.

The student develops a portfolio for transition through levels in the school.

Figure 4.1.   A Student Position Description

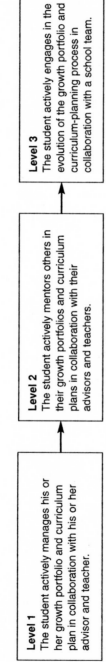

Level 1
The student actively manages his or her growth portfolio and curriculum plan in collaboration with his or her advisor and teacher.

Level 2
The student actively mentors others in their growth portfolios and curriculum plans in collaboration with their advisors and teachers.

Level 3
The student actively engages in the evolution of the growth portfolio and curriculum-planning process in collaboration with a school team.

Figure 4.2. The Trajectory of the Levels in the Student Career Path

tive. Students' feedback that can be articulated using the pattern language can play an active role in shaping the future of the schema and the school's design.

Similarity at Scale

The example described here pertains to just one class and just one teacher. However, as described in chapter 3, the existence of a school schema and design makes it possible to scale the innovation in Case 2 to many teachers and teams. A creative act by one teacher and a class of students sets in place the initial conditions (Gleick, 1987) for immediate scalable potential in an environment where all teachers know and use cooperative learning, where there is explicit teaching and peer mediation, and where (as illustrated in the last case) there is an organizational design capable of capturing and scaling such an initiative.

In this example, the schema scaled up to a class of students. In doing so, the distinction between teacher and students was diminished, albeit in just one class. The teacher created a new potential for many students, who, like their teachers, could ultimately assume active roles and a trajectory in the school as teachers and learners.

Dispersed Control

There can be no better example of the dispersed-control principle than the way in which the teacher employed the existing schema and design of the school to disperse control to students in his class. Expert group and teaching group meetings and tutoring moved from being an unstructured narrative exchange to become explicit instruction. This happened because the teacher dispersed control for the application of those pedagogies to students in ways that engaged them as partners in the teaching and learning process. Cooperative learning and peer tutoring evolved as a result of the initiative and in ways that their developers had not anticipated. In this case, the teacher's action provided the impetus for dispersed control, which in turn created the potential for all students to become agents of self-organization in the class and, possibly, the school.

From a theoretical perspective, students could develop facility with the school's body of practice by applying the same principles of self-organization described in the previous case. The students' work became an extension of the similarity at scale and dispersed-control principles as they became active agents in the system using the body of practice, reflecting and giving feedback. Students were able to use the pattern language and knowledge to explain their own learning, give feedback to their teachers, and actively contribute to the evolution of the school schema. In doing so, they became engaged with the cooperative learning process, addressing the overall engagement issues described in the last case, and making cooperative learning robust and adaptive as a result. This student engagement can ultimately stimulate the development of new roles for all students.

The case illustrates the way in which a design can evolve from its original iteration and the work of its developers in unanticipated ways. In this case, the evolution leads to new and sophisticated roles for a whole new group of agents: the students.

CASE 3: EMERGENT STUDENT FEEDBACK

The third case emerged during a review of the student feedback in the school's database during the fall of 2000. While reviewing large numbers of student feedback protocols, the following remarks were found in the comments section of different entries of a database:

> The class would benefit from more guided practice to go over specifics before homework.
> I think the jigsaws for this class are too much for some kids to handle. I think if you summarized each subject for each jigsaw group it would be easier to learn the material.
> He does overuse Inspiration and concept maps.
> I think this class is great and I love the STAD[3] and jigsaw groups.

Students provided feedback to their teachers in all classes every semester, using the electronic protocol described in Figure 4.3.

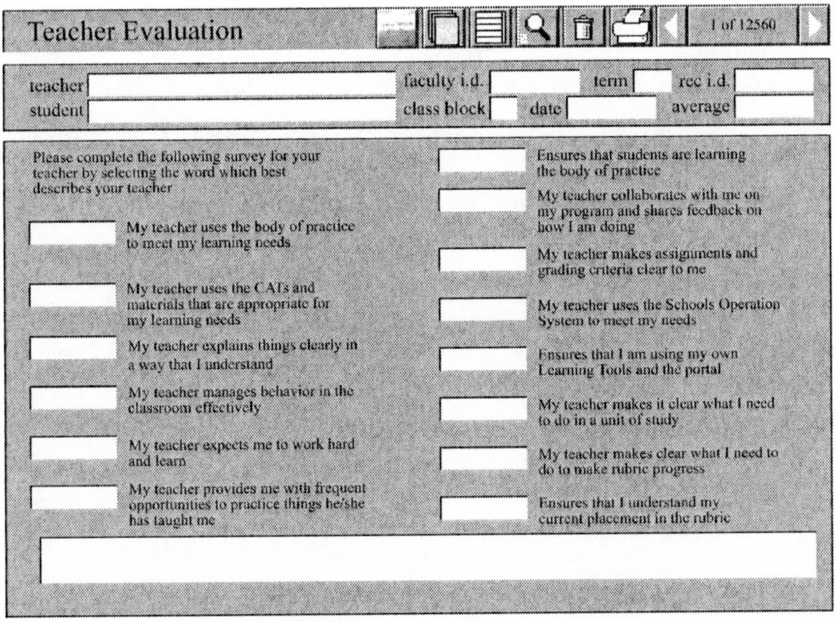

Teacher Evaluation

1 of 12560

teacher
student
faculty i.d.
class block
term
date
rec i.d.
average

Please complete the following survey for your teacher by selecting the word which best describes your teacher

My teacher uses the body of practice to meet my learning needs

My teacher uses the CATs and materials that are appropriate for my learning needs

My teacher explains things clearly in a way that I understand

My teacher manages behavior in the classroom effectively

My teacher expects me to work hard and learn

My teacher provides me with frequent opportunities to practice things he/she has taught me

Ensures that students are learning the body of practice

My teacher collaborates with me on my program and shares feedback on how I am doing

My teacher makes assignments and grading criteria clear to me

My teacher uses the Schools Operation System to meet my needs

Ensures that I am using my own Learning Tools and the portal

My teacher makes it clear what I need to do in a unit of study

My teacher makes clear what I need to do to make rubric progress

Ensures that I understand my current placement in the rubric

Figure 4.3. Teacher Feedback Survey Completed by Students

From the remarks, it is clear that students had developed facility with the pattern language of the school, as reflected in the use of professional terms and words. Although they may seem unremarkable given the previous case, what distinguishes this scenario from the previous one is the absence of active teacher involvement to stimulate student acquisition of the language used. The remarks were from different students and were presumably a result of repeated exposure to the school's pedagogies and related terminology in their classes. Like that in the previous case, the language reflects the existence and impact of the school schema and the way that it was beginning to migrate from teachers to students in the school.

Emergent Feedback at Scale?

As with the prior cases, the student feedback described here can be linked to all six principles in a manner consistent with that of Case 2. However, what is especially compelling about this example is its spontaneity and significance given the critical importance of emergent feedback in a self-organizing system.

When students and teachers in a school can speak a common language (as illustrated in Cases 2 and 3), the potential exists for learning to occur at a whole new level of sophistication based on a common metacognitive understanding of the teaching and learning process. Metacognitive capability has been shown to have a profound effect on the acquisition of skills, as diverse as learning to read and how to behave in stressful social situations (Flavell, 2000; Tunmer, Herriman, & Nesdale, 1988). It has also been shown to play a well-defined role in the practice of beginning and experienced teachers (Artz & Armour-Thomas, 1998).

When students and teachers possess this capacity, the learning environment can use feedback in new and powerful ways that put teachers and students on the same learning page. They can do many of the same things and share emergent feedback, as illustrated in Case 2. Under these conditions, teachers and students can work together to realize the educational power of the school's design. In doing so, they can exert school-level influence as the schema extends to everyone engaged in the learning process.

IMPLICATIONS

A self-organizing system disperses control and creates the capacity to produce spontaneous emergent behavior. From the perspective of the self-organizing school, this capability results from an intentional design process. That process creates the initial structures and network connections for the kind of self-organizing behavior described in the three cases. In those examples, the school and its agents were able to create a web of spontaneous transformations that captured current and past technology (in the broadest sense) to create something new (Johnson, 2001; Waldrop, 1993). This is what happens when self-organization occurs with a frequency and scale required to transform the system. At this point, a comprehensive school reform that is designed for self-organization can become indistinguishable from the school.

In the field of self-organization, researchers have observed that to generate the scalable effect described here, systems must possess a certain level of complexity for self-organizing behavior to occur (Waldrop, 1993).[4] That complexity is reflected in the application of the principles described in chapter 3 and the cases used to illustrate those principles featured in this chapter. Researchers have found that a simple system with sparse connections will just freeze up and sit there, and if the networks of connections are too dense, then the system churns away in total chaos (Waldrop, 1993).

In either case, the agents—in this instance, the students and teachers—never optimize their capacity in the system (Waldrop, 1993). Like the systems they compose, they are always unfolding, always in transition. The self-organization described in the cases occurred without top-down direction because of the deeply embedded structure and function in the system. It was also active and intentional (Waldrop, 1993). Over time, the repeated self-organizing action of agents evolves a schema to a point where the system may seem totally altered as it seeks to respond to the forces and drivers that it faces. Although the simple rules and schema provide a focus of the school's beliefs, values, and practice, that expression is constantly changing and adapting as a result of self-organization. In this way, a school's use of a second- or next-generation comprehensive school reform can evolve away from its developers.

Beyond Fidelity and Sustainability

If a school or comprehensive school reform increases its capacity for self-organization by applying what it knows to the point where emergent self-organizing behavior occurs spontaneously all the time, it becomes possible to think beyond the challenges of getting a school to implement a comprehensive school reform or any reform with fidelity. The reform model that consistently generates bottom-up self-organizing behavior should become responsive to the inevitable change that occurs in schools all the time. Under such circumstances, there is no clear beginning or end in terms of adoption, just a constant process of adapting. Practices change constantly in response to the needs of the school, its teachers, and its learners.

Case 1 illustrates this idea by showing how an iteration of cooperative learning can be fully satisfactory for a school's needs at a given point in time and then become problematic as the school's and the teachers' needs evolved. The original version of cooperative learning described in Case 1 was adequate and appropriate for teachers who were building an initial understanding of the pedagogy. However, the same teachers identified new issues and problems as they became sophisticated in their use of the approach. Those problems had to be addressed if cooperative learning was to remain viable. New technology tools and self-monitoring systems, which may have been overwhelming in those initial stages, became essential as the situation changed.

The self-organizing school project could have persisted with its original permutation of cooperative learning, but in doing so, it would have set in place the conditions for the demise of cooperative learning by failing to respond to the problems described by teachers in Case 1.

This interpretation of the case shows that there is no absolute endpoint in terms of adoption or implementation integrity in a reform, because there is no absolute or static set of needs and conditions in a dynamic system such as a school. From the date of an initial adoption decision, comprehensive school reforms are engaged in a race to build individual agent and organizational capacity at a rate that is commensurate with the changing circumstances of the schools in which they function.

There is no equilibrium condition in this situation, for the same reason that there was no viable "one best way" approach to cooperative learning in the self-organizing school project. In Version 1 of comprehensive school reform, equilibrium is pursued as a goal under the guise of implementation integrity. In self-organization and next-generation school reform, equilibrium occurs just before the demise of a system because if it achieves equilibrium, the system has entered into a relationship with an outdated set of conditions that no longer apply (Merry, 1995).

In the parlance of complex systems, this dynamic adaptive process of change is known as surfing the edge of chaos (Pascale et al., 2000). Successful "surfing" means negotiating the hard edge between the constant adaptation required for a system to be sustainable and the chaos that can emerge from failing to do so. In the current context, chaos can be seen as the unraveling of the comprehensive school reform process that was described as a frequent occurrence in comprehensive school reform implementation (e.g., Datnow, 2003a; Franceschini, 2002).

Needs shift over time, a fact that all school innovations must face. This may explain why fixed ideas about adopting change in schools leads to so many problems when it comes to implementation. It is also important to note that questioning fixed and enduring points of adoption and implementation does not dismiss the importance of implementation integrity. Comprehensive school reforms must know how well they are doing, even if what they do changes over time. They must also remain aware that what they do should be subject to constant change.

The most important takeaway from the examples and the ideas shared in this section is to emphasize the dynamic nature of schools and comprehensive school reforms and the broader milieu in which they operate. The long history of difficulty in reconciling reforms and schools makes this of particular interest. As a methodology for school change and improvement, it is clear that it is unproductive to have fixed ideas about reforms interacting unsuccessfully with fixed ideas about schools. As such, developers may wish to consider whether their models are capable of the levels of ongoing adaptation required to succeed in a dynamic environment. This means eliminating the race between capacity building and change over time by supporting teachers and leaders in schools to become agents in the evolution of their designs because of the way it is structured for self-organization.

For start-up schools and in-school model development efforts, this section instantiates what they already know. From the perspective of the theory described here, they too are surfing the edge of chaos and need to set a trajectory that crafts the schema, design scope, and similarity at scale required for self-organization and emergence over time. For all sets of stakeholders, this capacity-building capability must ultimately yield dispersed control where agents can truly work bottom-up in ways that extend beyond the vision of the developers and consultants.

It is important to recognize and acknowledge the possibility of alternative explanations and interpretations related to the transactions and outcomes described in each of the cases shared in this chapter. For instance, the second case was described as a product of a schoolwide schema, although it is altogether possible that the new roles for students could have emerged as a product of the initiative of just one creative teacher acting alone in an autonomous school environment. The Spanish teacher could have taught his students to be skillful explicit teachers, as a result of his own skills and as a product of his unique professional journey. The cases are not intended to represent causal evidence of the presence of the theory or to imply that the circumstances and events described here are possible only if the theory of the self-organizing school is in place.

As noted in the introduction to the chapter, however, the key takeaway from all of the examples relates to trajectory and scale and what is possible as a result of the creative actions of teachers and students. Because each case did emerge within the context of a schoolwide process and design, the software, the new program, and the new roles for students each possess a scalable potential that would not be possible had they been the product of idiosyncratic creativity in the acknowledged and well-researched autonomous culture and context of most schools. The potential offered by the theory is represented by the opportunity to assist many teachers and students, as illustrated in Case 1. In the absence of a schoolwide schema, such schoolwide effect is unlikely.

CONCLUSION

This chapter illustrates how knowing and applying the six principles of self-organization can produce self-organizing behavior. In the instances described here, teachers and students produced something new because of an emergent capacity with the school schema arising from the application of the six principles. Chapters 5–8 explain the principles in detail, including the way in which each principle was enacted in the self-organizing school project.

CHAPTER TAKEAWAYS

1. All schools exist in dynamic, ever-changing landscapes where change and adaptation are prerequisites for future viability.

2. Failure to change and adapt to the conditions that exist in those landscapes is a precursor to an equilibrium condition and the ultimate demise of the system (Waldrop, 1993).

3. The pursuit of a stable equilibrium condition is to seek a relationship with the past (Merry, 1995; Pascale et al., 2000).

4. In comprehensive school reform, ideas about implementation integrity and fidelity are dynamic. There is no clear beginning or end in terms of adoption, just a constant process of adapting. Practice changes constantly in response to the needs of the school, its teachers, and its learners.

5. Successful self-organizing systems are in states of constant change and adaptation, evolving their rules, schemas, and designs. It is this process that enables those systems to surf the edge of chaos (Pascale et al., 2000).

6. Repeated acts of self-organization permit a system to not only adapt to immediate change but ultimately emerge at a whole new level of functioning.

7. Emergence is what happens when a comprehensive school reform evolves from its developers in purposeful and sustainable ways.

NOTES

1. These examples of self-organization were developed by Bob Carter and Gerry Swan, who created the software described here and built a number of other components of the self-organizing school software system.

2. Eladio Moreira, Spanish senior master, built the student model described in Case 2.

3. STAD refers to Student Team Achievement Divisions, a cooperative learning teaching approach (Slavin et al., 1994).

4. The information described on this page and cited as Waldrop (1993) represents the content of interviews conducted by Waldrop involving leading complexity scientists Stuart Kauffman and John Holland. The core ideas represented here that relate to the concept of self-organization are theirs.

CHAPTER 5

Simple Rules

Wisdom lies neither in fixity nor in change but in the dialectic between the two.—Octavio Paz

A dialect or interplay of ideas is essential to translate theory into practice. To better understand this interplay, the next four chapters feature
a detailed treatment of each of the principles of the self-organizing
school and the way that they were applied. The focus of this chapter is
the simple-rules principle.

The comprehensive school reform adoption and needs-assessment
process provides a context for the chapter, which describes five steps
for getting started with comprehensive school reform or any site-based
reform, by developing simple rules. The five-step approach is designed
to address the next-generation design target of effective adoption. In
doing so, it describes how to reconcile content and process in the adoption or needs-assessment stage of comprehensive school reform. The
self-organizing school project is used as an example to show how
schools can use their simple rules to build the self-understanding necessary for informed decision making about comprehensive school reform or any site-based approach to change.

Model developers can use the chapter to reflect on their current practice in the areas of needs assessment and adoption. For start-up schools
or schools developing a site-based model, this chapter describes ways
to get the adoption process started by developing some simple rules.

Despite the ready availability of needs-assessment resources and
processes, the comprehensive school reform implementation literature

indicates that adoption initiatives and needs assessment may not be producing their intended outcomes (Appelbaum & Schwartzbeck, 2002; Asenio & Johnson, 2001; Zhang et al., 2005). For example, one of the most definitive findings of the Rand evaluation of the New American Schools project was the instability in teacher and school commitment to the comprehensive school reform models over time (Bodilly, 1998).

Decisions about these models, and reform in general, are often made hastily, without appropriate planning and sometimes without choice (American Federation of Teachers, 1999). Instability can appear shortly after an adoption decision, especially when it is forced or made too hastily. The implementation literature also indicates that commitment is much more likely to diminish the longer the model is implemented (Datnow, 2003b). These findings stand in contrast to the expectation that a school can arrive at a stable and sustainable adoption decision by engaging in a rational needs-assessment process (Mid-Continent Research for Education and Learning, 2006). Adoption decision making is much more a product of the ongoing dialect that exists between fixity and change than it is an absolute time-dependent decision.

From the perspective of the self-organizing school, effective adoption is about the beginnings of schema building and, specifically, the development of a school's foundational simple rules. This requires a realistic analysis of the complex and often contradictory circumstances of schools (e.g., Fullan, 2001; Hargreaves, 1995). A school needs to learn much more about itself to inform its commitment to a design or make major decisions about change. To do so means building stakeholder consensus around the simple before moving to the complex. This involves first coming to terms with what the school knows and values about such areas as research-based practice, standardized testing, and collaboration at the beginning of a comprehensive school reform needs-assessment process. These are seen as necessary prerequisites to the kind of big questions asked in many needs-assessment processes. For example, one of the key questions asked by the National Clearinghouse for Comprehensive School Reform Self-Evaluation Tool addresses whether teachers, administrators, and staff share a vision for the school (Hansel, 2000).

This seems like a sensible starting point for determining how much commonality there is in the views and perspectives of the members of the community. However, given the individualized engagement and autonomous cultures reported in the multigenerational ethnographic study of schools, what does such a statement really mean? And even if a community expresses a common sense of vision, what is the likelihood that a consensus at such a general and abstract level will actually translate into support for the highly specific change in the day-to-day teaching practice associated with a comprehensive school reform?

A shared vision needs to emerge from a common sense of value and priority about the meaning of teaching and learning. Statements such as "The school staff and administrators clearly and centrally focus on teaching and learning" (from the Self-Evaluation Tool) have limited value if the school has not explored in a deep and meaningful way what it means by teaching and learning as a total community. It is this interplay that is most important. The experience of implementing comprehensive school reform suggests that analyzing performance data or voting on comprehensive school reform designs without rigorously testing the underpinning assumptions means building a rationale for change on a shaky foundation.

FIVE STEPS

A needs assessment in a self-organizing school is first about identifying the simple rules that drive its schema. The process focuses on establishing the school's beliefs, values, and action about teaching and learning. This involves the following five steps:

Step 1—Identifying the drivers: Establishing the forces or events driving the school to change.

Step 2—Establishing "what works": Identifying what the school can do about its drivers by reviewing what is known about what works, those research-based practices and approaches that can help the school address its forces for change.

Step 3—Identifying needs and strengths: This step involves establishing a school's needs and strengths in light of its drivers and the direction offered by the literature on research-based practice.

Step 4—The match: In this step, the forces driving the school—and the potential resources available to address those forces—are matched with the school's strengths and needs.

Step 5—Task group validation: This step involves establishing a representative group of the school to validate the drivers, needs, and strengths as a preface to the development of the school's simple rules.

Steps 1–4 provide the requisite information for a school to develop a preliminary set of simple rules that express its beliefs and values about teaching and learning (at the level of the school) and as a term of reference regarding how it will act on those beliefs. The process is underpinned by the idea of a dialect around the interplay and connectedness among the steps. This includes the need to revisit one step based on what is found by taking another.

The simple rules are the cornerstone of a school's schema and, ultimately, its design. What follows is a detailed description of those steps, including examples of the product that arises from their application in schools.

Drivers

Drivers are forces or events that cause a different course of action to be taken (Gribi, 1995). They stimulate the interplay between ideas and actions, and they build an understanding of why choices need to be made. In schools, whether a need becomes a driver is all about the way that the school community chooses to act in response to its circumstances. In fact, the biggest presumption in school reform may be assuming that those areas that drive big policy and large-scale reform at the system level represent drivers in schools. The history of school reform suggests the contrary and that needs in schools do not necessarily turn into drivers (Tyack & Cuban, 1995).

Establishing drivers means positioning factors such as comparative test data, the Comprehensive School Reform Demonstration Program requirements, changes in student populations, and comprehensive school reform itself, as an expression of those things that are "out there" representing potential forces for change. For example, the following list describes an extract from the driver component of a needs assessment conducted at a secondary school.

Drivers Identified by Faculty

1. Site-based management initiative (a government policy to increase site-based planning, decision making, and accountability)
2. Increased student diversity
3. Technological cost and competitiveness with peer schools
4. Faculty capacity to deal with individual difference
5. Responsive curriculum (Bain, 2000)

In these drivers are examples of the pressing factors associated with system change, funding, student diversity, technology, and professional capacity. The first driver, the site-based management initiative, is an example of a nationally sponsored systemic reform—in this case, an effort to devolve management responsibility to schools (Ministry of Education, 2001). This initiative was driving the school to alter its management and reporting structure when faced with new and different accountability standards from the central authority, not unlike the reporting requirements associated with No Child Left Behind (U.S. Department of Education, 2005).

The school was also wrestling with the challenges posed by an increasingly diverse student population and the extent to which the prevailing curriculum was responsive to that diversity. Again, this reflected the central driving force of the paradigm crisis described in previous chapters and created drivers related to the responsiveness of the school's curriculum and a longstanding faculty.

The looming fiscal and curricular challenges of technology were also being recognized as a powerful force in the school. As such, the technology driver was strongly connected to the others. The faculty and administration recognized its crucial effect on the school's funding, curriculum, and faculty professional development. In each case, the drivers had risen to a level of demand that caused the school to do things differently. This example illustrates evidence of the commonality of circumstance across schools and common resonant themes—system change, student diversity, accountability, faculty capacity, funding, and technology.

Although drivers may connote a sense of urgency, the best way to increase the likelihood that these big factors turn into drivers may, ironically, be to take a step back and respect the community by avoiding the assumption that "we must change because. . . ." The history of school reform and the comprehensive school reform implementation literature suggests that "must" is a variable, not a definitive. Tyack and Cuban (1995), in their book *Tinkering Toward Utopia*, show the way in which the grammar of schooling has been profoundly resistant to mandated change over time. Mandates in education have a remarkable propensity for circumvention and ultimately rely on the individuals who implement them (Lipsky, 1980).

Community members need not and will not agree on all the drivers, just as they may not agree that there is a paradigm crisis. However, they should know that such conditions exist. It is especially interesting to divide the community into some of its traditional constituencies to see how people in different roles view the school's drivers. This process not only clarifies the many schemata operating in schools but also illustrates why presumptions about a unified response to forces for change are almost always premature and oversimplified and how important the dialog between fixity and change is.

What Works

After identifying the forces and events driving the school, it is timely to look at what the field offers schools in terms of research-supported ways to respond to those drivers. This step helps the community to see that there are resources "out there" that can help address the complex array of forces that affect the school. This step also draws the community's attention to things that have a proven track record of success in schools and, as such, are aligned with the Comprehensive School Reform Demonstration Program requirement that a school use research-proven strategies in its models. However, these approaches are not foisted on the school as lockstep solutions; rather, they are presented as contextual knowledge to clarify school values and priorities.

This step provides an opportunity for the school to look outward as well as inward to solutions to its problems. There is a dazzling array of resources available to schools that can be used in this step, including guides to what works in schools (Mid-Continent Research for Education and Learning, 2006; North West Regional Education Laboratory, 2004; U.S. Department of Education, 2005). It is important to anchor the introduction of these ideas within the existing strengths of the school. This includes identifying those who are advocates or possess expertise in particular areas to present innovative practice and attest to its value. Invariably, this step validates existing practice in the school and creates a sense of opportunity regarding what can be done differently and better.

Clearly, "what works" is a contested idea in the field of education, and, as noted in chapter 3, there will be different dialects and perspectives expressed in the selection of the content for the presentation described here. From the perspective of the self-organizing school, this is not a problem. More important is the follow-through that turns whatever practices and approaches the school values into a workable reality in the day-to-day lives of the school, teachers, and students.

Needs and Strengths Revisited

The preceding steps provide a context and an expression of the possibility associated with change. Drivers and new practice are juxtaposed as contextual influences. They are not rushed into position as rationales for comprehensive school reform as a plug-and-play solution. Needs and strengths can be given greater credence by examining them within the broader context of the drivers affecting the school and the resources available to address those drivers. For instance, instead of immediately trying to match the results of a school's perceived needs with specific comprehensive school reform models or to create a sense of urgency about test results, it makes much more sense to look objectively at the needs as they relate to the forces that are driving the school to change. In doing so, the school can look at its strengths in a meaningful context while needs can be expressed in an objective, less-threatening way as desired responses to forces or events influencing the school. Change can be represented less as a pressured reaction to imperatives and much more as an opportunity to grow and develop the school.

For example, when school community members are asked under nonthreatening conditions to describe what works and what is missing, they are invariably "right on the money" about the condition and needs of their schools. The following list is an extract from a needs assessment conducted with a whole faculty, based around two simple questions: "What do we do well?" and "What do we need to do differently?" The list describes some of the needs identified by the faculty:

- In-house sharing of expertise.
- Better match between students and curriculum.
- Identify latest research.
- Provide opportunities for teachers to be researchers.
- Maximize opportunities for student involvement in decision making.
- More collaboration among faculty.
- More peer evaluation and feedback.
- More information on individualizing instruction.

What is especially interesting about the examples is that they reflect an awareness of, and a perceived need for, a very different type of school culture and schema than the highly autonomous one in which the teachers worked at the time. Each of the examples implies a desire to break down the autonomous barriers of "private practice" teaching that was reported by teachers. The teachers identified the need for more professional skills and collaboration and a role for research. These were clearly valued despite the missing system capacity to address them in the school at the time.

Match

After identifying drivers, opportunities, needs, and strengths, it makes sense to build some connections across these areas and steps to help the school build a growing self-awareness about their current context, challenges, and possibilities. The matching-steps process respects the agents in the system by permitting them to make the connections that may result in a different course of action. Members of the community can work in groups at a workshop reconciling those forces, opportunities, and possibilities that can include the potential adoption of a comprehensive school reform design. However, this first involves assessing whether the school can become responsive to its drivers by building on strengths and addressing the needs. Will it do a better job in pursuit of its mission and values? Needs can become much more than a wish list when placed within a context of the school's drivers and current reality.

Task Group Validation

Needs identified in the type of process described here should not be seen as a valid expression of the total reality of the school community. The product of the process so far is an informed and thoughtful brainstorm, although a brainstorm is always a risky foundation for action. A conversation has begun, but it needs to go further.

To this end, a volunteer and representative task group should be established to research the drivers, strengths, and needs and to provide objective support for contentions about such factors as the degree of collaboration in the school, the changing enrollment profile, and the current student performance. The task group employs a methodology derived from the program evaluation literature (e.g., Fitzpatrick, Sanders, & Worthen, 2003), which involves the following:

- Generating questions for each strength, need, and driver
- Establishing criteria for answering those questions
- Identifying data sources for gathering information on the questions
- Analyzing and interpreting the data
- Reporting

This evaluative approach can include the careful use of the comprehensive school reform planning and needs-assessment tools identified earlier in this chapter, although the scope of such use needs to be aligned with the readiness of the school for such an approach.

The role of the task group is to generate a report that articulates the school's current condition with respect to its drivers, strengths, and needs. Using this step, assumptions are turned into data. For example, instead of starting the change conversation with the school's test results, the task group validation may use those test results to answer a bigger question about the needs and drivers facing the school, thus creating a substantial context for change. In conjunction with the workshop product and experience, the report is used to develop those simple statements of value that represent the school's simple rules. In this way, the rules become a positive expression of the school's beliefs and values, as opposed to the reaction to a problem.

It is important that the task group process model a seriousness of purpose about change. It is also important that the voracity of any claim about drivers' needs or strengths respects the opinions expressed at a workshop while establishing support for those opinions. The task group's constitution provides an additional opportunity to disperse control for change and adoption decision making by empowering a broad-based effort among members of the community to establish the current reality. An executive summary of the findings can be shared with the community as a whole, whereas individual members of the task group can process the findings, with smaller groups exploring drivers, needs, and strengths in detail.

SIMPLE RULES

Building simple rules is made much easier when the match between needs, strengths, and drivers is validated by an evaluation of the school's current circumstances. The data generated by the task group report can create a sense of urgency that is capable of turning needs into drivers in ways that no amount of persuasion can accomplish. Needs, strengths, and drivers can be translated into an original statement about the areas that the school believes affect learning. Such a statement will ultimately serve as the foundation of the school's schema. The community is faced with the straightforward question: "Given our driver's strengths and needs in each of the areas voted on as priorities, what do we believe and value about those areas?" Figure 5.1 provides an example of this process.

Notice from the example the way that the needs and drivers can build the foundation for a simple rule. The first box describes the need/strength. The second box describes the driver. The third box poses the task group question, and the fourth box describes the validation of that need/strength as represented in the task group finding.

But how can this finding be turned into a simple rule?

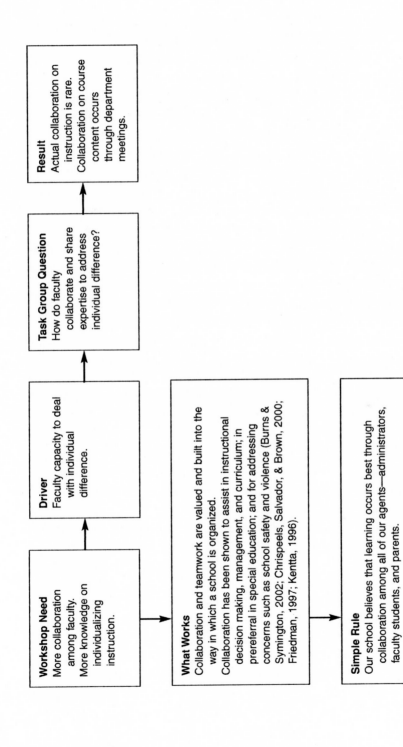

Workshop Need
More collaboration among faculty.
More knowledge on individualizing instruction.

Driver
Faculty capacity to deal with individual difference.

Task Group Question
How do faculty collaborate and share expertise to address individual difference?

Result
Actual collaboration on instruction is rare. Collaboration on course content occurs through department meetings.

What Works
Collaboration and teamwork are valued and built into the way in which a school is organized.
Collaboration has been shown to assist in instructional decision making, management, and curriculum; in prereferral in special education; and for addressing concerns such as school safety and violence (Burns & Symington, 2002; Chrispeels, Salvador, & Brown, 2000; Friedman, 1997; Kentta, 1996).

Simple Rule
Our school believes that learning occurs best through collaboration among all of our agents—administrators, faculty students, and parents.

Figure 5.1. The Trajectory From Workshop to Simple Rule for Collaboration

To do so, the community is asked to propose a simple statement that expresses the belief and value. For example, simple rules such as "Learning is cooperative" or "Decision making is collaborative" readily emerge from the process of matching the results of the validation process with drivers, strengths, and needs from the workshop. Consensus is sought for each statement (although it is not required), and the community makes an initial commitment to a universally held simple rule. Through this process, the statements are imbued with the knowledge of the drivers, needs, and strengths from which they emerged.

Consider a second example, to clarify the process. The needs assessment reveals that faculty members expressed a need for greater peer evaluation and feedback. Assume that the task group also identified feedback as something that occurs only informally and on a sporadic basis. Figure 5.2 describes how this second example plays out.

The first box illustrates that the faculty identified the need for greater feedback, something that was brought into a realistic focus and substantiated by the driver, questions, and results. The need was then substantiated by the task group and the review of what works, which established feedback as a key factor in all learning for students and teachers. The simple rule established feedback as an important priority, in line with the workshop outcomes and the forces driving the school.

The process described in the aforementioned steps is inarguably rational, which begs the question "Why are they not hyperrational with the attendant problems and concerns described earlier in the chapter?" The simple answer is that, under certain circumstances, they definitely can be. If establishing a simple rule became an end in a time-dependent process, as opposed to a means for clarifying the school's values, then the five-step process could result in the same instability and wavering commitment described in the comprehensive school reform literature.

The key distinction here is about what is expected from a needs assessment and, specifically, whether the magnitude of the commitment or the permission to change given by the community is realistic for the scope and nature of the process. The following description of the way that simple rules were developed in the self-organizing school project clarifies this distinction.

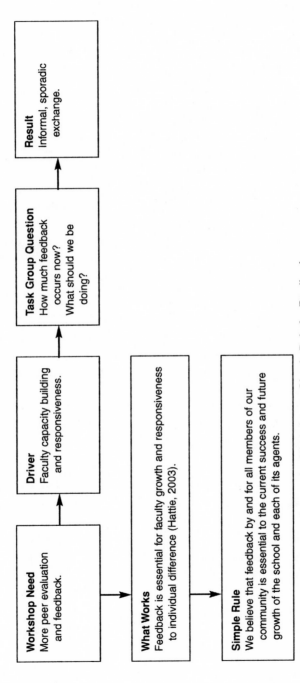

Workshop Need
More peer evaluation and feedback.

Driver
Faculty capacity building and responsiveness.

Task Group Question
How much feedback occurs now? What should we be doing?

Result
Informal, sporadic exchange.

What Works
Feedback is essential for faculty growth and responsiveness to individual difference (Hattie, 2003).

Simple Rule
We believe that feedback by and for all members of our community is essential to the current success and future growth of the school and each of its agents.

Figure 5.2. The Trajectory Connecting Workshop to Simple Rule for Feedback

SIMPLE RULES AND THE SELF-ORGANIZING SCHOOL PROJECT

The process of building simple rules for the self-organizing school project began at an end-of-year workshop in June 1992 and can be viewed as the starting point for the design/pilot phase of the self-organizing school project (described in chapter 1). The workshop involved an initial presentation by the school principal, in which he described the drivers that he perceived the school to be facing at the time. This activity was followed by a breakout activity that enabled the faculty to identify its drivers. The community voted on the list of drivers that emerged from the presentation, and the breakout process identified those drivers of greatest priority. They included a changing enrollment profile, the role of technology in the school, student and faculty retention, and facilities. The list is not unlike those identified in Figure 5.1. Note that those drivers came from a workshop conducted at another school (Bain, 2000).

The workshop also provided the context for a presentation about what works, the second of the five steps. The presentation drew on a number of sources available at the time—including Edmonds (1979), Rutter et al. (1979), and Fraser et al. (1987)—and yielded a list of characteristics and practices of effective schools. Examples from the list included the role of collaboration and effective instructional practices, maximizing learning opportunities and feedback, a commitment to diversity, and valid and authentic assessment.

The presentation did not seek to identify deficits, nor was it an admonition to the community about what it should do. Rather, it showed the group what tools and strategies were available "out there" to address the needs and drivers that the school faced. As such, it was an expression of the possibility that existed for the school, as represented in the professional knowledge of the field.

The effect of the presentation was to inject a practical perspective to the workshop program by illustrating the relationship between what is known about successful schools from "outside" and the school's drivers, many of which were seen to be from "inside" and much closer to home. As a result of juxtaposing the drivers with the "what works" presentation, the scope of the input was broadened when the members of the community were asked to respond to strengths and needs. As the program unfolded, it became clear that the working groups were informing their input with reference to the "what works" characteristics and practices. This was especially evident in relation to collaborative approaches to collegial activity and cooperative classroom practice.

After considering the input, the community worked in small groups to identify strengths and needs. Strengths were identified first, in a way that was uplifting to the group as a whole. The groups recognized what the school did well, and they acknowledged the fact that the community embodied many of the characteristics of an effective school.

As before, the work of all groups was shared and then validated using a voting process. Each member of the community was given a discrete number of votes and asked to use the voting process to prioritize the list of strengths. This approach provided additional validation beyond the face validity of the work of the groups, and it allowed the community to reflect deeply on their beliefs and values. The process was repeated to identify and validate needs.

With a base of consensus in place about drivers, strengths, and needs, the latter sessions of the workshop involved matching strengths, needs, and drivers using the process described in the previous section of this chapter. No attempt was made to go further without a broader validation of the content generated at the workshop. The community demonstrated a strong sense of commitment to the process and product of the day. However, the potential instability in attitudes and beliefs about change in schools suggested a cautious approach and a need for further validation of the workshop product before developing a set of simple rules.

A volunteer task group with broad-based membership that included teachers from different faculty groups and the school's leadership was established to validate the outcomes of the end-of-year workshop. The group committed to spend some time during the summer of 1992 to develop a picture of the school's circumstances with respect to drivers, strengths, and needs, using the evaluation process described earlier in the chapter. The work of the task group resulted in a report that became the subject of an opening of school workshop in September 1992. Their findings became the final step in the process of using drivers, research, needs, and strengths to identify simple rules.

At the September 1992 workshop, the executive summary of the report was presented to the school, and each task group member worked
with a small group of faculty members to process the report in detail.
In the afternoon session of the workshop, the results of the report were
used to extend the matching process undertaken in the June workshop
and to identify a set of statements that captured the commitment of the
school's moving forward, its simple rules. Statements were identified
for the role of

- Cooperation, collaboration, and teamwork
- Learning and continuous improvement
- Mastery of research-based practice at all levels
- Professional development
- Technology
- Differentiated learning
- Authentic assessment and evaluation at all levels

PERMISSION AT SCALE

The introduction to this chapter focuses on whether the information-
sharing process associated with comprehensive school reform is sufficient in form and methodology to result in a stable and enlightened
adoption decision. When the process is inadequate, there is a clear risk
of overreaching, trying to move a community too far, too fast, toward
an artificial consensus. In the case of the self-organizing school project,
the needs-assessment process was an attempt to give the community
the chance to reflect expansively about its circumstances while acting
in a much smaller and more measured way.

The process described here provided the school with an opportunity
to engage in the reflection and self-understanding required to make a
school- and community-level decision about simple rules. However,
that decision was not viewed as a universal commitment to those rules,
a comprehensive school reform model, or a site-based effort. Commitment at scale is an emergent phenomenon that builds over time as individuals and groups develop a deep engagement and understanding.

The result of treating commitment as an emergent phenomenon in the
self-organizing school project was a smaller school-level decision, a

commitment to a next step. That step turned out to be gaining the community's permission to use the simple rules to frame a yearlong design process that would most likely result in a pilot of that design effort.

A reflective and enlightened needs-assessment process can be energizing and highly productive for a school community. However, there is no reason to assume that there would be any greater commitment to a set of simple rules after undertaking this approach than there would be for a comprehensive school reform subsequent to the kind of needs-assessment process advocated in the reform literature. Getting to a consensus point during a workshop does not mean that all members of the community are necessarily "on board" or have bought in to rules, needs, strengths, or drivers.

At the beginning of any process that considers major change, there will be those who believe that simple rules represent an immediate and wholehearted expression of their current beliefs, those who are ambivalent, those who impersonate whatever is produced without a sense of commitment, and those who actively resist any change to the status quo. These responses are normal and well established in change processes and are a product of the awareness raising and reflection that ultimately yield an informed decision about comprehensive school reform or any change.

Over time, the most significant outcome of any attempt to assess school-level needs and values may be the way that the process occurred. Instead of a needs-assessment process that assumes a time-dependent homogenous view as an end product, a more realistic goal may be to simply invite a community into a conversation about change.

In the self-organizing school project, the workshops that generated the school's simple rules served two major purposes. First, the process modeled dispersed control by engaging the whole of the community in a bottom-up process of reflection and future thinking. There was no expectation that this would position individual members of the community to vote, adopt a model, or commit to a major change in their professional lives. Second, the process sought permission for a design year followed by a pilot. The latter was seen as a prerequisite for any schoolwide decision making that may have a sweeping influence on teachers' professional lives. Members of the community needed to experience the change "on their turf" to make an informed decision about participation.

The design year offered a way to demonstrate how a school can be configured to reflect those rules. The pilot program showed what that design would look like in practice, giving teachers the opportunity to see the potential impact on their professional lives while providing early adopters with an opportunity to sign on straight away after the design year. To this end, the simple rules became a powerful force in the lives of those early adopters who pioneered a new school design and schema, as represented in the pilot implementation. The pilot team experience is described in detail in chapters 6 and 7. However, the engagement of the whole school with those rules, design, and schema was iterative as the experience of the pilot process unfolded and generated new learning about the way that the rules were expressed in practice.

The experience of the self-organizing school project suggests that a measured approach is likely to result in engagement that has a sustainable quality. The next-generation design target of effective adoption is about a measured iterative process of knowledge and schema building.

USING THE SIMPLE RULES

Although the simple rules were only a starting point for a design process, they represent a powerful term of reference for making meaning of comprehensive school reform and evaluating existing models. A school that has built its initial simple rules can use those rules to investigate the content and adoption process of any existing comprehensive school reform model by probing the extent to which its design reflects the school's preliminary attempt to identify its beliefs and values. This can help a school further its understanding of its rules and the reform. For example, for a school that has developed rules in those areas described in this chapter, the following questions could be asked:

Feedback: How does feedback work in this comprehensive school reform? How is it gathered and shared? When does feedback happen? How is it employed?

Collaboration: What role does collaboration play in the design? What form does it take?

Professional development: What kind of professional development is necessary to implement this model? How is the professional development model connected to the way that feedback works and to the roles of community members?

Technology: How is technology deployed in this comprehensive school reform? How does it serve the way that feedback works, the roles, the rules, and the organizational support?

These basic questions allow a school that has developed some simple rules to explore the meaning and implications of those rules for practice. For example, feedback and technology have not been strong features of existing designs, and the scope of many models does not extend to organizational support. This knowledge can focus attention on areas that have been problematic in the past and should be addressed in the future. As a school expresses its priorities through these questions, it adds meaning to its rules as each comprehensive school reform shows its capacity in relation to those simple rules. The existence of those roles makes possible the dialog about the needs of the school and the prospects offered by change.

Existing comprehensive school reform models may not be able to answer all of these questions to the satisfaction of a school. However, there is much to be gained by asking the questions because the answers may help a school evaluate the risk potential of a design in its current condition and help it understand whether a comprehensive school reform is aligned with a given school's needs, drivers, and simple rules.

The process described here applies equally to a site-developed effort such as the self-organizing school project. In asking the question of existing comprehensive school reforms, a school can clarify what it believes is necessary to craft a design that addresses its values and beliefs as expressed in those simple rules. In doing so, it can reconcile its vision of content with the change process required to make the vision a reality.

CONCLUSION

This process of developing simple rules is the beginning point for reconciling the many individual teachers' schemata in a school community around a common set of ideas about professional practice. As noted throughout the chapter, this is a dialog about fixity and the nature and substance of change. Such a dialog represents the beginning of a school's journey toward becoming responsive to teachers and learners by focusing on what the school believes and values.

The process models a commitment to dispersed control by inviting a community to engage in its first act of self-organization. In this way, the principle reconciles content and process. It respects the views of a broad range of stakeholders and promotes the potential for a new way of thinking about collective capacity. In the absence of such a process, a vote on comprehensive school reform adoption cannot be assumed to reflect a stable commitment, a phenomenon that is aptly reflected in the comprehensive school reform literature.

As noted earlier, overreaching is risky in school change, even when a community receives an approach positively. There is a big difference between reflecting on the past or developing future prospects and expecting every member of a community to take on board the scope of change implied by a comprehensive school reform model. The application of the simple rule principle begins the process of reconciling content and process in a site-based reform; it frames the content of a reform within an inclusive and participatory implementation approach.

Chapters 6 and 7 show the way that the simple rules are catalyzed into action through the design process. Chapter 10 shares the longitudinal evidence in support of the outcomes that can be expected from the application of simple rules and the other principles of self-organization.

CHAPTER TAKEAWAYS

1. The research on comprehensive school reform implementation and school reform in general suggests that change processes in schools do not follow a rational order. Although a process may have steps, this does not mean that they will be followed in some orderly fashion.
2. Research on the nature of professional practice should inform any needs-assessment process that seeks to build cultures of professional practice.

3. The most important need faced by schools engaging in comprehensive school reform is to identify their core values, their simple rules. This is the first need to be assessed.

4. Building simple rules disperses control to the school community and represents the school's first act of self-organization and the foundation for engagement with comprehensive school reform.

5. Simple rules are a product of the school's needs, strengths, and drivers.

6. A needs-assessment process provides a school community with an opportunity to reflect expansively while acting in a much smaller, measured, and more circumspect way.

7. Scale is a measured and emergent accomplishment in a change process.

8. Applying the simple-rule principle is a first step toward reconciling the content and process of a site-based comprehensive school reform.

CHAPTER 6

Embedded Design

As soon as man gives a thing a name he ceases to see the thing, he only sees the name he gave it.—Miguel de Unamuno

From the theoretical perspective described in chapter 3, a school or comprehensive school reform model is expressed in the way that the principles of self-organization are employed to create a schema. The third of the six principles of self-organization, embedded design, provides the method required to create a school or comprehensive school reform schema.

Applying the embedded design principle means employing the school's simple rules, described in the last chapter, to articulate what research-based teaching and learning means in the classroom. This involves ensuring that the key features and content of the design are embedded in all of its parts. Further, it means embedding those design parts into each other in ways that translate the intention and naming associated with the school's simple rules into a structure or design for action.

This chapter unpacks the description of the embedded design principle, with a focus on the next-generation design target of being comprehensive. The chapter also explains how embedded design was applied in the self-organizing school project.

Developers can use the example to reflect on the comprehensiveness of their designs. In doing so, they can reconcile this key design principle with the specifications of their own models and those required for next-generation comprehensive school reform. For site developers, the chapter expresses the idea of embedded design through examples of the way that a school's specific comprehensive school reform design features are developed.

SIX STEPS

The six steps of embedded design are simple yet confronting in their detail. The rationale for the approach is driven by three equally simple yet confronting assumptions. First, the support required to sustain research-based practice in schools has been grossly underestimated. Second, if innovation of any kind is to scale beyond the classroom, it must become deeply embedded in the organizational fabric of the school. Third, when the time and energy associated with accomplishing the first and second assumptions are given serious and genuine consideration, the futility of engaging with thinly implemented innovation becomes self-evident. The rationale and evidence presented in chapters 1 and 2 provide extensive support for these strong claims, including the danger alluded to by the quote that opens this chapter. It is easy to give an innovation a name and say that it is happening, without attending to whether the name represents something deep and resonant in the total life of a school.

The six steps in the embedded design process are as follows:

Step 1—Vision building: Translating the big ideas and simple rules from the needs assessment into a vision of classroom practice.

Step 2—Articulating the simple rules: Establishing those teaching and learning approaches that best express the vision and simple rules in practice.

Step 3—Defining roles and trajectory: Embedding the teaching and learning approaches into the roles of agents in the school and into the growth trajectory of those agents.

Step 4—Identifying feedback sources: Establishing the way that feedback will be delivered about the teaching and learning approaches employed in the school.

Step 5—Designing tools: Designing the technological tools required to support the teaching and learning approaches.

Step 6—Designing professional development: Designing a professional development or capacity-building program that connects Steps 1–5.

Embedded design is a forward-mapping process that transforms the school's needs assessment and simple rules into a school design using the six steps.

AN EXAMPLE: COOPERATIVE LEARNING

What follows is an example of the approach applied to the simple rule "Student learning is cooperative and collaborative," described in chapter 4. The area of cooperation is pertinent for a number of reasons beyond its importance to the self-organizing school project.

Cooperative learning has received extensive research validation as a teaching approach, making it a useful expression of the proven research and strategies requirement of the Comprehensive School Reform Demonstration Program (Slavin, 1991; U.S. Department of Education, 2002). It is also recommended as a curriculum component in a number of existing comprehensive school reform models, including Success for All Foundation (2006), Co-nect (2006), and Modern Red Schoolhouse (Herman et al., 1999). The example shows how a simple rule drives the articulation of role, trajectory, feedback, professional development, and the deployment of technology, and it also shows how these design elements are embedded in each other.

Vision Building

Senge (1990) notes that a shared vision is a force that fosters risk taking and experimentation and encourages the organization to learn. In the self-organizing school, vision building involves turning the product of the needs assessment into a holographic vision of classroom practice. For example, a community can ask, "What would a classroom look like if we applied our simple rules?" More specifically, in the present example, it can ask, "What would cooperation look like in that classroom?"

In answering these questions, a school can begin to move its conversation about change, from theory into practice. This includes an exploration of what instruction might look like, to respond to the cooperation rule, to how technology might be used in cooperative learning, to the way that cooperative learning affects the role of the teacher, and how that vision differs from the current reality. Answering the questions in a workshop format provides the whole community with an opportunity to explore the possibilities afforded by the rule as it relates to classroom learning.

Vision building also addresses the problem identified by Leonard and Leonard (2001), whose research illustrated the gap between the way that schools express a commitment to the idea of practice and the articulation of what that idea means in the day-to-day life of the school. In the case of the self-organizing school, this gap bridging means giving form to the drivers, needs, and strengths that have been validated in the needs-assessment process and applying them to the core activity of the school—teaching and learning. Thus, visioning the simple rules in classroom practice represents the community's first step in translating its needs assessment into a schema for teaching and learning at the school level.

Articulating the Simple Rule

Vision building about cooperative learning or any part of a comprehensive school reform design can identify the way that students work together, the way that a classroom may function, and what a teacher may do. However, the term *cooperative learning* is used to describe anything from unstructured and much less successful group work to a highly effective structured and widely researched pedagogy. The simple rule "Learning is cooperative," like the term *vision building*, does not make a distinction between these interpretations, although the community can ask, "What do we need to learn or do to make the vision a reality?" For example, if a design is to capture the educational power of cooperative learning and incorporate such an approach into its schema, the rule needs to be articulated by identifying research-based cooperative learning approaches to express its role in practice. What are those approaches?

In the self-organizing school project, a review of the cooperative learning literature identified the student team learning approach (Slavin et al., 1994), which was selected for use in the school from those cooperative learning methods with the greatest educational power. Student team learning includes a number of well-researched approaches, including STAD, Jigsaw II, and Teams Games Tournaments (Slavin et al., 1994). Each incorporates the principles of task structure, individual accountability, group reward, and mutual interdependence, all well-established drivers of student achievement effects (Slavin, 1991). The three approaches also provide clear implementation guidelines for teachers, as well as sample curriculum materials. In the case of the self-organizing school project, these features of student team learning articulated the school's simple rule and added research-supported detail and depth to the vision of cooperative learning in classroom practice.

Articulation is a critical step in the broader self-organizing school design process because it represents the occasion where research-based practice is formally injected into the design. In many ways, the quality and scope of innovation and the educational power of any existing comprehensive school reform rest on this step because it defines all others. It is also the starting point for building the framework for action that assists each teacher to personalize his or her interaction with new practice.

Roles

In the self-organizing school project, student team learning clarifies the design of instruction, the teaching approach, the way that instruction is evaluated, and the roles of students, making it possible to define the teacher's role when using cooperative learning. Figure 6.1 describes an excerpt from a teaching position description related to cooperative learning:

Learning
Demonstrates excellence in the design and delivery of cooperative learning through its research-based characteristics.
Ensures that students demonstrate their roles and responsibilities as cooperative learners.
Can manage the cooperative learning classroom.
Can use the school's learning tools to implement cooperative learning lessons.
Can reflect upon and provide feedback to others related to the research-based attributes of cooperative learning.

Figure 6.1. Excerpt From a Teaching Position Description (adapted from Bain, 1996)

This statement about cooperative learning "actions" what the simple rule means. The first three points address the implementation of the pedagogy, whereas the last two illustrate how the role definition extends beyond what a teacher needs to know and do about cooperative learning in the classroom, including the use of technology and the way that feedback is shared. This excerpt shows how two additional elements of the design (feedback and technology) are embedded into another (role). Clear role definition requires thinking through what an innovation really means, understanding the full scope of associated demands, and trying to realistically address what the design means for teachers day-to-day.

Figure 6.1 illustrates the way that role is defined, based on the articulation of vision and the simple rule. Taking this step precludes the amorphous reference to "best" or "effective" practice that is common in teachers' role or position descriptions. When left in such an ambiguous form, such descriptions are impossible to support and provide only limited opportunities for feedback. In the contested world of educational theory and practice, such a reference has little meaning and may be more likely to cause conjecture and conflict than to provide direction (e.g., Furtwengler, 1995; Murnane & Cohen, 1986). In the example described here, the role definition includes the way that cooperative learning is reflected in the use of technology, as well as the broader role of feedback within the school. In an embedded design, using any new practice means using the totality of a design.

Trajectory

Building capacity with cooperative learning or any other pedagogy extends beyond the immediate "how to do it." It takes years of engagement with cooperative learning to become expert in its use (Jacob, 1999; Putnam, 1998). If a comprehensive school reform is to be realistically connected to the professional lives of teachers, the time frame and the nature of growth need to be recognized in the way that roles change and develop over time. Like the overall process of change, building professional capacity is, in part, an iterative dialog that occurs over time in nonlinear ways. Failure to recognize and understand this process is to invite an overly simplistic interpretation of what it means

Early Career Level

Demonstrates excellence in the implementation of cooperative learning and its research-based characteristics.

Ensures that students demonstrate an accurate understanding of their roles and responsibilities as cooperative learners.

Can use the school's learning tools to implement cooperative learning lessons.

Can reflect upon and provide feedback to others related to the delivery of the research-based attributes of cooperative learning.

Midcareer Level

Demonstrates excellence in the design and implementation of cooperative learning lessons and their research-based characteristics.

Ensures that students demonstrate an accurate understanding of their roles and responsibilities as cooperative learners.

Can use the school's learning tools to implement and design cooperative learning lessons.

Can reflect upon and provide feedback to others related to the design and delivery of the research-based attributes of cooperative learning.

Advanced Career Level

Demonstrates excellence in the development of curriculum incorporating cooperative learning and its implementation.

Can design processes that ensure students have an understanding of their roles and responsibilities as cooperative learners.

Can develop the school's learning tools to implement and design cooperative learning lessons.

Can design the processes by which the community reflects upon and provide feedback to others related to the design and delivery of cooperative learning.

Can teach cooperative learning in the school's professional development program.

Figure 6.2. Example of Cooperative Learning Career Trajectory (adapted from Bain, 1996)

to adopt new practice. This may lead to a breakdown in implementation as teachers encounter inadequate support and recognition. It also explains why "front-loaded" professional development in school reform frequently fades over time, when the ongoing support required to build capacity is unavailable.

Figure 6.2 describes how expertise with cooperative learning can be represented in the growth requirements for teachers at different levels in a career path. It describes the progress from an early career competence to a mastery level of competence with cooperative learning. Teachers advance from a role that focuses on implementation to one that becomes focused on cooperative learning design and development.

The career path creates an explicit trajectory for self-organization by creating the conditions for the schema to evolve, as the capacity of the agents in the system grows. For example, a teacher who has progressed to an advanced level in the career path (described in Figure 6.2) can be expected to generate the kind of solutions to the cooperative learning problems described in chapter 4 (i.e., new database and self-monitoring tools). The career path indicates a clear expectation that cooperative learning will change over time, adapting to the changing circumstances of the school and the capacity of the agents. There are no fixed ideas about the model and the school or the year-in, year-out use of the same curriculum materials. Change and adaptation are expected.

Feedback

The capacity of individual teachers to progress along this career path depends on feedback. Feedback drives the growth of the system through the growth of its agents. In the present example, feedback generates the professional growth that a teacher requires to progress from cooperative learning implementer to cooperative learning curriculum developer and, ultimately, to reform designer.

How does the school or comprehensive school reform enable feedback and formal recognition of the use of cooperative learning to occur? The simple answer is to embed the appropriate tools in the feedback system. Figure 6.3 describes one tool that has been used to share feedback about cooperative learning. This tool has been used for classroom observation and reflection, and it is part of a suite of software that was developed for the self-organizing school project. It uses technology to make it easier to gather, manage, and report feedback in a timely manner (Bain, 2005). The design and development of the feedback tool and other software in the self-organizing school project is discussed in detail in chapters 8 and 9.

Individual teachers, teaching peers, and supervisors use this tool to conduct classroom observations, reflect on the use of cooperative learning, and share perspectives. The tool is designed to focus users on whether the key characteristics of cooperative learning are present in classroom practice. Items in the tool consider individual accounta-

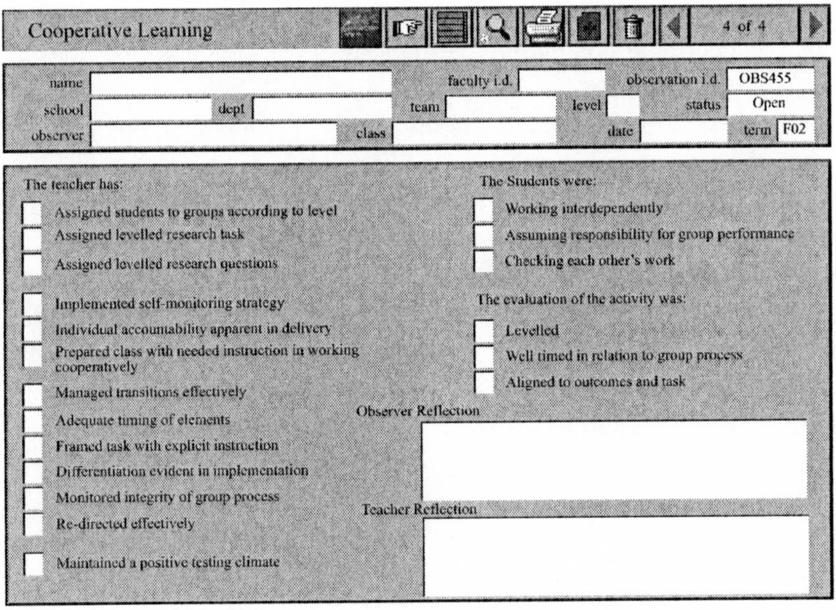

| Cooperative Learning | | | | | | | | | 4 of 4 |

name				faculty i.d.			observation i.d.	OBS455
school		dept		team		level		status	Open
observer			class			date		term	F02

The teacher has:

- [ ] Assigned students to groups according to level
- [ ] Assigned levelled research task
- [ ] Assigned levelled research questions

- [ ] Implemented self-monitoring strategy
- [ ] Individual accountability apparent in delivery
- [ ] Prepared class with needed instruction in working cooperatively
- [ ] Managed transitions effectively
- [ ] Adequate timing of elements
- [ ] Framed task with explicit instruction
- [ ] Differentiation evident in implementation
- [ ] Monitored integrity of group process
- [ ] Re-directed effectively
- [ ] Maintained a positive testing climate

The Students were:

- [ ] Working interdependently
- [ ] Assuming responsibility for group performance
- [ ] Checking each other's work

The evaluation of the activity was:

- [ ] Levelled
- [ ] Well timed in relation to group process
- [ ] Aligned to outcomes and task

Observer Reflection

Teacher Reflection

Figure 6.3.   Feedback Tool for Cooperative Learning

bility, the self-monitoring strategy described in chapter 4, and classroom processes that relate not only to the structure of the task but also to the nature and quality of student interactions. These items reflect the way in which cooperative learning is embedded in the feedback approach.

The items also address a number of important management issues identified by Jacob (1999) that relate to making cooperative learning work in the classroom (e.g., quality of student interaction, redirection, and instructional differentiation). Individual teachers can use this tool to develop reflections as well as receive objective and qualitative narrative feedback from peers who observe their classes. The fields on the bottom right of the layout are used for this purpose. Examples of the narrative are shared in chapter 10.

Designing Tools

The feedback tool describes how technology can serve as an accelerator by providing timely, response-contingent, and constructive feedback

(Brophy & Good, 1986) in ways that would be immensely difficult without it. The whole community can use software tools like the one described in Figure 6.3. Data gathered using the tool are immediately made available to all who participate in the exchange. Individual observations can be compared and contrasted. An interaction between the power of a relational database and the embedded design principle can gather, retrieve, and represent the knowledge of the school in time-efficient and flexible ways. Figure 6.4 describes a second example of the role of technology in the form of a cooperative learning lesson-planning and implementation tool.

Teachers plan, organize, and deliver cooperative learning lessons using the lesson design tool, which reinforces the same research-based characteristics that are embedded in the feedback tool. Both tools articulate what the tenets of the teacher's role actually mean. They embed the day-to-day transactions of cooperative learning in technology tools that can make "doing the design" easier for teachers, students, and administrators.

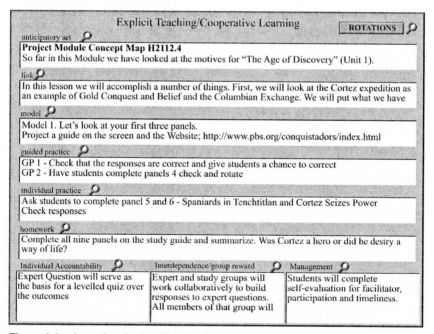

Figure 6.4.   Learning Design Tool for Cooperative Learning

Professional Development

Professional development is invariably what we think of first when considering the implementation of an innovation. How many times have we heard the admonition "We really need some professional development in this area," when something new appears on a school's radar? However, professional development is the last element in this example because capacity building is embedded in a self-organizing school. This means that all the skills required at different levels in the career trajectory (e.g., technology, feedback, teaching) required to fulfill that role become an integrated part of the professional development program.

Figure 6.5 shows an excerpt from the self-organizing school project professional development institute that incorporated embedded design in this way. In this example, the research characteristics and how-to's of research-supported cooperative learning practice are taught through the software tools (i.e., curriculum authoring tools). Thus, teachers are introduced to cooperative learning as they build curriculum and lessons in the tools (Bain, 1997; Bain & Huss, 2000).

In the self-organizing school approach, professional development represents a last step in the design process and a first step in implementation because it must capture the holographic nature of the design, as opposed to a jigsawlike training in the parts (Senge, 1990). Professional development is simply the beginning of the capacity- and pattern-language-building process. The role, ongoing feedback, teamwork, and use of technology tools together build capacity with cooperative learning. It is important to note that the example shared

---

Course Description
This course identifies the essential characteristics of a successful cooperative learning approach and teaches you how to employ those characteristics to create successful cooperative learning lessons in the Curriculum Authoring Tools (CATs) software. In order to successfully complete the course you will be required to demonstrate that you can successfully build a Jigsaw II Lesson in the CATs software and that you can apply all the essential components of a cooperative learning activity. Members of the group will describe their lessons to the class.

Figure 6.5. Sample Course Description From Self-Organizing School Project Training (from the 2003 summer institute schedule)

here shows how embedded design is applied to just one teaching approach. In the self-organizing school project, this approach is used to embed multiple innovations and connect them in a total curriculum and teaching model.

IMPLICATIONS

The cooperative learning example has four major implications related to the application of the embedded design principle and the broader theory of the self-organizing school. First, the embedding of key features of the design into all parts—and then all parts into each other—increases the likelihood that a design is complete, averting the problems of missing elements described in the comprehensive school reform implementation literature (e.g., Bodilly, 1996; Datnow et al., 2000). The rule; the teacher's role; and the trajectory, feedback, and technology tools are all reconciled to reduce the ambiguity in expectation about what constitutes cooperative learning practice and to produce the consistency and regularity necessary for a schema to develop. These embedded features also provide the support necessary for adopting change and to address the risks and challenges inherent in doing things in new and different ways.

For example, the professional development approach described here employs the school's technology tools. The learning that is gained from using one tool (e.g., the lesson design tool described in Figure 6.4) is reinforced by any training in the use of the feedback tool (Figure 6.3). As the teacher progresses in the career trajectory, new expectations for cooperative learning are developed. Teams meet and solve cooperative learning problems. Team members listen to one another, and the team learns from the collective intelligence that arises from the interaction. Team members use the feedback tools to exchange perspectives. Cooperative learning exists in all aspects of the design, and all aspects of the design are included in each other. The use of one part of the design reinforces another, thus creating the regularity required to make cooperative learning part of the schema.

Second, this interactive and continuous learning generates the self-reinforcing quality described in chapter 1. The embedding makes clear the connection between action and outcome in the teaching and learning process and the value assigned to those connections. The likelihood of sustainability increases because capacity building occurs all the time and is not solely reliant on professional development. In doing so, the approach addresses the known points of breakdown in comprehensive school reform implementation described in chapter 2 and the long-standing challenge of adequately supporting change in schools.

Those points of breakdown include the lack of feedback (Berends et al., 2002), the validity of implementation integrity evidence (Appelbaum & Schwartzbeck, 2002), and the alignment of a comprehensive school reform with the totality of the professional lives of teachers (Datnow, 2003a; Faddis et al., 2000; Franceschini, 2002; Hodge, 2003). Evidence in support of the assertions about embedded design is provided in chapter 10, where the results of the self-organizing school project are described.

Third, the embedded design process emerges from the needs assessment and the simple rules and thus expresses the school's position, turning what it believes into action. The design represents the school's articulation of its beliefs.

Fourth, the application of the embedded design principle is continuous and dynamic. It responds to the self-organization it creates. The new software and self-monitoring tools described in Case 1 of chapter 4 provide a useful illustration of this point. Those self-organized innovations changed cooperative learning from its original form as described in the student team learning materials. The changes emerged bottom-up and were then embedded using the same process described in this chapter.

That process is continuous in a self-organizing school. Embedded design is not a "one-off" to get a design implemented. There is no absolute endpoint in a reform, in terms of adoption or implementation integrity, because there is no absolute or static set of needs and conditions in a dynamic system like a school. An equilibrium condition cannot exist for cooperative learning, any other part of the design, or the school.

SELF-ORGANIZING SCHOOL PROJECT DESIGN, 1992–1993

This section describes the design and pilot year of the self-organizing school project, with a focus on the application of the embedded design principle. The account is deconstructed using the six principles of the self-organizing school as a framework.

Visioning

The embedded design process in the self-organizing school project started early in the first semester of the 1992–1993 school year with a vision-building workshop that began the process of articulating the simple rules. The presentation focused on representing three key concepts to the community as a stimulus for vision building: the nature of the differentiated classroom, the process of differentiation (which permitted the exploration of the simple rules, mastery, authentic assessment, cooperation, and technology), and collaboration and teamwork. The collaboration and teamwork components of the presentation addressed the role of teaching teams in the school and the nature of professional development and feedback.

The faculty members were asked to visualize students working in groups and with differentiated expectations, to focus on the role of the teacher and technology in the process, and to consider the layout of the classroom and how a lesson that they were visualizing was developed. They reflected on the way that they would work together, the kind of feedback that they wanted to receive, and the way that teams would function. Finally, the teachers considered what kind of growth experiences would be necessary to realize the vision.

The process drew heavily on both the content of the needs assessment report and the workshop product described in the last chapter, including what individuals said about collaboration, classroom learning, and technology. After the presentation, the teachers worked in groups to develop a vision. This made it possible for the vision to be expanded and tested from multiple perspectives. The following is an example of the kind of picture that emerged from the visioning process, as applied to a Spanish-language class.

The students are gathered into three groups as the teacher circulates around the room traveling from one group to another. She stops at a cluster of Spanish 3 students to listen as each member of the group recites a dialog for her evaluation. A second group of three sits around their desks, which are drawn into a circle around a computer. They are focused intently on a website where they are researching for a cooperative learning project. When the teacher approaches them, they explain that one of the students has prepared a PowerPoint presentation to teach his peers the forms of the present-progressive tense. The other two students have received the PowerPoint through e-mail, have downloaded it, and are working their way through the practice program. As they work through the program, they refer to the PowerPoint's author for confirmation of their answers. Another group of students is sitting toward the front of the room working on a CD-ROM program they have accessed from the CD tower located in the library. They are working through a lesson on formal commands, and, as each student finishes a set of sentences, he or she copies his or her final score with a special key on his computer and mails it to the teacher for review and feedback.

The teacher finishes listening to the recitations and continues to move around from group to group quizzing, interacting, encouraging, and answering questions in Spanish. The classroom functions smoothly as the students move through their groups' activities. Three different levels of Spanish are being taught, each with its own program, each keyed to the ability level of the student.

The visioning process as described in the example reflected the community's view of the simple rules in practice. This included a different and more facilitative role for the teacher, greater student cooperation and collaboration, a substantive emphasis on technology, and the existence of a multilevel curriculum taught in a classroom that was responsive to those different levels. It also implied a curriculum that was differentiated in content, teaching, and learning process as well as product (Tomlinson, 2001).

Vision building engendered many reactions, including expressions of fear, trepidation, and excitement. There were many questions as people began to think more practically about the way that the rules might guide teaching and learning in the school. As was the case with the needs assessment, the process was not driven by a perceived need for a hasty consensus about a vision. Instead, it was positioned as the first participatory act of design in an ongoing process. *Visioning* provided the term of reference required to search for well-researched teaching and learning approaches that respond to the kind of scenario described here and the school's simple rules. However, they were applied to only a pilot program.

Articulation

In conjunction with the results of the needs-assessment process, the vision building helped the community recognize the need to articulate the vision in practice. Practices were selected and then shared with management and the community in a series of demonstrations and workshops. The school's existing committee structures were used as dissemination and feedback vehicles. The existing management group, the department head's group, and full faculty meetings disseminated ideas and monitored progress.

The design process followed the sequence described in the cooperative learning example, progressing from practices to roles and from trajectory to tools and professional development. During the 3 months following the vision workshop, the school built a body of practice that reflected the rules and vision to include the following:

- Explicit teaching (Rosenshine, 1986)
- Collaborative problem solving (West, Idol, & Cannon, 1989)
- Cooperative learning (Slavin, 1991)
- Differentiated curriculum (Bain, 1996)
- Cognitive strategies (Huck, Myers, & Wilson, 1989)
- Peer tutoring (e.g., Greenwood & Delquardi, 1995)[1]

As was the case with the student team learning example, each practice had a defined way of being best used in classrooms. The practices and their research-based characteristics provided the basic elements that were necessary to expand the example of the teacher's role described in Figure 6.1 to a complete position description. Those practices became the basis for the school's differentiated curriculum model. See Bain and Huss (2000) and Bain and Parkes (2006b) for more information on the curriculum model. Although the design articulated what that curriculum should look like, actual curriculum materials were not developed over the course of the design year.

Roles and Trajectory

The second 3 months of the year (December to February) involved applying the forward-mapping process described earlier to develop a career trajectory, design the feedback approaches and technology tools, and frame out the areas for a professional development program.

The first task in this embedding process was to use the role definition to build a career path. The literature on the implementation of comprehensive school reform has frequently identified issues associated with work conditions as potentially confounding adoption and implementation (Little & Bartlett, 2002). However, building the roles and trajectory for the project helped answer the many questions about the potential impact of change on the professional life of the community. People often asked such questions as they emerged from the needs-assessment process.

It was also clear from the literature that human resource issues were not deeply embedded as part of existing comprehensive school reform designs and that the demands of those designs were often superimposed on existing work conditions (e.g., Asenio & Johnson, 2001). This was seen in the self-organizing school project as a critical point of breakdown that needed to be addressed as part of a design process.

After building the core position description and a four-level career path that ranged from graduate to master teacher, each level on the career path was given a timeline and a set of transitional portfolio requirements. This design element set into place the process for engagement with the model, including the way that new and experienced teachers would enter the trajectory. For example, teachers new to the school entered with a 1-year timeline to make their first transition in the career path, which was expected as a probationary step at the entry level. On the other hand, an experienced teacher was afforded 3 years to meet the portfolio requirements at the third level in the career path, although a number of teachers chose to confirm at the fourth, or master teacher, level.

Because the embedding of like features was central to the design process, portfolio requirements became the tenets of the role descriptions that were, in turn, embedded into the feedback tools; all of these elements constituted the focus of the professional development program.

The idea was to create a high level of transparency across role, feedback, and growth, thus creating the regularity and consistency that would create the self-reinforcing conditions required for schema development and the feedback that would eventually result in self-organization.

By reconciling role and trajectory before the development of a pilot, it was possible for the teachers involved to enter the process with a clear understanding of the terms of their engagement. For those who would observe the implementation, it was possible to extrapolate what their future involvement could mean.

Feedback and Tools

The last 3 months of the year focused on three major design tasks: the development of feedback and technology tools, the design of the professional development program, and the engagement of the pilot team. This also followed the process of forward mapping described at the beginning of the chapter. The teaching approaches employed in the pilot provided the content for the feedback tools. For example, the student team learning materials included checks for lesson implementation, as did the peer mediation materials. It was relatively easy to design similar approaches and tools for explicit teaching while classroom engagement was established using existing classroom observation methods (e.g., Shapiro, 1987).

Technology Tools

In the design and initial pilot phase of the program, the application of technology to the creation of lesson design and feedback tools took the form of spreadsheets and word-processing documents. Although the need for more sophisticated tools was recognized during the design year, they did not emerge until later in the project, at the end of the pilot phase, because of time constraints and the prioritizing of other aspects of the design. This put considerable pressure on the pilot phase because feedback was much more ad hoc than desired and there was only limited information available about the implementation process and effects.

The inability to provide these tools at start-up highlighted technology's importance to the design. For example, as more and more teachers became involved with the design, it became exceptionally difficult to manage the feedback and reporting process with spreadsheets and word-processing documents. They were difficult to interrelate and time-consuming to produce. This put the design at risk because feedback became less timely and more summative and certainly unlike the intended constant exchange necessary for self-organization.

SELF-ORGANIZING SCHOOL PROJECT PILOT, 1993–1994

Expressions of interest in the roles of team leader and team members in the pilot program were requested during the second semester of 1992. Descriptions of the positions and the program were shared to recruit a team that would serve the school's ninth grade. All current faculty members were eligible, and every candidate who expressed an interest in the position was offered an interview. The process turned out to be competitive given that there were more applicants than the number of positions available. Although there may have been a perception across the school that there was some value associated with getting involved early in the pilot process, the initial pilot team demonstrated a genuine interest in the simple rules and design. The successful team comprised an experienced team leader with a background in special education, the school's most experienced teacher, one highly experienced teacher, three moderately experienced teachers, and one early-career teacher.

Professional Development

The professional development program was conducted during the summer of 1993. The curriculum covered the core pedagogies, teamwork and collaboration, feedback, and technology. The pilot team received the program enthusiastically, and team members worked together in training sessions, discussing and problem solving as a group. The school's administrative team also attended the training. This was seen as being critical, if the leadership were to be credibly positioned to conduct the pilot program and lead the school that may emerge from the experience. The pilot team members and the school community viewed the presence of the leadership as an expression of commitment to the program. Overall, there was a strong sense that the effort was a collaborative one.

The professional development program also included an opportunity for the team to field-test its work with students who were invited to attend the training for short periods, experience the new forms of teaching, and give feedback. This injected a practical reality check into the training process and gave students a chance to be involved.

Despite its strengths and the benefits expressed in the course evaluations, which gave the program an average "A" rating over all sessions, the professional development program generated some initial signals that more work on the design was needed. For example, it became clear that lessons using cooperative learning and peer tutoring required careful attention, if they were to be implemented according to the guidelines provided by the presenters. They would take more time to develop than the lesson plans that most teachers were used to. There were also implications related to when the technology system would emerge as part the program. The needs assessment had focused on the promise and potential of technology, and although sessions were conducted on the use of a number of productivity software applications, there were no tools developed specifically for the pilot. In some instances, the questions reflected design considerations that had not been addressed.

Although the sessions on the feedback approach focused heavily on the observation of the collaborative process and the use of the pedagogies, there were questions about when observations would happen and what it would mean for teachers and the team. For example, the team members and administrators believed that they lacked the expertise required to give feedback. Everyone involved, including the leadership, had limited experience and expertise with the content and process of the design.

Except for the change agent, presenters in the professional development program came from outside the school. Although they were briefed on the circumstances of the pilot, including the results of the needs assessment and the design, they delivered programs that were largely about their own areas of expertise. The procedural knowledge associated with the core practices predominated, and despite the opportunity for the team members to work together, there remained considerable unfilled "white space" regarding how those practices would fit into the day-to-day reality of the pilot.

Despite the many questions, the pilot team emerged from the professional development with a high level of enthusiasm and positive energy about the year ahead. At this point in the project, there was a strong sense of alignment between the needs assessment, the vision building, and the way that the professional development embodied the vision. From the perspective of the team, the pilot program seemed to be on track in terms of the school's simple rules, needs, and the connection between the vision of a differentiated classroom (described earlier in this chapter) and what the professional development program had prepared the team to do.

Gaps

In reality, and from a change agent's perspective, the pilot year began with a program that tended to be more like a jigsaw than a hologram. Although most of the parts were designed at some level and were embedded "on paper," this was not always the reality in practice. For example, the team model, the pedagogies, the role descriptions, and the framework for the feedback approach were all in place, but how these elements fit together was much less clear.

The design year had produced guidelines and a protocol for curriculum development that described how instruction and assessment would reflect multiple achievement levels, how to employ classroom groups, and how to develop adaptations. These guidelines were assumed to be adequate for the production of curriculum on the fly. This was incorrect. There was an inaccurate view, held by all involved, that realizing the kind of classroom vision described earlier was much more about what a teacher did in "real time" than the product of a highly articulated and differentiated preexisting curriculum. The curriculum guidelines developed for the pilot were more visionary than practical and did not provide teachers with the materials that they needed day in and day out to provide an individualized experience for students. The design effort had given the curriculum a name and a form and then ceased to focus fully on what that naming represented in practice.

A lack of curriculum materials has been identified in the literature as a critical point of breakdown in comprehensive school reform (Bodilly, 1996), although in the self-organizing school project, it was assumed that materials could be developed over the course of the year. In the pilot year, all involved, including the change agent, lacked the experience to understand the full ramifications of a differentiated curriculum.

Without the required resources, teachers were compelled to do much more in the area of curriculum and lesson development than was the case in their prepilot roles and for their peers working in the school's existing model. The effect of this problem was to put undue pressure on the pilot team members and introduce high levels of variance to the implementation. Some teachers took on the immense challenge and worked tirelessly to approximate the expectations described in the guidelines. Others found the task overwhelming and began to engage in a modified version of their original prepilot approach to teaching. The variance in implementation described by Berends et al. (2001) in the analysis of the New American Schools project was beginning to play out in the self-organizing school pilot for many of the same reasons.

Fortunately, for the pilot, this issue did little to diminish the enthusiasm of the team. Its positive disposition was also consistent with the ebullience that characterizes so many start-up efforts, although the lack of curriculum sapped its energy over time. Although the small scale of the pilot made it possible to solve some of the curriculum issues on a contingency basis (e.g., providing some additional time for curriculum development and making adjustments to the time table), most of the big problems required more time and more design than was available.

Feedback Implementation

With team members working so hard on the many unanswered questions, there was an immense amount of feedback in the pilot year. The school had invested heavily in the program and was committed to making the pilot a success. School leaders frequently visited team meetings, and the pilot team had dedicated support. However, the feedback to the team tended to be less about the specifics of the design and implementation of the program and more about the ways to address gaps between the pilot's intent and the day-to-day reality. For example, it was difficult to apply the feedback model to the observation of lessons that were understandably incomplete due to the lack of curriculum. In contrast, the feedback derived from observations of team meetings was much as intended. Here the trajectory from design to training to implementation was far clearer, more complete, and self-reinforcing as a result.

Successes

Despite the difficulties described, the benefits of a team approach and better teaching practices became evident quite early in the pilot year. The teachers overwhelmingly supported the team collaboration that underpinned the design. There was a strong sense of a school-within-a-school that was interpreted by team members as a benefit for students. Team members believed that there was less chance for students to fall through the cracks in terms of their conduct and academic progress. The sense of community was also strong among students, and there was an overall improvement in conduct in and out of class (New England Association of Schools and Colleges, 1996).

Classroom observations, the feedback from team meetings, and informal reflection indicated that the team was making a solid effort to use the body of practice. However, the feedback really only attested to the effort. As noted previously, although emergent feedback was central to the design, it inevitably became a second-level priority in the drive to keep up. In large measure, classroom observations and reflections became a casualty of the time required to build tomorrow's differentiated lesson plan.

The design survived the pilot year, although the effort generated as many questions as it did answers about the program. The team worked diligently in the face of significant challenges, establishing that it was possible to implement a version of the school's new approach. However, the gaps between intention and reality resulted in significant variance in implementation from one team member to another, whereas the issues with curriculum, technology, and feedback produced an incomplete design overall. For example, differentiation existed on an implementation continuum from minimal to full, depending on the class and teacher. The result was an uneven student experience with the overall design. The same can be said about the use of technology. In the absence of the technology tools to power the design, the experience of students also varied greatly from class to class.

It was clear that from the pilot experience that the design could not be sustained if it was possible to do so with only an inordinate extra effort. The initial enthusiasm and energy would ultimately fall back to more sustainable levels, at which time something doable would need to replace something possible.

Unpacking the Pilot

Schema and Simple Rules

From a change agent perspective, the pilot emerged from a measured and inclusive adoption process, based on the school's simple rules. It focused on a relatively small-scale and manageable implementation of a new program for the school that was developed over a year of planning. From the perspective of the pilot team as reported in its evaluation of the professional development program and from feedback generated throughout the year, the design also reflected the simple rules and the broader needs-assessment process. The evaluation of all sessions in the professional development program was positive. Comments included as part of the evaluation feedback included many references to team process—"Looking forward to working on the team" and "The team will help me to learn the model"—as well as an appreciation for the way that the new pedagogies had broadened the team's capacity to differentiate instruction. Yet, those judgments were framed by the type of professional development that the team had experienced in the past. By those standards, the program seemed complete.

Despite the positive reaction, from a change agent perspective, the program bore too much similarity to the front-loaded and nonembedded model of traditional professional development that had been unsuccessful in prior reform efforts. Although, arguably, the self-organizing school project had gone further than most reforms in its needs assessment and design year, it had not gone far enough to realize the high-bar expectations and requirements of embedded design and the other principles of the theory.

The pilot team and leadership seemed prepared for what lay ahead. However, the incomplete nature of the curriculum, exacerbated by the lack of feedback and technology, made the design complex in the most unwieldy sense. There was a void in terms of the actual examples, tools, process, and product for curriculum development, and there was insufficient time to do the work. In terms of theory structure, the design fell into a space between its big ideas and the full complement of systems, instruments, and practices required for a complete theory and full implementation. All the design parts did not function in full self-reinforcing support of each other, because they were incomplete. As a result, the pilot failed to reach the threshold level of simple sophistication required for self-organization to happen in ways that enabled the whole pilot system to self-organize and adapt.

By way of contrast, the teamwork and collaboration dimension of the design seemed to produce a growing capacity with the pattern language of that process. The alignment in the design between the simple rule, the professional preparation, and the demands of practice were similar, and as a result, the pilot team built capacity and a shared level of sophistication in its use of the collaborative problem-solving approach. What was asked of team members (role), the opportunities and time for teams to meet, and the training process each functioned as intended. There was less formal feedback than desired about the pilot team's use of the meeting process. However, the pressing need to have team meetings to address the many issues that existed in the pilot created opportunities for feedback to happen, albeit in less structured ways. The success, more or less, of every meeting provided ongoing feedback about the process and the solutions it generated.

Overall, the schema development in the pilot mirrored the circumstances of the design. The team built capacity with the big picture, its components and elements, but implementing research-based practice at scale requires a detailed implementation that had not emerged from the pilot experience. The design was not sufficiently evolved to engender the regularity and consistency required for simple yet sophisticated schema development.

Embedded Design

As defined earlier in the chapter, embedded design is the key principle required to translate simple rules into practice and to build schema.

It was clear from the pilot design that its rules were not embedded into all of the parts of the design, nor were all those parts embedded into each other at a level required for a doable, self-reinforcing experience. This was partly a result of the lack of the feedback and technology steps described in the account of the pilot. Having an incomplete embedded design process led to an imbalance in the design and to a situation where role descriptions did not align with the reality of practice. In addition, the overall design process underestimated the meaning of curriculum and its scope. This was illustrated by the failure to embed the teaching and learning approaches in an actual curriculum design beyond a set of guidelines. The school's vision for differentiated curriculum, described earlier, required the creation of curriculum materials that would permit teachers to create multilevel classrooms by differentiating the content, process, and product of the curriculum (Tomlinson, 2001).

In practice, this differentiated curriculum was confused with the skills that teachers needed to create it and the somewhat naïve view that curriculum could be built on the fly. Complete curriculum would have pulled the content, process, and product of the design together. A full implementation of the embedded design process would have allowed teachers to properly develop curriculum rather than build it as they went.

By way of contrast, the success of the team process showed the potential of embedded design to generate high-integrity implementation, if a design could become complete. The contrast between incomplete curriculum and more complete collaboration generated an understanding of what was possible in the self-organizing school project and the work that needed to be done to build a complete design.

Feedback and Technology

The intent of the embedded design principle is to create the conditions for self-reinforcement; however, when incomplete, it can engender the discontinuity exhibited in the pilot. The tools and process were not in place to make feedback emergent, and as a result, the relationship between what was happening and its effects was unclear. Feedback was much more reactive and could not focus on the more timely process promised by the principle. Too much had to be done that was unrelated to the detail of the program. As a result, feedback was much more about what happened than what needed to happen next. The one exception to this circumstance was feedback about collaboration. That was more successful because the embedded design process was more complete.

Similarity at Scale and Dispersed Control

The adoption of a team-based model in the pilot made it possible for the school to take a powerful step toward dispersing control. The pilot set the foundation for a leveled network of teams and positioned the team as the key unit of collective intelligence in the school. Although there was still an immense amount of top-down intervention because of the incomplete nature of the design, the pilot stimulated a fundamental shift in both the operation and the psychology of the school, from an organizational perspective.

For example, throughout the pilot year, leadership scurried to provide the resources and solve the problems that would position the team to be the core unit of problem solving in the school. Instead of being the actual problem solvers, the leaders became the resourcers of the process. In large measure, this was consistent with the authentic role that they would play in a complete self-organizing school. In trying to make the design a success, the leadership set the foundation for the dispersed control that would scale up to multiple teams and levels, should the design move beyond the pilot. As such, this new relationship provided an early example of behavior that was indicative of what would happen in a fully functioning self-organizing school.

The success of the design's team dimension made it possible to see similarity at scale in the relationship between the roles of individuals and teams. For example, it became clear that a team-based classroom management plan needed to be a scaled-up version of individual accountability in that domain. This required team members to work together, finding mutual accommodation in their approach to classroom management, to build a common and advantageous team plan. The benefits of a team approach were reflected in the improved student conduct experienced by the team (New England Association of Schools and Colleges, 1996). However, overall, the ongoing need to manage other incomplete aspects of the design limited the opportunities to experience the broader potential for self-similarity.

Risk

Despite a thoughtful design effort and a community adoption process that was generally well received, the pilot year was difficult. The result was the kind of tenuous circumstance described in chapter 2, where the project had survived a year in which the quality of implementation was largely untested in any objective sense. To scale up under these circumstances risked further within-school variance in implementation and the energy sapping effort required to sustain an incomplete design.

From both perspectives, change agent and team member, the pilot generated a clear account of what was missing and what work needed to be done. This awareness was partly the product of the discrepancy between the intent of the design process and its outcomes. Although there was only limited consolation in knowing what was needed for success, such understanding did create the likelihood of a better result further down the road if the design gaps could be addressed. Of course, this was a promise that would need to be realized if the design was to scale successfully. Remarkably, given the stresses that they were under, the pilot team members retained their commitment throughout the year. Their resilience was largely a result of the team's breadth of experience, but even the most experienced team members were suffering some signs of burnout. Counterbalancing the fatigue was a visceral feeling and view that the pilot represented a more successful way for the school to operate. This was expressed to the change agent and leadership repeatedly in downtime, informal conversation that occurred during vacation breaks, when there was an opportunity to reflect. The team felt the responsibility to create what it believed could or would be a healthier school. Whether this was possible remained an unanswered question.

In replicating many of the problems of the existing comprehensive school reform literature, the first-year pilot of the self-organizing school project had succeeded in creating a "warts and all" opportunity for the community to observe change in action. The school's teachers had an opportunity to witness the added time involvement, the changes in roles that resulted from the team approach, the stresses of building curriculum on the fly, and the lack of technology. An incomplete design, limited feedback, and diminished educational power creating a high level of risk in terms of the project's future viability.

SUMMARY

This chapter presents a set of contrasting circumstances that reflect the gap between the intent and frequent reality of site-based comprehensive school reform. In theory, the embedded design principle calls for and ultimately creates a full account of the systems, instruments, and practices associated with a design. Yet, the first attempt at implementing the process in the self-organizing school project fell short, only approximating those characteristics. As a result, the pilot process set in place the tenuous conditions common to so many reform initiatives. The design had gone much further than giving the pilot a name, yet it had not gone far enough to ensure that the name represented something complete. Teachers were overburdened by an incomplete design as the pilot progressed over the course of the year.

The big ideas of team and research-based practice were in place, but the incomplete nature of the design diminished the potential for the regularity, consistency, and self-reinforcing conditions that are required for feedback and self-organizing behavior. It became clear why the usual suspects of time, resources, and professional development, described in chapter 2, were so commonly identified as points in breakdown in the literature on comprehensive school reform and broader school reform (Asenio & Johnson, 2001). The problems were real. If there was no curriculum and no time to develop it, then time was a problem. The design had not evolved to a level where a more sophisticated analysis of these problems was either needed or possible.

Despite the many challenges and reservations, the school remained committed to the big ideas and the way that the intent of the program expressed its simple rules. However, the design list for the summer of 1993 was long, and it required serious attention, if the second year of the project was to be an improvement on the first. The most obvious concern was the risk of an incomplete program getting bigger and more unwieldy as more teams were added. The ability to manage contingency and build on the fly would diminish as the scale increased. The summer of 1994 proved to be a critical period, during which curriculum would need to be developed and professional development improved.

CONCLUSION

Few comprehensive reforms lack vision and the belief that there is a better way to respond to the diverse needs of individual students. Where those reforms all too frequently falter is in their underestimation of what their visions mean in practice. The self-organizing school project articulated its vision in a framework of practice, although it did not go far enough to satisfy the demands or realize the benefits of embedded design.

The articulated approach associated with embedded design is uncommon and certainly represents a challenge to the autonomous and loosely coupled tradition of most schools. The application of this principle is not about reducing or shrinking the scope of a school's base of practice to accommodate ideas about schema development. From the perspective of the self-organizing school, it is a process that realistically reflects the time, knowledge, skill, and support required to build scalable capacity with research-based practice.

In its application, embedded design is the principle that generates the order to give up control. It creates the conditions enjoyed by the surgeon and the firefighter described in chapter 3, who possess the regularity and consistency in their roles and the pattern language needed to create a clearer relationship between what they do and what happens. As illustrated in the self-organizing school project pilot year, embedded design requires immense effort, if it is to address the widespread difficulties in comprehensive school reform implementation and the instability in levels of support within individual schools. Those levels were not forthcoming in the pilot. Even with a theory and strong design perspective, it is easy to replicate the issues and problems of past efforts when a design is incomplete.

Chapter 7 includes a description of the way that the pilot scaled up, ultimately achieving an implementation level that directly reflected the principle and processes described in this chapter. At the core of that transition was simply finding the energy to stay the course with the design approach to make it complete.

CHAPTER TAKEAWAYS

1. Embedded design is the principle that makes it possible for the school to possess a schema.
2. Embedded design provides the trajectory and connectedness necessary for comprehensive school reform sustainability over time.
3. To be self-organizing, a design must be complete. Roles must be articulated; technology tools built; and feedback effectively shared, understood, and valued.
4. Embedded design reiterates and reinforces the educational power of a pedagogy and the totality of a school's body of practice by ensuring that key research-driven characteristics are represented in all aspects of the design.
5. Feedback makes embedded design a continuous and dynamic force for change in a school.
6. Technology catalyzes the embedded design principle into action by providing the tools that make the design work on a day-to-day basis.
7. Professional development should express the integration of the elements of a comprehensive school reform, teaching new skills in a holographic, as opposed to a jigsawlike, manner.
8. Embedded design creates the self-reinforcing conditions required for self-organization.

NOTE

1. This more recent citation captures the basic principles employed in the self-organizing school project and is more accessible than the others.

Scaling Up

Snap back to reality. Oh, there goes gravity . . . —Marshall Bruce
Mathers III

The first year of the self-organizing school project was a snap back to
reality for the pilot teaching and learning team, the school's leadership,
and the change agent. The design was incomplete, and the prospect of
scaling up was a daunting one given the many issues described in the
last chapter.

To exert school-level influence, the self-organizing school project
needed to build the organizational capacity required to do so. In its first
year, the project had neither the complete embedded design nor the organizational capacity to exert an influence at scale. This chapter describes the way that a school or comprehensive school reform builds
the organizational design required to support what it believes and does
about teaching and learning.

Building organizational capacity begins by first showing that a design can successfully scale within an individual school. This involves
scaling up the embedded design process, described in the last chapter,
to all levels of the school. This occurs when the school's simple rules,
roles, trajectory, feedback, and technology, initially applied to teachers
and classrooms, are applied to decision-making teams. Those teams are
then networked at multiple levels to create an organizational design.
The result is the similarity at scale and dispersed control required for
self-organization. The approach addresses the next-generation design
target of school-level influence, and it includes a discussion of the way

that the resilience of a network addresses the turnover of teachers that is common in school reform.

This chapter describes how the self-organizing school project scaled up from one pilot team to seven over a 3-year period. The challenge for the self-organizing school project was in bringing a design to scale that was not yet fully embedded at its most basic pilot level. Comprehensive school reform developers can use the chapter to reconcile their classroom vision and practice with the organizational design necessary to support it. For site-initiated efforts, the chapter provides a framework for reconsidering the organizational structure of a school in a way that supports new approaches to classroom teaching and learning.

MISSING LINK

The ability to get to scale in many schools (Elmore, 1996) has become a defining characteristic of established comprehensive school reform models. However, one of the most alarming findings is the limited impact that comprehensive school reform has had on the organization of individual schools (Berends et al., 2001; Cook et al., 1999; Datnow & Castellano, 2000). Most models do not address the reform of the organization in their overall design approach, and evaluations of comprehensive school reform have not focused on this dimension. Those models that include an organizational design approach have experienced only limited success (e.g., Berends et al., 2001; Cook et al., 1999). Further, there are no studies that show the organizational effect of comprehensive school reform, despite the importance of schoolwide influence in this reform.

In reality, and for many of the reasons illustrated in the last chapter, getting to scale remains the unresolved challenge of comprehensive school reform in particular and school reform in general. The experience of the self-organizing school project in its pilot year provided an apt description of just how difficult the process of getting to scale turns out to be in practice. We can expect high levels of within-school variance in implementation and drift from the values, principles, and practices of a comprehensive school reform in the absence of an organizational design or method for getting to scale. School-level design is needed if school-level influence is to lead to innovative classroom practice.

TWO STEPS

The process of scaling up for dispersed control and self-organization involves two steps:

Team design: Applying the embedded design principle and process to the development of teams.

Team networks: Establishing the network of teams at different levels of the school to create an organizational design.

What follows is a detailed description of these steps, including examples of the product that arises from their application in schools.

Team Design

Teams are the basic unit of scale in the self-organizing school because they scale up what individual teachers do. An extensive literature exists on the roles, goals, and importance of teams in instructional decision making, management and curriculum, prereferral in special education, and in addressing concerns such as school safety and violence (Burns & Symington, 2002; Chrispeels, Salvador, & Brown, 2000; Friedman, 1997; Kentta, 1996). According to Dieker (2001), teams work best in positive learning climates where instructional approaches focus on active learning and high expectations and where there is time for planning and the creative evaluation of student performance.

In the self-organizing school, teamwork provides the context for the exchange of feedback at multiple levels within the school. This exchange draws on the research-based practice, the pattern language, and the professional capacity of individuals. Teams are established as the basic organizational unit of the school by using what is known about the power of collaborative process. This involves applying to groups the embedded design approach as it relates to the roles, trajectory, feedback, and tools for individuals. A summarized version of the process described in chapter 6 is reiterated here.

For example, if a school possesses a simple rule—"Decision making is collaborative"—then that rule needs to be put into practice by selecting a research-based approach that translates the rule into a method that teachers and students can use to work together. In the case of the self-organizing school project, the work of West et al. (1989), *Collaboration in the Schools,* was selected to articulate the rule. *Collaboration in the Schools* is a team process that defines the roles of individuals, a meeting model, the size and role of effective teams (6–12 people), and a collaborative problem-solving method of team functioning. According to West et al. (1989), this includes strategies for consensus building, the use of personal collaborative skills, the development of professional solutions, and the active monitoring of those solutions.

Team meetings also follow a problem-solving methodology, which involves problem definition and description, solution generation and evaluation, action planning, and evaluation of implementation.

These features of the *Collaboration in the Schools* process make it possible to define the role of a team in the self-organizing school in a similar manner to the way that student team learning defined and then articulated the roles of individual teachers. For example, Figure 7.1 describes an excerpt from the position description for a team in the self-organizing school that shows how the simple rule created the role description for a team.

The role description for the team is a scaled-up collaborative version of the roles of individual teachers. The team applies the research-based practice, pattern language, common approach to feedback, and technology tools embedded in the school's classroom design, described in the last chapter, to improve the performance of individual students and the team overall. All teams apply the same approach, irrespective of whether they are working with a group of students or managing the school as a whole.

Team Networks

School-level influence is about scaling up teams and team process. This involves applying the team structure described in the first step to

---

Teaching and Learning Team in the Self-Organizing School

Responsibilities

The Teaching and Learning Team is responsible for the classroom implementation of those beliefs and values about learning expressed in the school simple rules. The team should model excellence in the implementation of all aspects of the program—learning, sharing, growth, and feedback, bringing those capacities to the students and teams they serve, in pursuit of student growth and the current and future benefit of the school.

Sharing

Demonstrates excellence in all aspects of the collaborative process.

Takes responsibility for assisting each member of the team to make the best possible contribution.

Uses the team structure and process as a problem-solving and solution-generating opportunity.

Deals directly and openly with all members of the community

Works collaboratively toward the achievement of personal, team, and school goals.

Uses the sharing tools in the school operating system to maximize collaboration and effective solution generation.

Delivers on all learning and team responsibilities and action plans in a timely fashion.

Seeks assistance from peer teams, team leader, and the administration.

Ensures ethical computer and network participation.

Demonstrates advanced problem-solving skills with respect to computer hardware and software and can apply those skills to student difficulties.

Figure 7.1. Position Description for a Teaching and Learning Team in the Self-Organizing School (adapted from Bain, 1996)

a small and efficient network of school teams. Those teams provide every teaching and learning team with the support required to sustain the design. Figure 7.2 describes a simple three-level team-based network structure.

Level 1: Teaching and Learning Team

In a self-organizing school, the teaching and learning team constitutes the first, or base, level of the network. These are the groups of teachers described in the previous section and in the example of the self-organizing school project pilot that work directly with the students. They are the locus of self-organization in the school because their focus is the core activity—classroom teaching and learning. Teaching and learning teams make it possible for individual teachers and students to pool their collective intelligence by building a pattern language and by evolving the school schema.

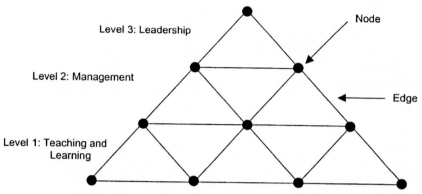

Figure 7.2.   Leveled Network of Teams

However, those teams engaged in the day-to-day challenge of meet-ing students' needs do not always have the time or influence to act on their experience and findings at scale. Their bottom-up problem solv-ing may generate the prototypes for new software tools or a change to a professional development program or the adaptation of teaching ma-terials, although the creation of the tools, processes, and products at scale requires additional support.

Level 2: Management Team

The second level in the network provides the support required to scale up the work of the teaching and learning teams. A second-level management team assumes primary responsibility for this work. This group comprises the leaders of each teaching and learning team. The leaders work together at the second level to pool the intelligence of each of their teams at scale. This involves processing the innovations, issues, and challenges produced by each of the Level 1 teams that they represent. The management team makes it possible for information to flow readily over the network, and it precludes the need for every Level 1 team to communicate independently with every other. All teams func-tion with the same common schema, have compatible roles and trajec-tories, and derive overall benefit from the school's embedded design.

Level 2 also includes specialist groups, like a technology team or a personnel team. These teams respond to the needs of the teaching and learning teams by assuming responsibilities related to innovations and changes that emerge across the network. For example, a technology team may assume responsibility for the development of a piece of software; a professional development team may manage the school's professional development program, career trajectory, and portfolio process. The role of Level 2 teams is not solely responsive. They also identify needs that create agendas for Level 1 teams. The flow and effect of self-organization over the network, though predominantly bottom-up, are multidirectional.

Level 3: Leadership Team

The third level in the structure is the leadership team. This group includes representation from all Level 2 teams and the school's executive. The leadership team is the keeper of the school schema. The process of embedded design means that any change in one aspect of the design will affect all others. The leadership team manages any domino or cascading effect that may be caused by any acts of self-organization produced by the Level 1 and 2 teams.

The leadership team is also responsible for prioritizing initiatives, for managing the school budget, and for the evolution of the design overall. By assuming the responsibility for maintaining the school's focus on its simple rules, the leadership team ensures that the cascading effect of change retains a connection to a constantly evolving schema, pattern language, and professional capacity.

Network Features and Advantages

The three-tier network is designed to reflect the characteristics and advantages of networks in self-organizing systems. For example, there are frequent opportunities for members of one team to communicate with others because their edges or boundaries are shared or close together. Team meetings permit this communication to occur at all levels. They make possible the nonlinear communication and near-neighbor interaction that characterize successful self-organizing systems (Barabasi, 2002). The examples of self-organization described in chapter 4 illustrate the product of this near-neighbor communication. For instance, the teachers who developed the self-monitoring tool and database first used their own teams and then the Level 2 management teams for their initiatives to be implemented schoolwide.

Because the network is not widely dispersed at just one level, the distance between nodes (individuals) is shortened (Stocker et al., 2002). The hierarchy described in Figure 7.2 illustrates this concept. The distances between teams at Level 1 and 2 are shortened because the subsequent level provides a place for all of those teams to meet. In combination with the common schema, this leveled approach creates the conditions for clustering, as the short edges increase the probability of more related connections (Newman, 2003). The same teachers who built the self-monitoring and software tools described in chapter 4 were able to share their knowledge of the tools with teachers on their own team and other teams. Those initiatives may stimulate similar problem solving by teachers at other levels in the system (e.g., the technology team). That work will also be given a trajectory by the leveled network structure. The way that the network helped these teachers share and work together in the past increases the likelihood that they will work together in the future and involve others in the process. The close proximity of teachers and their common pattern language and schema makes an increase in network connections possible.

A simple network of teams configured in a three-level structure encourages the commonality of purpose and action that is the intended hallmark of comprehensive school reform. The pilot team in the self-organizing school project alluded to this potential in its descriptions of a school-within-a-school and in the way that teachers and students created a stronger sense of community during the pilot year. One team of teachers working in a dedicated fashion with a discrete group of students creates the small-world communication potential that increases the frequency of purposeful exchange within a learning community. The network structure makes it possible for that purposeful small-world communication to scale up, extending across multiple teams and, ultimately, to multiple levels influencing the school as a whole.

THE NETWORK IN ACTION

Chapter 4 describes two examples of the way that students built capacity with the school's pattern language and schema in the self-organizing school project. The following scenario extrapolates from those examples to show how students could stimulate self-organization at scale because of the organizational support provided by the three-tier network of teams.

Consider a group of students working on a Jigsaw II cooperative learning task (Slavin et al., 1994). Each student has researched a specific question and is meeting with other students, who have become experts with the same question. As the students meet, they indicate that their question was hard to understand. The group decides to address this issue using the *Collaboration in the Schools* problem-solving approach. Like their teachers, all students were taught how to use this approach as part of an orientation at the beginning of the school year. The students built capacity with the pattern language because of their common ongoing classroom experience with collaboration and cooperative learning.

The students identify the issues associated with the cooperative learning question that they have been asked to address. They note that the question is unclear and does not seem to relate to the materials that they were directed to use. Instead of the more common individualized engagement with teachers and the likelihood of an individualized response, the students are pooling their perspectives in ways that are likely to yield benefit for their group and their teachers.

They invite the classroom teacher to be part of their process just as the teacher described in chapter 4 originally invited the students to engage with the school's schema. The teacher takes a passive role and listens to the students as they clarify and problem-solve. They use their knowledge of the design and pattern language to express a need in a manner that is less about criticizing the teacher or the curriculum and more about self-organizing to solve a problem.

The students also use a classroom computer and the software tool described in Figure 7.3 to record their meeting process. They respond in text fields that correspond to the elements of the problem-solving model. Those fields provide space for describing the problem and solutions and for making a plan of action. In using the tool, the students provide a clear account of their process and its outcomes. They recommend that the cooperative learning question be revised or that new questions and resources be identified. They also provide important detail related

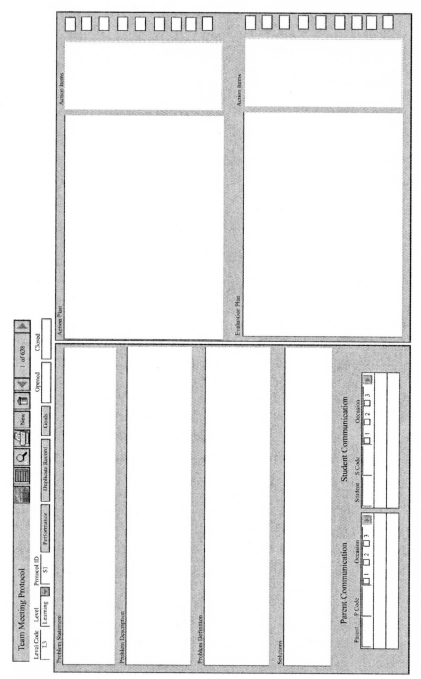

Figure 7.3. Collaboration Tool

to why the question does not work from a student perspective. After using the software, the group returns to its expert group task and exchanges the information that it has found by answering its cooperative learning questions. Technology captures the students' interactions in a manner that can be used by other teams.

At the conclusion of the lesson, the teacher places the students' feedback on the agenda for the next meeting of her teaching and learning team. In doing so, the teacher serves as a link to the other teachers on that team, thus shortening the distance between a group of students in one class and all other teachers on the team. At their next team meeting, all teachers use the software to review the students' issue. On reflection, the teachers report that the students' concern may be more widespread. They indicate that a number of the team's additional curricula have general expert questions, and they conclude that the issue may extend beyond the case in point to other curricular areas and teams.

The Level 1 teaching and learning team uses the *Collaboration in the Schools* problem-solving process to expand on the students' initial solution. They confirm the student issue and explore some additional possibilities. These include the identification of better research resources for the students and more specific and scaffolded expert questions. These solutions are recorded in the software on the same record used by the students. In this way, the teachers directly add their collective intelligence to the students' solutions. They agree to implement a plan of action, and they also recommend that the school management team take up what may be a broader curriculum design issue. The teaching team functions in the same manner as the student team. This similarity at scale allows the solution to scale up from classroom to team.

In the school's three-tier network structure, the leader of the teaching and learning team serves as a member of the school management team. Like the classroom teacher, he or she serves as a bridge that shortens the path between his or her team's teachers and students and between the leaders of other teams and the school leadership.

In preparation for their meeting, the management team members log on to the collaboration software that now has input from students and teachers. At its meeting, the management team solicits input from each team leader, using the problem-solving approach to identify the scope of the curriculum design issue first identified by the students. In this way, the whole school has become part of the students' small world because of the way that the network structure, with its links and bridges, shortens the path between a group of students and the school's leadership. The benefit to the school is derived from the active engagement of students, teachers, and leaders as agents in the process of self-organization.

All team leaders commit to taking the problem back to their respective teaching teams and to audit the scope of the issue. The management team agrees to make a decision at its next meeting, regarding the need to plan for a curriculum modification across teams or, possibly, the whole school.

In this example, a problem identified by students scaled up to address what may be a whole-school need. Instead of languishing in one classroom or producing a one-off solution, the problem was given a trajectory because of the self-similarity in the design. This happened in a manner fully consistent with the way that the new software described in chapter 4 came about. An innovative idea or need scaled up through the school because of the common schema, pattern language, and existence of a network of self-similar teams. In the example, the networking of teams and the sharing of information placed teachers who may have never worked with the students in a position to help them solve a problem. Leaders from different teams engaged directly with a classroom that they may never have visited.

This small-world effect is driven by the short paths between members of the community, and it is an expression of a commitment to cooperative and collaborative learning expressed in the school's simple rules and schema. Everyone, including the students, can reasonably be expected to understand the form and pattern language associated with the discussion about cooperative learning and collaborative problem solving. However, it is the dynamic interaction between the agents and the pathways of communication that enables the small-world phenomenon to play out. The content of the conversation, as well as the process and structures for having it, is in place across the school. Control is dispersed, solutions emerge, and the network allows the potential of those solutions to be scaled up. The result is school-level effect because the school has the organizational capacity to exert school-level influence. Evidence in support of this assertion is presented in chapter 10.

Tools at Scale

In the collaboration example, students, teachers, and leaders pooled their collective intelligence with the help of technology. The software for reporting on collaborative meetings made the common action plan possible. Teachers and leaders accessed the input of students by using the collaboration software, and additional information was added as the solution traveled over the network. This resulted in a more sophisticated outcome as the information passed through different levels in the organization. The software tool was readily available, and all groups could access it, either at meetings or in preparation for the meetings.

The technology was used to make the connections between the teams and among all of the individuals involved. The technology also ensured that teachers and administrators could build on the initial self-organizing behavior of the students by enabling the collaborative work of all groups to be saved, stored, and made accessible over time. Consequently, the likelihood of the same problems recurring at a smaller scale elsewhere was reduced.

Network Implications

The effect of the meeting, planning, and feedback tools described in the book so far is to create a virtual "hyperedge" between every node or individual on the network. A hyperedge is a link that connects two or more nodes (Barabasi, 2002). When network-based technology tools are deployed to help agents in the community work together, they make it easier for more agents to communicate effectively and efficiently about more issues.

This communication has the effect of shortening the edges or links in the network. For example, the school's principal may not have visited the class from which an original problem and solution emerged, yet by logging on to the software and reviewing the student and teaching team solution, he or she could meaningfully engage with the process. Links that would normally represent long pathways in the school's communication network can be made short by the technology. This is possible only because the software embodies the school schema and the principal, teachers, and students all possess the professional understanding and pattern language required to play an active role in the process.

The application of the similarity-at-scale and dispersed control principles through team development and networking provides the organizational capacity to exert the kind of school-level influence that is frequently missing in comprehensive school reform. The principles described in this and preceding chapters make it possible for all members of the community to participate in the bottom-up self-organization that makes school-level influence happen. The responsibility for the constant evolution of the teaching and learning process is dispersed to all members of the school community.

NETWORKS AND DESIGN RESILIENCE

Staff turnover is synonymous with significant change in schools, and it is a major challenge for comprehensive school reform. According to Fullan (2001), turnover diminishes school-level capacity because skilled teachers are lost to the system, reducing its resilience and making it difficult to sustain an innovation. From a network perspective, resilience is defined by what happens to a network when one takes an edge or link away and, in doing so, increases the length of the paths between nodes (Newman, 2003). Faculty attrition can be conceptualized as the loss of nodes and edges in the network as a result of the loss of key individuals.

For example, if one or more of the students or the teacher described in the preceding scenario were absent or left the school permanently, he or she could be temporarily or permanently lost to the network. This would extend the length of the links between nodes. However, the successful functioning of the network is not precluded in such a situation. Unlike environments where control and expertise are highly focused on a few individuals or are a function of an autonomous engagement with the system, in a self-organizing school, expertise is dispersed. In the current example, a student absence or a change of one teacher on the team will not exert a debilitating effect on the self-organizing capacity of the group, because all members possess a common pattern language and schema.

In terms of the sustainability of a reform, a self-organizing school can remain immune to the effects of cyclical turnover. Of course, if a whole team of teachers were to leave, then the result would be prob-lematic, although not catastrophic, as members of other teams could be deployed to reconstitute the network. The common schema and design mean that members can leave a team and join another without a criti-cal breakdown in the network. A self-organizing school can take ad-vantage of this feature in ways unavailable to schools or comprehen-sive school reforms that involve highly individualized, as opposed to collaborative, engagement with a reform.

As noted in chapter 3, school-level influence occurs bottom-up through the networking of teaching and learning teams charged with re-sponsibility for the core activity of the school. These teams make it possible for a self-organizing school to address the content and process of those factors, described in chapter 1, that are highly amenable to school-level influence. They include classroom learning, the type and quality of instruction, the role of feedback, and the deployment of tech-nology at scale. The capacity to influence these things at the level of the organization is the key to bringing research-based practice to scale in any school.

SCALING UP THE SELF-ORGANIZING SCHOOL PROJECT

The Decision to Proceed

The scaling-up process for the self-organizing school project started at the beginning of the 1994–1995 school year when two new grade-level teams were added to the original pilot team. To scale up the proj-ect, two teams were added each year, starting in 1994–1995 and con-cluding with the full school adoption of the model (seven teams) in 1996–1997.

At the conclusion of the 1993–1994 academic year, the leadership and the faculty jointly decided to scale up on the basis of three factors. First, the pilot indicated improvement in the students' academic and so-cial behavior. The school's leadership thought that this could only im-prove further, given the known limitations of the design in the project's first year (New England Association of Schools and Colleges, 1996). Despite the many reservations caused by the challenges and stresses of the pilot, there was a subjective view that the school was becoming a healthier place in terms of its mission to maximize the academic and social growth of each student. This improvement aligned with the stated intentions of the community, as expressed in the needs assessment and simple rules.

Second, the pilot team members were supportive of the decision to scale up. Team support was seen as an indicator of the project's viability. The team believed that the challenges expressed during the first year would diminish as the design became established. To establish itself and diminish the challenges, the design needed permission to scale up.

The third factor was abstract, and it related to unfinished work. The missing features in the pilot were generally well understood by all involved. It was believed that there was a trajectory or way forward if those areas could be addressed. Not to pursue the design under these circumstances would be tantamount to giving up prematurely.

Together, the three factors took precedence over the long list of problems and issues that emerged from the pilot and, especially, the concerns described in chapter 6 about workload, time, technology, and curriculum. Although there were no guaranteed solutions to these problems, the school nonetheless committed to move forward. This type of decision is common in many school reforms. A preexisting investment of time, resources, and reputation drives a reform forward even when key issues remain unresolved.

Scaling the Network of Teams

From 1995 to 1997, the self-organizing school project transitioned to the three-tier network of teams described in this chapter. Over this period, existing departmental and school committees morphed into the three-tier approach and created a new organizational design for the school. The ad hoc change agent leadership, described in the last chapter, continued during the second year of the pilot, and it was not until the third year that the team infrastructure began to align with the new program. The sequence is illustrated in Table 7.1.

This transition was particularly challenging for the leaders who were responsible for conducting two programs within one school.[1] During the 1995–1997 transition period, teaching and learning teams replaced departments at the critical first level or tier of the organizational design,

Table 7.1.   Transition of the Self-Organizing School Project to the Three-Tier Network (1995–1997)

1993–1994 (1)	1994–1995 (3)	1995–1996 (5)	1996–1997 (7)
Pilot team (9)	Two teams (10)	Two teams (11)	Two teams (12)
Existing	Existing	Transition	Team network
management	management	management	

Note. The number adjacent to the year represents the total number of teams; the number adjacent to the team is the grade.

whereas the roles assumed exclusively by the management committee of the school (principal, assistant principals) were dispersed to other Level 2 teams. These included teams for technology decision making, curriculum, and personnel. The management committee became the leadership team in an expanded form and included the leaders of the new Level 2 teams (e.g., technology, personnel).

The new three-tier structure replaced the high-contact ad hoc management of the first two pilot years with a formalized near-neighbor approach, making it possible to employ the network to actively scale up the design. Although this retained many of the benefits of the ad hoc approach, it was much more proactive and less crisis oriented in the way it contributed to the design's completion. Benefits included the refinement of the curriculum model, the development and refinement of portfolio guidelines, and the management of the implementation of new technology, all of which emerged from the work of teams. The successful work of these teams indicated the existence of the kind of distributed leadership and dispersed control that has been much advocated yet elusive in practice in the reform literature.

Initially, the teaching and learning team leaders were better positioned than the Level 2 management team to develop solutions to the day-to-day problems faced by their teams and the program overall. Given the incomplete design, they could capitalize on the bottom-up problem solving that was occurring day-to-day on each of their teams. However, the introduction of the Level 2 management team was critical as the design scaled up. It became the formal embodiment of the shift from the traditional top-down leadership to a network of teams as the primary locus of problem-solving in the school. In the three-tier model, the school's leadership team formally assumed a role similar to the one that evolved during the first year. They became enablers and resourcers of the self-organizing initiatives of Level 1 and 2 teams but at scale.

In the first year, members of the leadership group made on-the-spot decisions about curriculum and schedule. However, as the project scaled, the preferences and circumstances of different teams had to be considered, making it more difficult to make those immediate contingency-based decisions. The management team provided a venue for team leaders to pool their collective perspectives and capacities. As the project scaled up, leadership began to focus specifically on the missing pieces of the design.

New Initiatives, 1994–1995

As described in chapter 6, the pilot year had not been easy. The school's leadership committed immense organizational energy to the pilot, although even the most creative contingency management could not satisfactorily address the difficulties caused by an incomplete design and, especially, the lack of curriculum.

Two initiatives were undertaken to respond to the curriculum problem. First, a complete 5-week module of the curriculum was developed to give members of the teams an opportunity to define a differentiated curriculum and see what one looked like. The demonstration module included descriptions of the way that groups of students could rotate through different classroom activities, how time could be managed, and how lessons could be adapted to address learner differences.

A second initiative provided more time for curriculum development in the summer training sessions. These sessions now focused on producing curriculum materials using both the existing guidelines and the new model. This initiative fit well with the theory, given that the professional development program was intended as a holistic integration of all of the design's parts. By developing curriculum, the team members could embed their understanding of the simple rules and new teaching approaches in a meaningful context that would give them a head start on the year ahead.

Additional improvements were made over the summer of 1994. Although there were still no sophisticated technology tools, a greater commitment was made by the school's leadership to provide formal feedback, albeit using the spreadsheets and the word-processing approach described previously. Further, the original pilot team members were available during the summer training to help new team members prepare to enter the program. This was especially helpful in teaching collaboration. Team members could model the process using realistic challenges and problems that were meaningful for new team members.

In Play, 1994–1995

The goal of the second year was to build on the key milestones that were accomplished during the pilot year, including team process and the use of the research-based pedagogies. The curriculum model progressed the design from the initial guidelines and expectations referred to in the last chapter. This was a major step forward, although it also represented a double-edged sword. The design seriously underestimated what was required to make a multilevel differentiated classroom a workable reality for all teachers. The pilot experience had shown that the kind of classroom envisioned by the community required multiple lesson plans, adaptations, instructional outcomes, and assessment, each integrated into a total plan and process for classroom delivery. This level of curriculum adaptation was unprecedented at a secondary school level, and it became clear that a preexisting curriculum and delivery plan were required to genuinely respond to the variability in learner needs that existed on all of the pilot teams. The Pandora's Box of addressing individual difference in a secondary school classroom had been opened, and this required a realistic response that extended well beyond one-size-fits-all instruction.

The demonstration model made clear exactly what was involved in developing such a complete curriculum and just how difficult the process would be for the majority of faculty members who were becoming increasingly aware of and conversant with the magnitude of the curriculum problem. The development of the demonstration model was undertaken by one of the school's most capable teachers, who found the high cognitive load associated with the task to be demanding and the actual development process time-consuming and difficult.[2]

Despite the improvement efforts, the curriculum was still incomplete for the three teams who began the 1994–1995 school year. In the time available during the summer, the members of the two teams who participated in the second iteration of the training program could, at best, only develop one 5-week module. This lack of curriculum continued to be the project's major Achilles' heel in its second year.

Arguably, the second year of the pilot was even more difficult than the first. Although much had been learned during the first year, the project still lacked a complete feedback process and feedback tools, technology, and complete curriculum. Further, the most experienced team members had been in the program for only 12 months. As a result, the nodes of mastery and expertise that they represented were not fully developed, thereby diminishing the resilience of the network as a result. The network of three teams was also growing faster than the school's capacity to support it, especially in the absence of the feedback tools and the full implementation of the three-tier organizational model. Under duress, the teams functioned in an autonomous and introspective manner, focusing on their immediate within-team needs.

Not surprisingly, the two new teams encountered similar difficulties to those experienced by members of the original pilot team, although they found it harder to maintain the same positive approach to the overall effort. With only one team in place, it was much easier to solve problems as they appeared and to provide the high-contact small-world feedback and mentoring that helped team members through difficult periods. With three teams in place, many of the problems remained, but the growing scale of the project meant that issues could not be easily solved using the highly personalized approach employed in the pilot. This resulted in high levels of dissatisfaction among some teachers. The world of the self-organizing school project was getting bigger, but the gaps in the program and the lack of a network infrastructure meant that the problems of the pilot year were magnified.

Although the feedback system was incomplete, it had nonetheless advanced significantly and was creating an additional unanticipated problem. The commitment to higher levels of feedback was considered threatening by some team members. Some teachers felt insecure about their abilities, given that they had such little experience with the design. Scrutiny of their teaching under those circumstances exacerbated that sense of insecurity and discomfort. This concern was flagged in the first professional development program and, without resolution, grew in magnitude. Despite the anticipated benefits of frequent feedback, in practice it was overwhelming for teachers who did not have all of the tools and experience that they needed to do the job. The feedback expectations could not be reconciled with the reality of their role and the available resources, thus creating an imbalance. This sort of imbalance generally occurs when the embedded design process is applied inconsistently or in an incomplete state. The overall effect was to inject a source of discontent into the teams resulting from the variability in the comfort levels of individual team members with the feedback process. This added additional stress to the teams overall.

Progress

By the end of the 1994–1995 school year, the pilot teams included over 20 teachers with some experience in the project. More curriculum modules were developed, although not nearly enough. Student conduct continued to improve, with an ever-increasing schoolwide impact as more students participated in the project (New England Association of Schools and Colleges, 1996). The two new teams also reported the positive effects of the school-within-a-school phenomenon and improved academic achievement. Members of the original pilot team were still building experience, although the lack of detailed design limited the overall effect.

Despite the stress placed on teachers, there was a general perception across the school that a tangible benefit was accruing for those students participating in the new design. There was also a view that the cost, in terms of teachers' time and strain, was too high.

Unpacking the Pilot: Year 2

Schema and Simple Rules

Overall, the second year of the pilot exacerbated the challenges of the first year and constituted a step backward for the project. On one hand, more teachers were involved in a project designed to express the needs and simple rules of the school community. However, the nature of that involvement was compromised by the incomplete design, which left teachers to self-invent as opposed to self-organize in the absence of a complete embedded design and schema. The result was greater complexity, greater variance in implementation, and limited opportunity to redress the situation. In its second year, the original pilot team should have been positioned to evolve the schema, but the limited progress on the design significantly constrained this process. This also affected collaboration. Although it was still a redeeming strength of the pilot, it was nonetheless diminished in the second year.

Feedback, Embedded Design, and Technology

In the second year of the project, feedback became a focus with the intent of strengthening the connections across the elements of the design. However, in practice it served to create disruption. The expanded feedback approach was supposed to provide opportunities for teachers to reflect on practice, but instead it led to concerns about teacher readiness and fairness, when so much of the design was a work in progress.

The reaction of the teams to increased feedback illustrates how the problems of an incomplete embedded design are magnified when a project scales up. The expectations related to one aspect of the design (feedback) were not commensurate with the support available from others (articulation of curriculum). The result was the opposite of the expected self-reinforcement; the imbalance created a negative destabilizing force across elements in the design. This effect added stress to the professional lives of teachers and the community in a manner that is similar to the cases of incomplete design reported in the broader comprehensive school reform literature (e.g., Bodilly, 1996).

Unfortunately, the problems of uneven implementation experienced over the summer of 1994–1995 weakened the self-organizing school project overall by placing more teachers in the role of implementing an incomplete design. The continued absence of technology exacerbated the project's difficulties. Time delays made feedback more summative than formative, and those delays were partly caused by the lack of appropriate tools. Further, the promise of technology to make the design accessible and capture its core transactions remained unfulfilled. Again, as was the case with the curriculum, the type of deeply embedded technology promised to the project was unprecedented in schools and could not be procured off the shelf. Its importance for promoting communication, for encouraging collaboration, and in making the design less complex was also underestimated, as was its overall importance to the viability of the project. Moreover, the failure to produce this kind of technology was becoming emblematic of a failure to deliver on a promise made in the needs assessment, thus creating a fundamental credibility gap for the project.

Similarity at Scale and Dispersed Control

Even under duress, the team-based model continued to be a strength of the design. The lag in the implementation of the three-tier structure during the first 2 years made the team role even more important as it provided support that should have been available from Level 2 and 3 teams. Teams tended to function as small autonomous schools. The implementation was increasingly getting ahead of the design, resulting in the kind of dispersed control that was much more consistent with the tradition of autonomy than that of a self-organizing system. In the absence of the intended common schema and pattern language, this kind of dispersed control was more likely to produce the self-invention and variability in implementation so commonly described in the comprehensive school reform literature.

Crisis

With the conclusion of the second year of the pilot, it became increasingly apparent that the incomplete design and the inability to keep up with the curriculum demand threatened the viability and future of the self-organizing school effort. The process of scaling up had moved at a much faster rate than the capacity of the project to produce curriculum materials. Much more design effort and product were required at a time when energy, resources, and effort had begun subsiding.

The project was reaching a critical juncture. As is so often the case in change efforts, several years of hard work had been invested with only limited returns. There was an ongoing need for effort, resources, and persistence. It is not uncommon at this point in a change process to claim victory and move on. Some key or more successful features of the innovation are typically left in place (e.g., the collaborative model and teams in the case of the self-organizing school project) as the basis for such a claim. However, the victory claim invariably signals the beginning of the return to the way that things were, albeit with a modified lexicon.

The best alternative to moving on from the self-organizing school project was to accelerate the development of the design to catch up with the implementation. This required adding resources to the process in key areas, including curriculum, technology, and feedback.

Initiatives, 1995–1997

The additional resources that were needed to catch up came from several sources. Over the 1995–1997 period, the school successfully employed three improvement grants that made catch-up possible. Two of the grants were used to employ teachers from existing teams to develop curriculum.[3] A third grant was used to develop the promised suite of software tools for the project.[4] The suite included an authoring system for reducing the cognitive load associated with developing differentiated curriculum.

The first initiative, curriculum writing, supported a summer program that was similar to the initial professional development training. The funding made it possible for teachers who had graduated from the initial training to work as teams building curriculum modules for the forthcoming year. Teachers new to the project could then begin the year with these modules and build ahead for when the preexisting curriculum ran out. Over time, a full year of curriculum could be completed in this iterative fashion.

The curriculum development experience provided an excellent follow-on for teachers who had completed the initial summer training, and it gave them an opportunity to accelerate along the career path by becoming curriculum developers. The curriculum-writing program also demonstrated to the community that there was a solution to the curriculum problem. As a result of these catch-up efforts made possible by the grants, the school produced over 1,200 hours of curriculum between 1996 and 2001.

The second major initiative made possible by the grant funding involved the creation of a suite of software authoring tools that would make it easier to develop differentiated curriculum and integrate it with the whole design. It was clear from the program's pilot years that even with complete curriculum and technology, the design was always going to be complex for teachers who were used to working autonomously within a school using their self-invented schema.

Technology was seen as the key to making a sophisticated school accessible, not just for curriculum, but for all of the transactions associated with the design. The technology, although making the design workable, would serve to instantiate the key transactions of the theory in practice. This could not happen without the tools that would embody those transactions. As a result, the failure to deliver the software was especially problematic. Its omission impeded schema development creating the same kind of imbalance caused by the lack of curriculum.

For example, throughout the pilot, teachers reported that it was difficult to manage all the detail of curriculum development, including levels, grouping, and adaptation in outcomes, as well as assessment and instruction at multiple levels (module, unit, and lesson). Technology could reduce the cognitive load of linking objectives, instruction, outcomes, and classroom process and free teachers to focus on the development of creative differentiated instruction. The goal of the software development was to make the classroom vision of the design, as described in the last chapter, an accessible reality at scale across the school. The curriculum was seen as the most urgent gap in this regard. As such, the software development initiative began with the development of the curriculum authoring tools (Bain, 1997; Bain & Huss, 2000; Bain & Parkes, 2006b). The curriculum authoring tools use technology to make complex connections and relationships between differentiated outcomes, assessment products, and lesson plans.

Figure 7.4 describes examples of layouts from the tools, including tools for framing modules and units, for differentiating assessment products, for managing differentiated classroom instruction and resources, and for building lesson designs (including the example described in Figure 6.3). The software created a circumstance in which teachers could generate much-needed curriculum at an accelerated rate. For a complete description of the tools and their use, see Bain and Huss (2000).

Teachers could use the tools to develop the materials that would make a differentiated multilevel curriculum possible. This included the

Lesson Plan

Classroom Management Resource

Menu

Curriculum Framing

Authentic Assessment

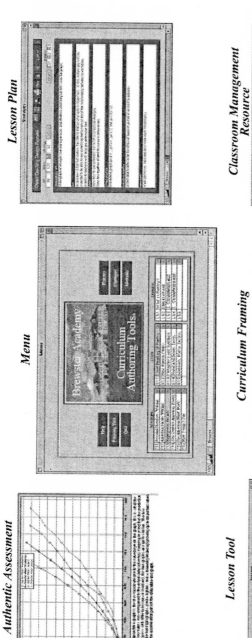

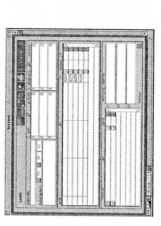

Lesson Tool

Figure 7.4.   Layouts From the Curriculum Tools Software

way that different levels of Spanish (as described in the last chapter) or any other subject could be taught in the same classroom. Further, the tools could help manage the complexity associated with delivering a curriculum differentiated for content, process, and product. This included the management of multiple lesson plans, diversified classroom activities and roles, as well as differentiated assessment. For example, the figure includes a tool that would permit teachers to plan and manage the rotation of different groups through different levels at different times and store adapted resources for use in each lesson. These practical tools made unambiguous connections between the design and its implementation and reduced the load on teachers.

With the curriculum authoring tools in place, work began on a suite of feedback tools, including the examples described in Figure 6.2. Tools were also developed for managing student performance and records. A specific description of the software tools is, in part, the subject of the next two chapters.

Getting to Scale, 1995–1997

By the beginning of 1995, the third year of the pilot process, the design had become a substantive reality in the school. With five teams now in place, there was a sense of inevitability about the trajectory of the project in the school. This did not mean that support was universal or that the many problems had been resolved. The time required to produce curriculum and software precluded such an overnight transformation. However, the substantive initiatives underway in both of these areas altered the disposition of the community.

Where formerly there was only a long list of apparently unresolved issues, large steps were being taken to address those problems. Light could be seen at the end of the tunnel. The convulsive effects of change were subsiding. The new curriculum and software initiatives were also combining with some additional positive effects of the change that emerged at scale. They included improved standardized test performance on PSAT and SAT measures and much improved student conduct that made the general work environment for teachers less stressful (New England Association of Schools and Colleges, 1996). It was becoming clear that even an approximation of the design was more effective than the preexisting program. Nonetheless, the risk of dilution and regression were ever present given the continuing incomplete state of the project. There was no premature declaration of victory or a drive to turn back although many challenges remained.

By the end of the 1996 school year, the total self-organizing school effort had crossed a viability threshold. The leaders of the initial pilot team were emerging as future leaders of the school with deep experience of the design, whereas each team included a core of experienced individuals who were now involved in developing curriculum and conducting the training. These individuals were represented on management teams, and there was a much-diminished sense of crisis management in the broader culture.

Curriculum was coming online at an accelerated rate. Teachers with experience in the project recognized the huge difference in the demands of their job with and without curriculum materials. Every new module brought the pressure down.

The network of teams enabled new teaching and learning team leaders to emerge from an expanding core of experienced individuals. If necessary, it was possible to adjust or reconstitute teams with a balance of experienced and new team members. From a personnel perspective, the design had reached a point of critical mass. The growing expertise of individuals was generating a threshold level of resilience in the network of teams throughout the school.

By the beginning of the 1997 school year, the three-tier model was in place. It served a full-school complement of seven teaching and learning teams. The tools became a complete software system, creating the kind of self-reinforcing and embedded footprint promised by the theory. For example, during 1997, the professional development program first used the tools in training sessions.

Over the ensuing 3 years, the training program became much more specific and contextualized by the experiences of the teams who had filled in the white space described in the last chapter. It had progressed from the typical training in teaching practices in Year 1, to the approximation of the model curriculum in Year 2, to the embedding of the curriculum development training process in the software tools in Year 3. This 3-year trajectory exemplifies the overall progression of the design through successive approximations toward the realization of the theory in practice.

By the third year, there were large numbers of teachers involved in delivering the program. Experienced team members took responsibility for delivering sessions and leading teams of beginning curriculum developers. The career trajectory that expected this kind of engagement from experienced teachers was becoming a reality. As the multiple elements of the design gradually moved to become a whole, levels of expertise and self-reinforcement began to increase. One effect was a reduced concern about feedback. In the context of a more complete design, the level of feedback seemed more appropriate and reasonable. As a result, those teachers who had been concerned about feedback now felt that the level of support was commensurate with the level of scrutiny. Where feedback was initially the source of imbalance and disruption, it became the key to self-reinforcement and, ultimately, self-organization. This happened because the design began to catch up with its implementation. Evidence in support of this assertion is shared in chapter 10.

The introduction of the software tools represented a critical milestone for the project. Along with the professional development program and the network of teams, their implementation marked 1997 as the beginning of a complete theory and practice of the self-organizing school. After 5 years, theory, instruments, systems, and practices were all in place. At this point, the design began to assume the qualities and characteristics described earlier in this book. The implementation was now delivering on the promised effects of a common schema and the self-reinforcing conditions required to rapidly shift responsibility away from the leaders/developers. Even though building software and curriculum models were technically complex, their overall effect was to simplify the design. The detail of those processes could exist in the background of a school schema that demonstrated the consistency needed if it was to be accessible for the community.

The successful curriculum, feedback, technology, and team network initiatives became the tipping point (Gladwell, 2002) for the self-organizing school project. Just as the compounding negative effect of incomplete embedded design exacerbated the difficulties in the early pilot years, the positive initiatives exerted an equally rapid and compounding positive force that was catalyzed by the existence of the embedded design process. As the gaps were filled, the benefits of embedded design became profound. Professional development, role, trajectory, technology, and feedback each and all began to exert the self-reinforcing effect intended by the embedded design process.

Attrition and Resilience

Attrition was a major factor in the scale-up period from 1994 to 1997 and one reason for the discussion of resilience in this chapter. The pilot phase is the most vulnerable point in any reform, given that an immense amount of new knowledge and capacity-building effort is invested in a small number of individuals. Those individuals may underestimate what is involved, whereas developers and proponents may not be able to adequately represent the magnitude of the challenge to participants. At the conclusion of the pilot year, two of the seven faculty members on the pilot team left the school for opportunities elsewhere. In one instance, the loss was simply the result of a new opportunity, but in the second instance, the decision to move was heavily influenced by the pilot experience.

The decision to continue with the project initiated a process of self-reflection among all faculty members and affected career decisions across the school. Now, all faced the inevitability of involvement in the new design. Over the pilot phase, the faculty turnover rate accelerated because the programs raised serious questions about all faculty members' future involvement in the project. Further, in some instances, faculty members did not want to continue after participating in the project. Not surprisingly, the pilot years disrupted the professional lives of most faculty members. Although the pilot was a detractor for some, it is important to note that the majority of teachers decided to stay the course through this period.

That said, the findings of the needs assessment in relation to the future of the school were severely tested. As emphasized in chapter 5, it is exceedingly difficult for teachers to commit to a change that they have not experienced and cannot fully understand. If universal support for a new model had been presumed at the outset of the project, based on the largely positive needs assessment process, the school may have initiated a simultaneous whole-school change that would have been unsustainable. It would have been impossible to manage the issues and challenges described in the last two chapters in any one year at a whole-school level.

SUMMARY

This account outlines the way that the self-organizing school project scaled up in the highly stressed and extremely challenging circumstances experienced by nearly all reforms. The theory did not immunize the project from these circumstances. However, there was always a vision and intended design behind the effort throughout the scaling-up period. When things were not working, there was an explanation and a course of action that, though immensely difficult, was nonetheless plausible and understood.

The gap between the prevailing reality and the intention of the design was enormous. This was reflected in the difference between the examples of self-organization described in chapter 4 (which occurred in 2000) and the circumstances of the 1993–1994 pilot year. Both sets of conditions reflected the radical changes in the school over a 7-year period. Looking forward from the pilot year, it was difficult to see how the self-organizing circumstances described in chapter 4 could be possible. This was especially the case given the record of fading implementation integrity over time that is so commonly reported in the comprehensive school reform literature.

The examples described in chapter 4 were possible because the theory, systems, and practices were in place for the design to be complete. In the summer of 1994, before the beginning of the project's second year, this was definitely not the case. As it turned out, the design struggled in an incomplete condition for another 3 years. Getting there had been a complex undertaking. Despite the problems, it is fair to say that the implementation improved year over year instead of regressing (New England Association of Schools and Colleges, 1996). The risk of failure was ever present. However, the gap between theory and practice kept narrowing over time in ways that contrast to the accounts described in the comprehensive school reform literature.

CONCLUSIONS

The theory and practice descriptions included in this chapter demonstrate the importance of a complete design in any site-based school reform. Despite the immense effort represented in the account of the embedded design process, the issues described in the last two chapters show that the design was incomplete and that much had to be done to make it capable of producing a school-level schema. Many reforms never get this far. Proponents run out of energy, and the programs, though frequently retaining the rhetorical features of an altered school, regress toward the preexisting model.

The major conclusion from the scale-up period of the self-organizing school project is a simple one: It is near impossible to build a jumbo jet in flight or change a tire on a moving vehicle. These analogies are often used to indicate just how hard it is to do reform on the fly. However, the history of school reform suggests that they are really much more apt descriptions of the crash that is all but inevitable.

In hindsight, the curriculum problem and its solution showed that it is impossible to build the components required to seriously reform a school while trying to run one without the addition of significant resources. This is especially the case if a school is to be profoundly altered to support research-based practice and differentiated instruction with high levels of implementation integrity.

The self-organizing school project ultimately scaled successfully because additional resources were brought in to do much more than was normally possible. These included the software and curriculum development undertaken over summer breaks and the introduction of the network of teams to support the growing design. As the curriculum, professional development, and tools averted a crisis, the network of teams and organizational design emerged to support the new approach, thereby validating the efforts occurring in classroom and on teaching and learning teams.

The most important takeaway from this chapter is to ask and answer for every reform "What does the term *complete* mean to make a reform viable at scale?" and "What is the relationship between being complete and providing teachers with a reasonable and doable role?" These ideas are intertwined and ultimately determine the viability of a reform (e.g., Bodily, 1998).

Although the scale-up phase of the self-organizing school project was far from a picture of seamless theory into practice, the account shows why theory needs to drive reforms and emerge from experience. The theory systems and practices that underpin the project explain what a design needs to be. This provides a pilot process with a vision of what is needed for success and a map for how to get there. Few theories provide an immediate seamless account of a phenomenon of interest. They develop over time by the trial and error that tests and retests their assumptions, key ideas, and details.

In the self-organizing school project, the schema produced by the theory was at first a vision, then a 5-year process of successive approximation, before finally assuming the regularities and consistencies required for self-organization. The process was perilous, and the project surfed the edge of chaos (Pascale et al., 2000). Even in its incomplete form, there was sufficient integrity of purpose and design during the scale-up period for the project to progress toward a complete schema. The scale-up process was not an end in itself but simply a beginning for the self-organizing capacity necessary to make the design sustainable.

The account described in this chapter reinforces an assertion made in chapter 2. The stress and challenge of the initial implementation process form a major reason for the limited data on implementation integrity in comprehensive school reform. This was certainly the case for the pilot phase of the self-organizing school project and explains why the account described in the last two chapters is largely anecdotal.

Just getting the design into place consumed the energy of all involved. However, this circumstance changed completely in the adoption phase when, with a complete design in place, the self-organizing school project was able to produce extensive emergent feedback. In this way, it diverges significantly from the existing reform literature. Although these data do not confirm the details of the account described in the preceding chapters, they do lend support to the stated outcomes of the pilot phase and the existence of a fully implemented design.

Chapter 10 describes the implementation integrity data and results of the project for the 4 years that followed the pilot phase. The following two chapters address missing or underutilized parts of comprehensive school reform or site-based reform. They highlight the need for the systemic use of feedback and technology and illustrate the relationship between these essential features.

CHAPTER TAKEAWAYS

1. Teams exist to execute the school's schema at scale.
2. The design of teams is subject to embedded design, scaled up to all levels of the school.
3. A successful network of teams has a small-world effect, the way that a friend of a friend becomes a friend (Barabasi, 2002).
4. Links that would normally seem to represent long pathways in the communication network of a school can be made short by the school's technology.
5. The likelihood of a small world in the professional sense is predicated on a commonality of action and purpose that extends beyond a shared sense of mission. A strong schema will enable professional friendships to occur and grow the network so that self-organization can happen.
6. Theory provides the conditions for the testing, successive approximation, and progressive development that can bring a design to scale.
7. The immense challenge of getting to scale in the self-organizing school is simply the precursor to a process of constant dynamic change.
8. The level of fragility and resilience in a reform can be established by determining how rapidly the removal of nodes and edges would threaten the overall sustainability of the implementation.
9. You cannot build a jumbo jet in flight.
10. It is better to do all of a design on a small scale than to try to implement an incomplete design on a large scale. The reason is that the self-reinforcement that can ultimately emerge from a complete design can catalyze the process of scaling up. A large-scale incomplete design is much more likely to exacerbate the critical effect of missing parts and create problems that are too large to manage and redress at scale.

NOTES

1. Particular credit goes to David Smith and Pete Caesar, the school's academic leaders at the time.

2. Adam Man developed the demonstration curriculum module.

3. Two grants from the EE Ford Foundation were instrumental in completing the self-organizing school project curriculum.

4. A grant from the Carlisle Foundation made the software development possible.

CHAPTER 8

Emergent Feedback

To live only for some future goal is shallow. It's the sides of the mountain that sustain life, not the top.—Robert M. Pirsig

According to Hattie (2003), feedback holds the number one position on the list of things that influence student learning. Feedback provides the ongoing "mountainside" sustenance necessary for all learning, including the essential understandings required for the successful implementation of comprehensive school reforms. As described in chapter 2, the design of systems, processes, and methods for giving feedback has been a significant weakness in most comprehensive school reform models (Berends et al., 2001).

The gap between the important contribution of feedback to classroom learning and the difficulty in making it work at the level of the school represents yet another example of the challenge of scale in school design and reform. The difficulty bridging this gap was clearly illustrated in the description of the scale-up of the self-organizing school project described in chapter 7. This chapter is about how the design and implementation of effective feedback systems can close the gap between classroom feedback and its unrealized potential at scale in schools.

The chapter explains in detail the emergent feedback principle introduced in chapter 3, with a focus on the next-generation design targets of being comprehensive and providing emergent feedback. It defines emergent feedback and shows how and why it is different from traditional approaches to school feedback and evaluation. The chapter also reconciles the many discrete examples of feedback described throughout the book, to provide a total picture of emergent feedback in a self-organizing school. This involves explaining how the feedback tools described in earlier chapters are represented in a total emergent feedback system. The chapter also provides an example of how the emergent feedback principle functions in a self-organizing school.

Developers can use the chapter to reflect on the feedback approaches currently used in their designs. In doing so, they can reconcile this key design principle with the specifications of their own models and those required for next-generation comprehensive school reform. For site developers, the chapter presents examples of the way that a school's feedback system is developed.

CRITICAL OMISSION

Chapter 2 highlights the need for comprehensive school reform to include internal mechanisms for generating feedback. However, Berends et al. (2001) note that none of the seven competing models that reached the scale-up phase of the New American Schools project had complete formative evaluation and feedback measures included in their designs. The chapter also highlights the limited attention that is given to feedback in comprehensive school reform evaluation in general and the heavy reliance on external evaluation to detect implementation integrity and effects. As described in chapter 2, those approaches frequently lack the time and resources to get more than a snapshot of what is going on in a comprehensive school reform.

The debilitating effect of poor feedback was aptly illustrated in the early years of the self-organizing school project, where the scaling of the incomplete project made feedback difficult and sometimes contentious. The implementation in those years was a far cry from the promise of the theory.

EMERGENT FEEDBACK DEFINED

In successful complex systems, feedback is defined as a network of constant exchange among individuals and groups referenced to the system's schema (Waldrop, 1993). The schema is constantly revised as a result of the feedback exchange. Feedback makes it possible for agents to grow in their capacities and for complex systems to produce self-organizing solutions (Pascale et al., 2000).

The student problem-solving activities (described in chapters 3 and 7), the development of new software and the roles of students (described in chapter 4), and the way that innovations scale up (described in chapter 6) each emerged from feedback. When a self-organizing system learns to talk to itself through the constant exchange of feedback among individuals, an overall benefit accrues to the system as a result (Gell-Mann, 1994; Johnson, 2001; Pascale et al., 2000; Waldrop, 1993). From this theoretical perspective, a school can get smarter over time by producing higher-order behavior. Johnson (2001) claims that such behavior emerges from the collective activity and response of the individuals involved in the feedback exchange. This constant exchange is the essence of emergent feedback. It is deep instead of shallow because it emerges from the actions of many agents and because it happens all of the time. It also provides the full explanatory account of what is going on in a system that is necessary to explain any summative, or "mountaintop," finding of success or failure. What, then, makes feedback emergent in a school or comprehensive school reform, and how is it different from traditional forms of feedback and evaluation in schools?

First, an emergent feedback system represents what the school believes about teaching and learning (its schema). The cooperative learning example described in chapter 6 demonstrates this idea, by showing how a feedback practice and tool emerged from the simple rules and the six steps of embedded design.

Second, an emergent feedback system provides information that everyone involved in a system needs in order to successfully fulfill their day-to-day roles. This characteristic is described in chapter 7 in the way that three levels of school teams used feedback from students to evaluate and problem-solve a day-to-day issue with cooperative learning.

Third, an emergent feedback system disperses control to teachers and students, which results in self-organizing solutions to the school's needs and challenges. This characteristic was highlighted by the way that the database and self-monitoring solutions described in chapter 4 emerged bottom-up from the disparate action of agents in the system. It is also highlighted in the example of student-initiated problem solving described in the last chapter.

Fourth, and as a consequence of the previously mentioned characteristic, information collected by and about students, teachers, and administrators is never targeted solely at the summative performance of any individual. Rather, it first and foremost creates the conditions for individuals to make a purposeful and satisfying ongoing contribution to their personal success through the growth of the school as a learning community. At any given point in time, a snapshot can be taken of that mountainside contribution for mountaintop, or summative, purposes. However, the latter never precedes the former.

Fifth, feedback amplifies successful activity in a system and dampens actions that are unproductive (Johnson, 2001), thereby clarifying the relationship between values, intent, and action. In the early years of the self-organizing school pilot, the inability to amplify and dampen made the pilot complex, whereas the incomplete design hampered the development of the self-reinforcing relationship across values, intent, and action.

Sixth, and as described in chapter 3, emergent feedback drives constant change in the system. It captures, reflects, and reinforces the consistencies in the relationship between teaching and learning in a school. In doing so, it creates the conditions for changing that relationship as the system learns (Gell-Mann, 1994). The result is an evolving and dynamic order. One iteration of a school schema gives way to another as a result of the self-organizing and emergent behavior that results from feedback. Part of this process also involves change in the feedback system and tools.

FIVE STEPS

In a self-organizing school, emergent feedback is a low-inference next-step forward from how the simple rules define the roles and trajectories of individuals and teams. There are five steps in building an emergent feedback approach:

Step 1—Identify approaches: Identify the methods used to gather feedback (e.g., observations, surveys).

Step 2—Identify perspectives: Establish the sources of feedback (e.g., students, teachers).

Step 3—Build tools: Build the content of the tools included in the feedback system.

Step 4—Scale up the feedback tools: Identify how feedback for individuals scales up to other units and levels in the school (e.g., teams).

Step 5—Design technology: Design the technological approach required to gather, manage, and use the feedback.

What follows is a detailed account of the steps and the way that they interact.

Identify Approaches

Multiple feedback approaches make it possible for a school community to use different methods to determine what is happening. The many facets of comprehensive school reform cannot be adequately captured by the ratings of a supervisor or peer, a small sample of classroom observations, or student performance on an annual high-stakes test. Each of these feedback methods has well-documented technical limitations, not to mention the face validity concerns expressed about them by teachers, especially when they are used in isolation (Foster & Cone, 1980; Hoge & Coladarci, 1989; Skiba & O'Sullivan, 1987).

However, when viewed collectively—and empowered by a professional culture of practice, surveys, and ratings—observations, reflections, and standardized performance data offer a powerful picture. These are used in the feedback process in a self-organizing school. Sometimes referred to as *360-degree feedback* (Manatt, 1997), this approach recognizes that, to get a clear and useful picture of the implementation and effects of comprehensive school reform, objective and subjective measures that can be cross-referenced or triangulated are required. The use of those approaches may produce convergent or divergent information, yet they always provide the basis for a more complete understanding of what is actually occurring.

Identify Perspectives

What a group of students sees in a class varies from what an administrator or a teaching peer sees. In an emergent feedback system, perspective matters. Feedback becomes rich when multiple sources and methods are included in the feedback conversation. Administrators, teachers, parents, and students can participate in an approach that triangulates perspectives through the different lenses of many agents. In every case, the perspective of individuals about their own performance is the cornerstone for all of the feedback. The strength of a self-organizing school rests with many agents at many levels using multiple methods to fuel a conversation about growth, adaptation, and performance.

Build Tools

In chapter 6, articulating the simple rules with research-based practices is described as the critical step in the embedded design process. The reason is that the characteristics of those practices defined or articulated all other parts of the design, including the feedback approach. The practices that are chosen to reflect the school's beliefs and values and to define roles and trajectories generate the content of emergent feedback tools. For example, with the dimension of a school's innovation (e.g., teaching and curriculum approaches, organizational innovations), the feedback methods (ratings, observations, reflections), and perspectives of interest (students, teachers, administrators), it becomes possible to build the tools for an emergent feedback system.

Building an emergent feedback tool in that system involves drilling down to examine aspects of selected research-based practices that will constitute the priority sources of feedback that, in turn, become items on feedback tools. The items are then connected with the methods and perspectives described in the previous sections of this chapter. What follows is a detailed description of that process.

Figure 8.1 describes the trajectory of two items. One item appears on an observation protocol for cooperative learning. The second appears on a team survey. Their trajectory is mapped from the simple rule through to the feedback tool.

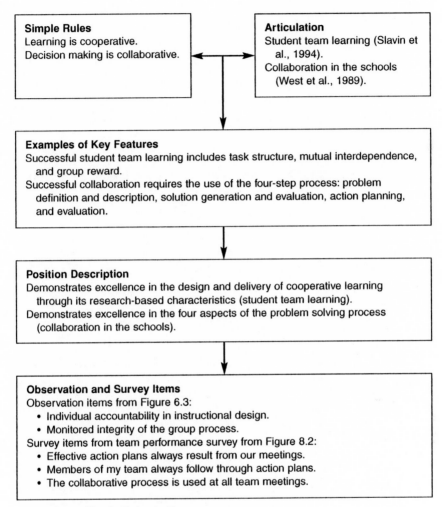

Simple Rules
Learning is cooperative.
Decision making is collaborative.

Articulation
Student team learning (Slavin et al., 1994).
Collaboration in the schools (West et al., 1989).

Examples of Key Features
Successful student team learning includes task structure, mutual interdependence, and group reward.
Successful collaboration requires the use of the four-step process: problem definition and description, solution generation and evaluation, action planning, and evaluation.

Position Description
Demonstrates excellence in the design and delivery of cooperative learning through its research-based characteristics (student team learning).
Demonstrates excellence in the four aspects of the problem solving process (collaboration in the schools).

Observation and Survey Items
Observation items from Figure 6.3:
- Individual accountability in instructional design.
- Monitored integrity of the group process.
Survey items from team performance survey from Figure 8.2:
- Effective action plans always result from our meetings.
- Members of my team always follow through action plans.
- The collaborative process is used at all team meetings.

Figure 8.1.   Simple Rules to Items

In this example, we see how simple rules about collaboration and co-operation and the content of selected approaches such as student team learning and collaboration in the schools were embedded in the roles of individuals and teams. That content then provided items for an observation tool and a team survey. A complete survey or observation protocol like the one described in Figure 6.3 becomes a simple extension of the process as more items are developed.

Scale Up the Feedback Tools

The example described in Figure 8.1 shows how feedback items can scale up to different levels of the school and how items are developed for the feedback shared by teams. The description of team role provides the definition required to develop feedback tools for use at the team level. In the same way, the definition of cooperation allows for the development of an appropriate feedback tool that focuses on cooperation for individual teachers. For example, Figure 8.2 describes an excerpt from a feedback tool used by teams to give feedback on their performance. It includes the items described in Figure 8.1.

Team Performance   return

name		faculty i.d.		record i.d.	
school	dept	team	level	average	
evaluator		type		date	term

notes

School Policy Goals:

- Our Team does a good job of implementing policy
- Our Team has a clearly defined role
- Our Team spends sufficient time to make everyone aware of the agenda and functioning of the group
- Team members have a sense of understanding of the goals of the Team
- My Team does a good job of student problem-solving
- My Team does a good job of scheduling
- My Team does a good job of instructional decision making

Implementation:

- Our Team meetings begin and end on time
- The collaborative process is used at all meetings when appropriate
- The role of recording, reporting and time-keeping are handled effectively
- The roles are rotated regularly
- My Team works with others to achieve school goals
- My Team leader does a good job of monitoring the Team process
- Effective Action Plans result from our meetings
- Members of my Team are interested in their own continuing education and model the active interest in learning that we hope to instill in our students
- Action Plans are followed through by members of my Team

Figure 8.2.   Team Performance Feedback Survey

The areas described on the tool reflect the emphases of the school's approach to collaboration. The items on the tool correspond to the example of the team position description in Figure 7.1. The leap of inference from rule to role to feedback to its expression in tools at scale is minimal. This is the essence of the regularity and consistency required for schema development.

Design Technology

The first three steps in the development of an emergent feedback system show how tools can be developed that use multiple methods to capture perspectives of agents at different levels in the self-organizing school. However, if emergent feedback is distinguished by its capacity to genuinely inform individuals about what to do next, then the information generated by those tools must be gathered, managed, and made available in the most efficient and timely fashion.

The research on feedback described in the introduction to this chapter indicates that to be successful, feedback needs to be frequent, timely, and informative (Hattie, 2003). However, most schools do not allocate extensive resources to feedback systems. This means that to be emergent, a system not only needs to accurately represent the school's beliefs, values, and actions about teaching and learning but must also avoid adding excessive burdens in terms of time, personnel, and cost. In the self-organizing school project, this challenging set of circumstances creates the drivers for a low-maintenance information technology solution.

In the self-organizing school, the day-to-day implementation of the emergent feedback system is based on deploying the same relational database technology that is used to build the curriculum tools described in the last chapter. The total community can access those tools. Specifically, the information technology tools designed for the self-organizing school project comprise 21 interrelated databases that are used to gather, manage, and report on the feedback occurring in the school. The files include the following:

- Classroom observation tools related to the body of practice (e.g., cooperative learning — see Figure 6.3 — as well as explicit teaching, classroom engagement, peer tutoring, math mastery teaching)

- Teacher surveys (peer, supervisor, and self)
- Teaching team survey (see Figure 8.2)
- Management team survey
- Indirect peer feedback and self-analysis for individuals and teams
- Reporting multimethod student feedback (e.g., portfolios, curriculum-based measures, standardized tests, social growth)
- Providing student feedback to teachers (see Figure 4.3)
- Integrating the aforementioned for reporting and portfolio development at the levels of individual, team, and school

Figure 8.3 describes the menu for the emergent feedback system tools. The system is designed to do the following:

- Stand alone without any designated personnel implications (e.g., manager or "reporter" of feedback information)
- Provide immediate access to all information (e.g., any survey, observation, or report can be seen by those involved as soon as it is entered on the database system)
- Scale up information (i.e., to automatically produce summaries of feedback at the level of teams, departments, or the school as a whole)
- Ensure appropriate transparent access (i.e., all members of the community have ready access to the tools and information required to do their jobs)
- Make rich feedback information available to all stakeholders at all levels of the school—including parents and students who have electronic access to information on how students, teachers, teams, and the school are doing—in a transparent fashion that respects privacy and confidentiality
- Be sufficiently open-ended in their architecture to adjust to changes in the design of feedback tools

Chapter 10 describes some of the implications associated with the feedback-gathering capability of the system. This includes gathering thousands of surveys, classroom observations, and reflections by students, peers, individuals, and supervisors.

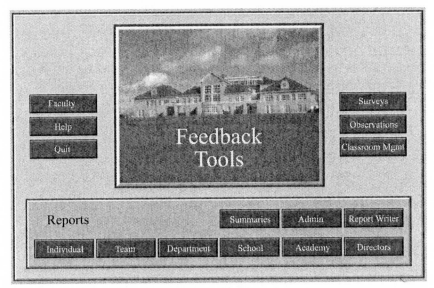

Figure 8.3.   Menu Layout for the Feedback Tools

FEEDBACK IN THE SELF-ORGANIZING SCHOOL

Individual and Team Growth

How are the emergent feedback system tools put to use to provide emergent feedback in a self-organizing school? The following examples describe the use of the tools at multiple levels, including a description of some of the reporting capabilities associated with their use.

The first and most obvious form of feedback at scale relates to the way in which team members employ the team as a venue for sharing their personal growth. Teachers use scheduled team meetings to present their reflections and the feedback that they have received from others. At those meetings, individuals use the schema and pattern language to describe needs, problems, and successes. Their personal experience evolves the schema and pattern language through the dialog with peers afforded by the network of teams. From their fellow team members, they can seek solutions to difficulties and confirmation for action and raise concerns or issues with the design. They can also discuss how each team member believes that he or she is contributing to the growth of the team. As teachers explore their practice, they not only reflect on their own growth but, by sharing their perceptions, build pattern language and evolve the schema. Figure 8.4 describes a feedback tool used by teachers at team meetings for individual reflection about pedagogy and student growth.

The fields on the right, under the heading "Open Faculty DB," contain summary data that describe teachers' use of the school's body of practice, including the cooperative learning approaches described in the last chapter. The fields also describe class engagement and feedback from peers and students. By clicking on the fields, the teacher can drill down to a lesson to look at quantitative data and a narrative reflection. This information can then be related to the student grade and social growth data described on the lefthand side of the layout. Those fields describe data on student growth, including grades, citizenship, attendance, curriculum-based measures, and class grouping. From this layout, teachers can link to specific student evaluations, lesson observations, and reflections.

By drilling down from this summative layout, teachers can use further objective and subjective sources to explore their feedback and look at relationships between their teaching and learning. After presenting a summary to their peers, it is possible to look at a lesson where a difficulty was encountered or where a success occurred and invite the team to comment or generate a solution to a problem. This kind of exchange invites teams into a self-organized and collaborative problem-solving process that provides opportunities to develop and share new approaches and solutions to a challenge or issue.

When combined with the team process, the emergent feedback system tools provide a stimulus for a conversation that can move rapidly from the general to the specific to pool the intelligence of the team and generate new knowledge. Self-organization happens through this process. New ideas emerge from the collective input of the group, and feedback informs the whole team because the open sharing process leads to the development of new ideas and solutions. The products of that sharing can be used in other classes and, based on their successes, may ultimately inform the simple rules and body of practice at the level of the school.

The second dimension of team feedback pertains to how the sum of individual feedback permits the team to look at the totality of student

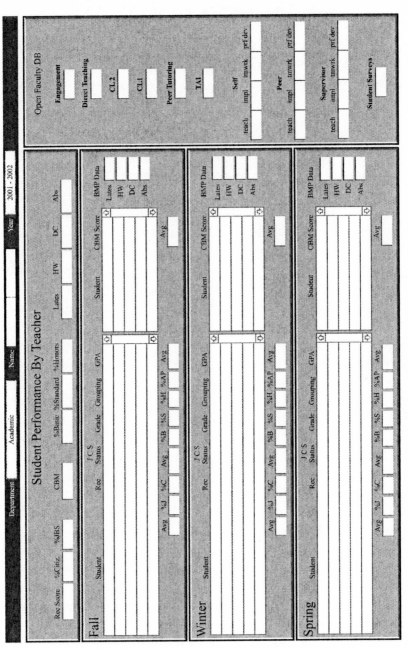

Figure 8.4. Report Layout for Student and Teacher Growth

or teacher performance across the team. Figure 8.5 describes a tool used by the team to look at overall team performance.

The figure describes summary data from the cumulative performance of students on the team. This tool scales up the student data described in Figure 8.4 to the level of the team. The layout is used in situations where the team needs information relating to student performance.

Students

Chapters 4 and 7 share examples of the potential for students to become active agents in the core activity of the self-organizing school. Those chapters describe how students built capacity with the school's pattern language and schema in ways that encouraged their active involvement in teaching and problem solving. For students to be fully empowered in these roles, they need access to feedback and the tools that enable them to partner with their teachers as active agents. This includes the tool described in Figure 4.3, which provides teachers with feedback. However, students also require access to the curriculum, to tools for the management of their own performance, to tools for sharing school benchmarks, and to the kind of collaborative productivity tool described in the last chapter. Figure 8.6 describes the menu from a set of student tools that are part of the overall technology system in the self-organizing school project. These tools mirror teacher access and enable students to have access to the just-in-time knowledge required to fulfill the role of a student in a self-organizing school.

School-Level Feedback

Much of the discussion to date about the role of feedback has focused on its capacity to enhance the growth of individuals and teams. So far, the examples of self-organization have shown how bottom-up activity that starts on a small scale can emerge to influence the whole school. However, the community can also use the accumulated knowledge generated by the emergent feedback system to manage and deploy the school's knowledge on a larger scale. For example, school-level feedback is a product of all feedback from individual and team levels.

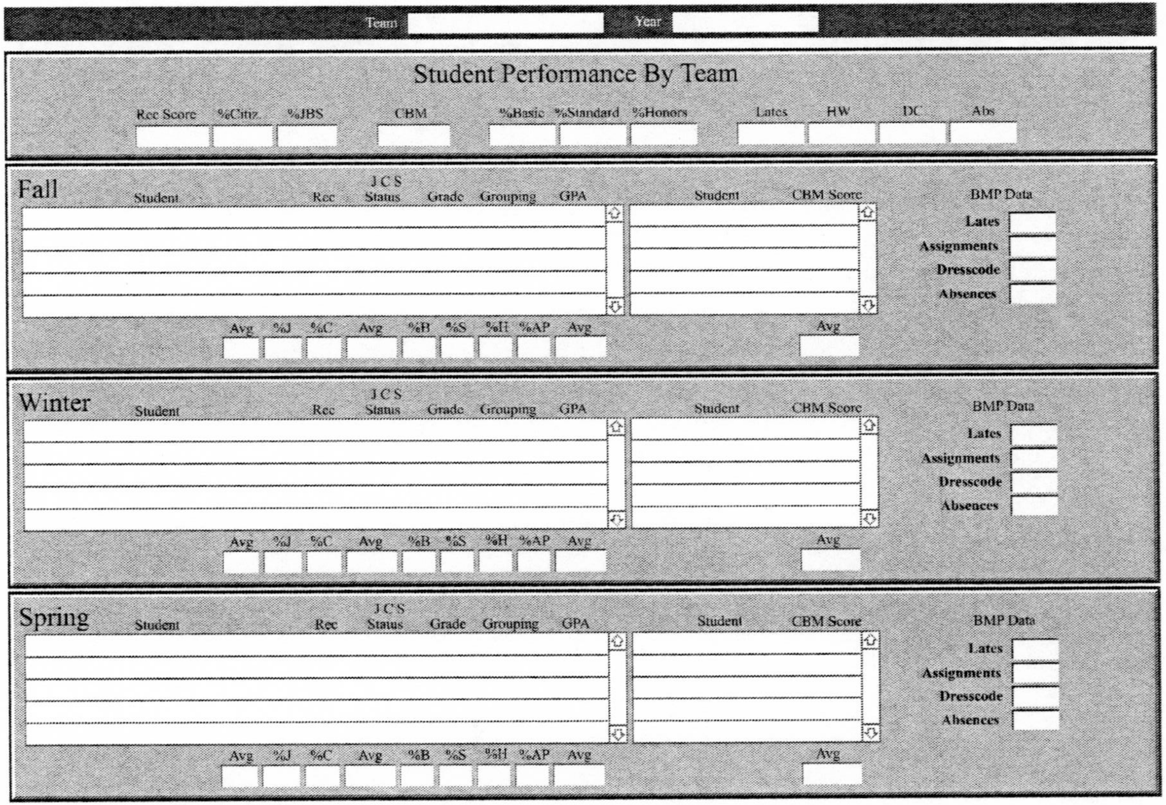

Student Performance By Team

Team   Year

Rec Score   %Citnz.   %JBS   CHM   %Basic   %Standard   %Honors   Lates   HW   DC   Abs

Fall

Rec   JCS Status   Grade   Grouping   GPA   Student   CBM Score   BMP Data
Student

Avg   %J   %C   Avg   %B   %S   %H   %AP   Avg   Avg

Lates
Assignments
Dresscode
Absences

Winter

Rec   JCS Status   Grade   Grouping   GPA   Student   CBM Score   BMP Data
Student

Avg   %J   %C   Avg   %B   %S   %H   %AP   Avg   Avg

Lates
Assignments
Dresscode
Absences

Spring

Rec   JCS Status   Grade   Grouping   GPA   Student   CBM Score   BMP Data
Student

Avg   %J   %C   Avg   %B   %S   %H   %AP   Avg   Avg

Lates
Assignments
Dresscode
Absences

Figure 8.5.   Layout for Team Performance

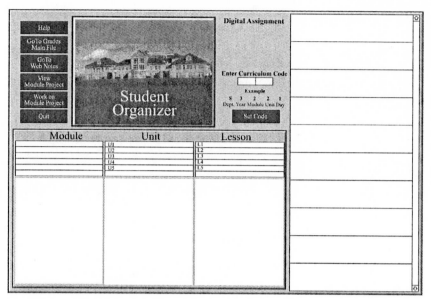

Figure 8.6.   Student Curriculum Tool

When this feedback is viewed at the level of the school, it becomes possible to ask some big questions about the community overall. Is the body of practice and curriculum working effectively across the school? Is student growth occurring at a rate and level commensurate with the school's expectations? Are teachers making satisfactory progress in the career path? Overall, how do students feel about their school? All of these questions can be answered at the school level. Figure 8.7 describes overall school performance in a number of key areas, including student feedback, classroom engagement, and the implementation of the body of practice.

Substantive answers to the big questions are made possible by answering smaller ones, using the emergent feedback system tools for sophisticated data mining and analysis. The scenario that follows illustrates how data mining can happen with an emergent feedback system.

The school's management or leadership finds that teaching and learning teams in the lower school seem to be experiencing lower levels of classroom engagement than those reported by other teams. The issue is raised at a leadership team meeting where some preliminary explanations are offered to account for the situation. The personnel team

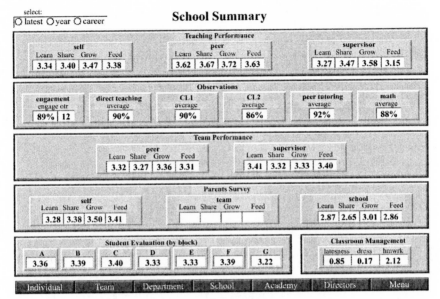

Figure 8.7. Layout for School-Level Performance

leader notes that there have been four new appointments on the junior school teams and all of those teachers are relatively inexperienced. This seems to be a plausible explanation for the engagement issue, although the leadership team can use the feedback system tools to test the veracity of this preliminary assessment.

The assistant principal engages in some data mining to explore the initial hypothesis by using the tools to first look at classroom management levels across teams and individual teachers. She finds that the lower levels of classroom engagement seem to be consistent across teachers and teams and are not explained by differences related to the new appointments. She decides to browse the curriculum tools (described in the last chapter) to get a sense of what kind of instruction has been occurring in recent weeks. She notes that students in both English and math have been engaged in a 5-week project-based module taught using cooperative learning.

After checking the curriculum tools, the assistant principal decides to review all observations of cooperative learning (e.g., Figure 6.3) undertaken during the 5-week cooperative learning module. As she reviews the observation protocols, she notices that that the overall implementation levels for cooperative learning seem to be lower than expected and that those lower ratings seem to be attributed to classroom management dimensions of the cooperative learning process. This includes whether or not the self-monitoring tool (described in chapter 4) is being used by students and teachers.

The assistant principal also reviews student feedback (see Figure 4.3) and notices that a number of students are finding the expert questions in the module difficult to understand. They do not seem to be closely linked to the resources made available for their research.

Finally, the assistant principal browses the recently completed records in the collaboration tool described in the last chapter and notices that some issues and solutions with cooperative learning have been on the meeting agenda of the lower-school teaching and learning teams and the school's management team. There seems to be some recognition of a problem.

The total process of mining the emergent feedback system took 40 minutes, during which a general idea about teacher inexperience as the cause of lower classroom engagement has turned into a highly detailed and potentially actionable account of the problem. The feedback indicates that the difficulties experienced by the lower-school teams are related to the use of cooperative learning and some additional issues related to curriculum design. The data mining produces information that can be the subject of team-based action to address the needs, not unlike the scenario described in the last chapter where student feedback resulted in a change to cooperative learning.

The findings may also stimulate development of the curriculum and team-based problem solving related to the use of cooperative learning. The assistant principal can contribute to the curriculum solution, although this does not occur in the form of top-down intervention. Feedback from the leader is shared with the teaching and learning team members who have the added benefit of a deep understanding of the context in which the problem is occurring. They may incorporate suggestions from the leader or generate a number of additional solutions that can be tested and evaluated as part of the ongoing team process. The processes of testing and evaluation are made possible because of the common pattern language and schema and transparent access to tools that shorten the distances across the network of teams in the school.

This example emphasizes how data mining and knowledge discovery can be employed to produce an emergent multifaceted solution to a need or problem. Such data mining is possible only because there is a common culture of practice and schema embedded in the school's emergent feedback system tools and curriculum software. These tools provide an accessible qualitative and quantitative data source that is amenable to the kind of deep analysis described in the example. The data emerges bottom-up to be used at scale. The approach also illustrates how the kind of decisions that so often proceed on assumption in schools can be subject to a more rigorous process of investigation and analysis that yields more accurate solutions. These solutions can inform the whole school as well as the team.

The more sophisticated solution is the product of the cumulative effect of the design empowered by the feedback that makes it dynamic. In the self-organizing school pilot, this kind of solution became possible only when the design and its implementation reached a threshold level of simple sophistication required to generate emergent feedback.

CONCLUSION

This chapter describes the way that emergent feedback provides the deep ongoing account of the behavior of a system required to instantiate and evolve its schema. The feedback exchange occurs at all levels in the system and is empowered by the network of teams over which the exchange occurs. Feedback amplifies what works in a system, and it dampens those things that do not (Johnson, 2001).

In the self-organizing school, the effect of feedback is to make explicit those areas that are helping and those areas that are getting in the way. In doing so, feedback clarifies the relationship between teaching and learning. This more predictable relationship between what a school does and its outcomes is necessary for the design to possess the self-reinforcing quality described in chapter 1.

This is the way that the essential features of a comprehensive school reform can be woven throughout a design so that those key ideas, processes, and practices are reinforced irrespective of which part of the design is engaged. Feedback makes self-reinforcement happen in a way that is necessary if comprehensive school reform is to produce the kind of timely and ongoing reflection necessary for sustainability. Waiting for external evaluation of complex innovations in school settings may be inviting a postmortem.

The chapter also illustrates the role of technology in catalyzing the effects of feedback. The emergent feedback system tools make feedback immediate, whereas the relational database technology permits data mining at all levels of the school. This technology addresses some of the biggest barriers to the provision of feedback in schools, including time, personnel, and cost. The feedback system tools are self-organizing, generating data at multiple levels and for a broad range of purposes without the need for active database management. They also sit at the center of a network of relational database software that includes the curriculum authoring software described in the last chapter.

The process and tools described in this chapter played a critical role in bringing the self-organizing school project to a sustainable position. Although they were part of the original vision, they took 5 years to develop. Their full effect on the project is illustrated in chapter 10.

CHAPTER TAKEAWAYS

1. Emergent feedback makes self-reinforcement possible by amplifying what works in the school and dampening what does not.
2. Emergent feedback in a self-organizing school is a low-inference next-step forward from the way that the simple rules defined the roles and trajectories of individuals and teams.
3. Emergent feedback happens bottom-up, although it can emerge at scale by mining the knowledge of the school.
4. The alignment between rule, role, trajectory, and feedback tools diminishes the ambiguity about feedback. In doing so, it strengthens the relationship between teaching and learning.
5. To be practical, emergent feedback systems need to be practical and self-organizing. Technology makes this possible.
6. Emergent feedback alters the schema that it creates and, in doing so, changes itself.

CHAPTER 9

Technology

A little neglect may breed great mischief.—Benjamin Franklin

The preceding chapters focus by way of example on the critical role that information technology plays in the self-organizing school. In every case, the content of the school's design was embedded in technology tools that were essential for its implementation. This defining role for technology in the self-organizing school project is unprecedented in comprehensive school reform, and it precluded the acquisition of an off-the-shelf solution to meet the project's needs. In comparison, chapter 2 describes information technology as an underdeveloped resource in comprehensive school reform and an important next-generation design target. This chapter is devoted to the role of technology because of these contrasting circumstances and the need to highlight the power of information technology in school reform.

This chapter unpacks the role played by technology in the self-organizing school project, with a focus on what makes technology educational. The frequent failure in school reform to reconcile practices that possess educational power with the inherent potential of information technology breeds the "mischief" described in the opening quote. The chapter defines educational technology and reconciles the many discrete examples described throughout the book to provide a total picture of the systemic role of technology in a self-organizing school.

The chapter has three specific purposes: First, it describes the relationship between information technology, self-organization, and knowledge management. This includes a discussion of the opportunities created when information technology is deeply embedded in the transactions of teaching and learning across a school. Second, it explains how the tools described in earlier chapters are represented in a total technology system that can create the conditions for self-organization and knowledge management. In doing so, this chapter presents an overall account of the way that information technology can be used in comprehensive school reform. The third purpose of the chapter is to show how the self-organizing school design is employed for technology planning.

Comprehensive school reform developers can use the chapter to reflect on the role that information technology currently plays in their designs and the way that it may be deployed in the future. Site developers can consider the role of the school's current and future technological infrastructure in their reform designs.

INFORMATION TECHNOLOGY, SELF-ORGANIZATION, AND KNOWLEDGE MANAGEMENT

A recurring theme common to the successful application of information technology in professional fields is the way that technology is used to advance the core activity of those fields. This phenomenon is seen in the application of technologies to surgical practice in medicine, computer-assisted design in engineering, and the management of inventory in business. The surgeon uses the arthroscope to trim a cartilage; the structural engineer uses modeling software to simulate the stresses on a bridge; the inventory manager predicts future needs based on current sales using inventory management software. In each case, technology enables, empowers, and accelerates the essential or core transactions undertaken by those professionals. The technology tools are a "pointy end" expression of the pattern language, the schema, the cumulative research, and the knowledge in the professionals' respective fields.

Not surprising, the connection between technology and professional practice that is evident in other fields remains a largely unrealized objective in the application of information technology at scale in schools and comprehensive school reform (Becker, 2001; Cuban, 2001; Gipson,

2003; Hasselbring, 2001; Hofstetter, 2001; Weston, 2006). Studies seek to establish the differential effects of information technology on school teaching and learning under conditions where there is no agreed-on understanding of what that teaching and learning is or means. This is the neglect that breeds great mischief in the use of technology in schools and school reform. As noted throughout the book, the problems of establishing and sustaining cultures of practice at the level of the school make it difficult to build those scalable pointy-end applications of technology that help teachers with the core transactions of teaching and learning and establish its role in the teaching and learning process.

When used at scale in schools, information technology is much more commonly employed to automate current practice. We see evidence of automation in the use of web pages for content acquisition, instead of books; in the electronic management of attendance, where formerly there was paper; in teachers' use of PowerPoint instead of the whiteboard; and in server-based content management as a replacement for filing cabinets. All of these applications are purposeful, yet none actually addresses how teaching and learning is transacted using the research-based professional practice of the field. They are not unlike the surgeon or restaurant owner who employs software to manage his or her day-to-day activities. The software may shorten the time in the waiting room or make for faster service, but the relationship of those automating tools to better surgery or better meals is less clear and requires a much greater leap of inference.

In addition, it is important to recognize that the transformation from automation to pointy-end application can be subtle and is not necessarily inherent to the characteristics of any particular technology. For example, an electronic grade book that simply transforms the scores and weightings of assignments from paper to spreadsheet can be viewed as relatively straightforward automation. However, if that grade book included functions for calculating improvement points for cooperative learning or for managing the mastery of objectives in a mastery teaching model, the situation changes. The inclusion of an improvement point calculation feature or a way to manage mastery objectives represent the embedding of educationally powerful research-based practice in a software tool. Two electronic grade books similar in overall intent—one represents an example of automation, whereas the other captures well-established research on teaching, learning, and assessment.

A second key issue or question relates to whether the research-based grading software sits idiosyncratically on just one or three teachers' computers or turns out to be located on a server used by all teachers. This distinction expresses whether the pointy-end use of information technology is idiosyncratic or an expression of the way that research about cooperation and mastery is part of a schoolwide approach that scales up to exert school-level influence.

The theory, systems, and practices described throughout the book are proposed as a solution to the problem of embedding research-based practice in information technology tools used at scale. When expressed in the school's design and information technology, the theory empowers the school to act in specific ways, to transact its views about teaching and learning and how it gives feedback.

By applying the principles of self-organization, a school or comprehensive school reform can position itself to benefit from information technology in a manner consistent with its successful deployment in other fields. For example, a school that has assigned value to cooperative learning or collaboration and then defined that value in practice can design software to enable the key transactions of its practice in the same way that a doctor can capture the potential of laser technology or that an engineer can do so with the power of three-dimensional modeling. This potential is only available to a school that has an articulated culture of practice defined at the school level.

KNOWLEDGE MANAGEMENT

The opportunity afforded by this scaled-up educational technology extends beyond the benefit that many teachers gain by using tools for more effective teaching and learning. It is about what happens when information technology is used to share the collective knowledge created by those teachers.

A school can use relational databases to gather, manage, store, and use the results of teaching observations, the ratings of team performance, the outcomes of collaborative meetings, and the information included in teacher and student growth portfolios. Information technology makes it possible to manage, cross-reference, and use this accumulated knowledge for problem solving at all levels of the school.

The power of knowledge management is illustrated in the data-mining example from chapter 8. It shows how the data derived from a set of interconnected tools for delivering feedback and curriculum, as well as for reporting student performance, can be mined to explain changes in student engagement. A school leader accessed multiple databases to investigate a problem and in doing so produced a deep and actionable account of a set of circumstances that existed on multiple teams.

The key to successful knowledge management is making the critical work processes and patterns of an organization explicit (Petrides & Nodine, 2003) so that relevant data can be gathered and acted on. The most basic unit of data in a knowledge management system is known as atomistic data (Thorn, 2001). In schools, atomistic data usually comprise student attendance, behavioral incidents, and the results of high-stakes tests (Cileo & Harvey, 2005; Petrides & Nodine, 2003; Sallis & Jones, 2002).

When taken at face value, these seem to be logical examples of atomistic data. Clearly, students need to be present for learning to occur. The timing and location of behavioral incidents may point to ecological factors that contribute to behavior problems. Variability in student performance in high-stakes testing may point to curricular needs, strengths, and weaknesses. However, in every case, these examples provide data that are one or more steps removed from the core transactions of teaching and learning. Understanding and articulating core transactions are described throughout the book as being essential for implementing research-based practice at scale. They include the way that students and teachers use the steps in a collaborative process, interact with the elements of research-based practices such as cooperative learning, and respond to the way that a lesson or assessment item is adapted.

When knowledge management is confined to data derived from a general level, the analysis and subsequent problem solving are invariably speculative and likely to produce general solutions or perpetuate false assumptions (e.g., that low classroom engagement is caused by inexperienced teachers). For genuine knowledge management, a school needs to capture data about the core transactions of teaching and learning that happen day-to-day in classrooms.

In short, the success of any knowledge management approach for schools requires the collection of data directly related to teaching and learning. Such data will exist only if a school has articulated its educational practice at scale.

A school or comprehensive school reform can define its core transactions and atomistic data by applying the six principles introduced in chapter 3 and described in the subsequent chapters of the book. The application of these principles makes it possible to articulate a school's essential teaching and learning transactions and to generate the real atomistic data required for knowledge management in ways currently unavailable in comprehensive school reform.

FROM TOOLS TO SYSTEM

How are the technology tools connected to make the aforementioned educational use of technology possible? The purpose of information technology in the self-organizing school is to translate the school's schema and embedded design into an operating system for everyday practice. That system connects the tools for managing and monitoring student growth with tools for sharing feedback and designing and delivering instruction. The end product is a practical toolbox that can be used by everyone in the school. The connectedness creates the potential for knowledge management and self-organization.

Every time that a community member uses any or all of the tools, he or she builds capacity with the school's schema. This includes the use of lesson design tools in professional development described in chapters 3, 6, and 7; the use of the curriculum design tools described in chapters 6 and 7; and the use of the collaboration tool described in chapter 7. In each example, the tools expressed the school's simple rules, embedded design, similarity at scale, and feedback. All of these elements comprise a school schema. Earlier in chapter 7 we saw what can happen when a design that is predicated on a deeply embedded and critical role for technology failed to produce the necessary tools to make a design work. In the case of the self-organizing school pilot, the arrival of a full suite of tools was a tipping point for the entire effort.

Figure 9.1 describes the menu fields for those tools that were developed as part of the self-organizing school project, from which most of the examples used throughout the book are drawn.

The figure shows the scope of the software system. It includes databases that exist in every school for gathering student demographic information, attendance, transcripts, and grades. This information is contained in the admissions or student records database shown in Figure 9.1. However, there are also differences, including the database for the design, management, and delivery of curriculum; the database for feedback; and the database for instructional support. The database for instructional support manages all of the information and resources related to the adaptation of instruction to address individual difference.

All of these databases connect with one another, enabling the school to talk to itself as a system. Just as it makes sense for a traditional transcript database to connect to a database for reporting grades, in the self-organizing school the databases connect to others for designing curriculum, gathering feedback on classroom practice, and much more. The reason is that the totality of the self-organizing school is embedded in and embodied by its information technology.

PORTALS

One of the benefits of the software tools described here is that they make the complex simple. This idea is illustrated in chapter 7, where the development of curriculum tools made the process of building a differentiated curriculum more accessible. The design became simpler yet more sophisticated with the tools. This example can be extended by considering how the suite of tools described in Figure 9.1 is best represented to members of the community in the most sophisticated yet simple way.

From a technical standpoint, it may make sense to organize databases around the data relationships described in Figure 9.1 (e.g., student records or school performance tools). However, such an organizational design does not necessarily reflect their use from the perspective of teachers, students, and parents who use those tools day-to-day. Given the self-organizing school theory and the idea of simple sophistication,

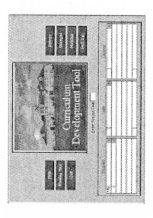

Figure 9.1.   Menus From the Database System

Teacher Menu

Setup	Learning	Sharing	Feedback	Growth	Our School
Password	Curriculum Tools	Team Meeting Protocol	Reflections	My Portfolio	Learning Statements
Logout			Gradebook	Class Growth Snapshot	Curriculum Benchmarks
	Classes and List	My Goals	Opinion Surveys		
		Team Goals		Individual Snapshot	Our Teaching
	Homework Builder		Obervations	Yearly Performance (Teacher/Leader)	Nichies, Levels and Growth
	IS Tools	Management Goals	Me This Week		
		SLT Goals	Student Summaries	Current Performance	Feedback
		Progress by Team	Learning Environment Summary	Team Performance Hub	Technology
		Progress by School			The Institute
				School Performance Hub	

Figure 9.2.   Teacher Portal

it makes more sense to organize them to suit the roles of individuals in the community. For example, Figure 9.2 describes the way that the databases described in Figure 9.1 could be represented as portals on a web page that faculty access as part of the school's intranet. This representation organizes the tools around four dimensions: learning, sharing, feedback, and growth.

The first dimension, learning, includes the tools for the design and delivery of classroom curriculum and lessons—for instance, student portfolios, guidelines for growth in the curriculum, the tools and resources required to complete authentic assessment products, and homework organizers. That is, it includes everything that a teacher needs in order to go to class and then act on what happens after he or she has been. For example, a teacher can send and receive homework, review grades, and open the day's lesson using tools from the learning dimension of the portal.

The second dimension, sharing, refers to the use of technology to capture and record the roles, goals, and progress of all the agents and teams in the school. This is where agents see how the school is functioning at all levels on a day-to-day basis. The meeting protocol described in chapter 6 is an example of this dimension. A teacher, student, or parent can use the sharing dimension to look at school or team goals and the action taken in relation to those goals.

The third dimension, feedback, is where the tools are located for sharing feedback. It is where teachers go to self-evaluate their progress in the career path. It is also the access point for the classroom observation tools, surveys, and reflections. The feedback dimension is where the self-organizing school acts on its small-world capability and shares perspectives on how it is doing. It is where feedback is turned into something that can be used and developed to help teachers plan a new piece of software or build an action plan to help a student grow effectively in the curriculum. These tools are used when a teacher agrees to observe a colleague's class or a student provides feedback to a teacher.

The fourth dimension, growth, is the access point for reports about all aspects of the school's performance. It is also where teachers log on to look at their classroom observations or student feedback; it is where they see how all of their students are growing in the curriculum. This place in the portal provides the source of the information that is required to decide what happens next. The reports that exist here are dynamic; they represent the latest feedback from ratings observations and ongoing reflections. Overall, the portal is a workplace, the location for accessing the tools required to do a job.

The portal illustrates the idea of simple sophistication. Although a large number of databases and relationships exist behind or underneath the tools represented on the portal, its configuration is simple. Thus, the design is accessible by linking the tools directly to the everyday roles of members of the community.

The access to a school's technology tools need not be confined to teachers. The second example of self-organization described in chapter 4 (i.e., the way that a teacher shares the schema and feedback with students) shows how a school's schema and design can engage students as active teaching and learning agents in the self-organizing school. Clearly, for this to happen at scale, access to the school's technology tools needs to be extended to students if they are to successfully fulfill their new roles as teachers and learners. Figure 9.3 describes a student portal, also organized under the four areas of learning, sharing, feedback, and growth.

This portal is where students go to look at their day-to-day-progress, review their grades, and give feedback to teachers and teams. In using

StudentMenu

![Setup] Setup	![Learning] Learning	![Sharing] Sharing	![Feedback] Feedback	![Growth] Growth	![Our School] Our School
Password	Learning	My Goals	My Grades	My Portfolio	Learning Statements
Logout	My Curriculum	Team Goals	Opinion	Class Growth Snapshot	Curriculum Benchmarks
	My Classes	Team Meeting	Me This Week	My Team Snapshot	Our Teaching
	Homework	Progress by Team	MySummary	This Year	Nichies, Levels and Growth
	Support			Last Year	Feedback
	Career Ladder			Team Performance	Technology
				School Performance	The Institute

Figure 9.3.   Student Portal

the portal, they become active agents in the totality of the school as a learning community.

In a similar fashion, parents can become meaningfully engaged with the school's design through their own tools. Figure 9.4 describes a parent portal that can be used by parents and caregivers to follow the progress of their children and the school, give and receive feedback, and share their perspectives on the growth of the school.

Each portal organizes the tools in a way that best reflects the roles of teacher, student, and parent. The roles that they fill differentiate their portals, but the portal design aims to be transparent and provide a timely flow of feedback among agents that is necessary for self-organization.

Parent Menu

![Setup] Setup	![Learning] Learning	![Sharing] Sharing	![Feedback] Feedback	![Growth] Growth	![Our School] Our School
Password	Learning	Goals Hub (Student, Team. School)	Grades	My Portfolio	Learning Statements
Logout	Curriculum		Opinion	Growth Snapshot	Curriculum Benchmarks
	Homework	Team Meeting Record	This Week	Team Snapshot	Our Teaching
			Summary	This Year	Nichies, Levels and Growth
				Last Year	Feedback
				Team Performance	Technology
				School Performance	The Institute

Figure 9.4.   Parent Portal

The tools described in previous chapters come together in one accessible place. In the examples described here, the portals represent the principle of similarity at scale. Parent tools are similar to teacher tools and student tools. Because all agents have access to individual, school, and team performance, they can share goals and feedback and talk to each other and the school.

SYSTEMIC EFFECT

This brief account of the role and organization of technology describes how individual tools that are deeply embedded in the school's design can become a whole system. Every time that teachers or students share their perspectives or reflect and collaborate, the conditions for self-organization occur in ways that support their understanding of the existing schema and create the conditions for what will happen next. Information technology engages the six principles of self-organization to become the virtual hyperedge, described in chapter 7, that shortens the connection in the three-tier network of teams and makes the school's world small.

The preceding chapters illustrate this phenomenon in the examples of the collaborative meeting tool that enabled agents at all levels in the network to exchange ideas, in the way that students and teachers share common access to the curriculum, in the way that the curriculum authoring tools reduced the cognitive load associated with curriculum development, and in the way that lesson observations were shared immediately with all involved in the process. In these roles, information technology instantiates what is, makes the intelligence of the school simpler and more accessible, and helps accelerate the process of making it all different.

THE SELF-ORGANIZING TECHNOLOGY PLAN

How does a self-organizing school plan for information technology? Traditional technology planning is a forward-mapping process. Barnett (2001) describes 10 essential and commonly cited elements for successful technology plans:

1. Building a vision
2. Ensuring stakeholder involvement
3. Gathering data
4. Reviewing research
5. Building curriculum integration
6. Committing to professional development
7. Developing sound infrastructure
8. Allocating appropriate resources
9. Planning for ongoing monitoring and assessment
10. Preparing for the future

In the self-organizing school, this forward-mapping process is inverted because the school does not need to build a separate vision of technology and research, find idiosyncratic ways to involve stakeholders, or collect data uniquely for a technology-planning process. Steps 1–6 of the traditional process are already deeply embedded in the school's design, its simple rules, schema, collaborative process, feedback, and research-based practice. They are reflected in the school's day-to-day operation and do not have to be reinvented for technology decision making.

The development of the new software for managing cooperative learning, described in chapter 4, illustrates this point. A need to manage cooperative learning was identified, based on the school's feedback tools. This passed through the school's teams and ultimately altered the school's design, leading to the new software being introduced and the school's professional development program being adjusted. Figure 9.5 describes the process in more detail.

Spontaneous self-organization scales up through the school's network of teams, and leadership decisions relate to broad-based implementation. The second-level technology team is responsible for making the changes happen through designing new software as well as through implementing changes to the network infrastructure. Professional development needs are represented in the cycle, although there is no specific technology training, given that training related to new technology is addressed within the context of the overall embedded design.

The figure reflects the way that the six principles of self-organization interact to produce a different approach to technology planning. For

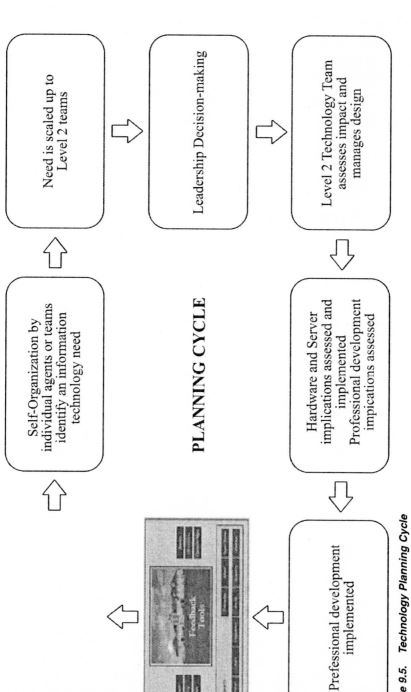

Figure 9.5. Technology Planning Cycle

example, the school's vision exists in a dynamic form that is expressed in simple rules and schema. It does not need to be developed for the purposes of technology planning. The network of teams exists all the time to ensure the bottom-up involvement of the community. All members of the community are stakeholders and active participants through the three-tier network, so there is no need to create a separate process to build a plan. By applying the embedded design principle, curriculum integration and professional development are included from the bottom up in the school's educational technology.

When information technology is a product of the self-organizing school's design, a much clearer picture emerges of where, when, and how often technology will be used. This creates an opportunity to be far more specific, focused, and fiscally confident when entering a discussion about hardware, software, and infrastructure. Instead of a conversation about counting classes, teachers, and students to determine network access, the plan would ask the following:

How often do students need to access their portal and from where? How has this changed since the last plan?

What do we need to add to the lesson design tools to make them more accessible for new teachers?

How do changes to cooperative learning affect the design of observation tools?

How can we make tools for writing reflections more efficient?

How can the curriculum descriptions on the parent tools be made more dynamic?

What type and model of computer or network are required to run the tools and associated applications?

Decisions about access, software, and connectivity get much easier in this context. The process is emergent. The design creates the conditions for a genuine educational technology, as expressed in its information technology tools. Because the tools are an embodiment of what the school is all about and are part of the school's design, decisions about whether to purchase site licenses for productivity software or upgrade the system hardware are embedded within broader decisions about the school's educational technology.

The six principles create the conditions, content, culture, and process for constant planning and adaptation. In this way, the technology plan is a microcosm of the school's design—everything in it embodies everything in the school. When the school decides what it means by teaching, learning, and curriculum, technology decisions can occur in a context.

CONCLUSION

In summary, this chapter describes how tools used by individuals in a self-organizing school can scale up as a technology system to have school-level influence. In doing so, they can have a profound influence on the conduct, viability, and sustainability of a comprehensive school reform. This occurs in three ways. First, the process builds connections across the tools that help individuals fulfill their roles. Second, the tools create the conditions for managing knowledge and using the school's professional knowledge at scale. Of particular importance is the way that school-level influence emerges bottom-up by paying greater attention to individuals through the use of information technology. Third, the systems for planning, growth, and change are an embedded part of the organizational design in a self-organizing school, so planning is not a separate event.

This chapter emphasizes the role of technology as a product of and catalyst for the six principles of the self-organizing school. Every time that members of the community use the information technology system, they rededicate themselves to those principles and the school design they created, while also establishing the conditions for that design to change.

The following chapter provides an account of the results of the self-organizing school project and includes two studies that show how technology can help a comprehensive school reform exert schoolwide influence and improve the educational power of the school's approach to teaching and learning.

CHAPTER TAKEAWAYS

1. Information technology in the self-organizing school reconciles the content and process of a comprehensive school reform in a

total system that articulates the school's schema in day-to-day practice.

2. Information technology advances professional fields by representing their professional knowledge in technology tools.

3. The real power of information technology in schools is in the management and deployment of classroom knowledge at the level of the school. Knowledge management is synonymous with school-level influence and the educational power of a design.

4. The application of the six principles of self-organization generates the atomistic data required for knowledge management.

5. In a self-organizing school, technology planning happens all the time.

CHAPTER 10

Results

A prudent question is one-half of wisdom.—Francis Bacon

This chapter describes the longitudinal study of the self-organizing school project. The findings represent the product of the challenging pilot process and the 5 years of scaling the design. They address implementation integrity, student achievement effects, and the roles of technology and collaboration using data gathered during the adoption phase of the design.

CENTRAL QUESTIONS

The central questions of the book frame this chapter. They pertain to the implementation of research-based practice at scale in schools within the broader context of the implementation and effects of comprehensive school reform:

Did the self-organizing school project possess the feedback system, methods, and practices required to gather adequate evidence of implementation integrity? How does the approach compare with existing comprehensive school reform feedback methods?

Did the self-organizing school project produce evidence of sustained implementation? How does this compare with existing evidence from comprehensive school reform?

Did the self-organizing school project produce achievement effects commensurate with those attained from the longitudinal study of classrooms described in chapter 1 (e.g., Hattie, 2003; Rowe, 2003)? How do those effects compare with existing evidence from studies of comprehensive school reform?

The answers to the central questions are used to connect the self-organizing school project with the nine next-generation design targets described in chapter 2 and to lend support to the six principles of the theory of the self-organizing school. The questions are answered in five sections:

Feedback: This section describes the scope and amount of feedback gathered using the emergent feedback system described in chapter 8.

Implementation integrity: This section describes the data produced using the feedback system and practices that relate to the project's implementation.

Collaboration and culture: This section describes a study of collaboration and faculty culture using a measure external to the project. The findings are linked to the implementation integrity data described in the second section.

Technology: This section describes two studies that support the role of technology in the self-organizing school project.

Achievement effects: This section describes a longitudinal study of student performance on the SAT-1.

The narrative makes the findings of the self-organizing school project accessible by limiting research jargon while providing enough technical detail to make the account meaningful. Each of the studies described in the third, fourth, and fifth sections is reported under the headings of Assumption (i.e., the driving idea or expectation upon which the study was based), Purpose, Method, and Results. Additional sources are cited throughout for readers requiring more information.

It is also important to note that the description of the type, amount, and process of data gathering in the self-organizing school project is separated in the presentation of results from the actual findings or results produced by the feedback system. This was done because every reform first needs to demonstrate that it has the capacity, the systems, and practices as part of its design to gather the feedback required to monitor implementation and identify needs and problems. Limitations in this area have been a critical concern in first-generation comprehensive school reforms (Berends et al., 2001), creating the need to make a distinction between the method for generating feedback and an analysis of what that feedback says.

FEEDBACK

This section focuses on the first question, whether the self-organizing school design generated the feedback necessary to make a determination of implementation integrity.

Observations of Classroom Practice

In sum, 1,614 classroom observations of key teaching approaches were gathered from the classes of all 114 teachers in the project over 5 years, from 1997 to 2001. This includes the cooperative learning approach employed as an example throughout the book. The cooperative learning data are shared here, along with the results for mastery or explicit teaching, peer-assisted learning, math mastery teaching, and classroom engagement.

The observers comprised department heads, team leaders, the school's administrators, and teaching peers. They recorded the presence or absence of the characteristics of each practice, using an electronic protocol. Each observation included an extensive narrative, examples of which are described later in the chapter. The observations occurred during a 50- to 55-minute class session. Table 10.1 describes the frequency of observations for each teaching approach in the self-organizing school project. Over the 5 years, approximately 55,500 minutes (925 hours) of classroom observation were completed.

Peer, Supervisor, and Self-Feedback

In comprehensive school reform, the views of the teachers involved are the most common form of implementation measurement. In many

Table 10.1. Frequency of Observations by Year, Teaching Approach, and Engagement

Year	Observations	Type				
		Mastery	Cooperative	Math	Peer	Engage
1997	155	55	18	12	8	62
1998	263	116	44	22	8	73
1999	288	99	35	60	7	87
2000	458	211	47	47	22	131
2001	450	203	51	25	20	151
Total	1,614	684	195	166	65	504

instances, those views represent the sole integrity measure (Berends et al., 2001; Faddis et al., 2000). In the self-organizing school project, self, peer, and supervisor surveys were administered at the middle and end of each year and then compared with the ongoing observations described earlier.

Each survey included 30 items in four categories: student learning, implementation of the design, teamwork, and professional growth. These areas represent key features of the school schema and simple rules. Raters were asked to judge whether the dimension of interest was *never* (0), *rarely* (1), *sometimes* (2), *mostly* (3), or *always* (4) present. For example, in the student learning category of the self and peer surveys, ratings were made on the use of the teaching practices described in the previous section, the extent to which the classroom was differentiated and whether technology was used effectively.

In the implementation section, ratings were made of the implementation of team plans, knowledge of the school's processes, and the roles taken in collaborative decision making. Items under the teamwork heading of the self and peer surveys included making expectations clear, the effectiveness of communication, and the quality of problem solving. In the professional development section, items focused on translating professional development into practice and seeking support and resources.

All items reflected a key feature of the school schema. Teachers nominated a peer to complete the survey, who observed classes before completing the form. Peers were usually selected from members of the same teaching team. The team leader and administrator responsible for the learning team on which the teacher served undertook supervisor feedback. The surveys, like the observations, included a field for sharing narrative reflections.

Team Surveys

Each member of the teaching and learning team completed a separate survey on the team process, using the protocol described in Figure 8.2. The survey included items in four categories: school policy goals (i.e., simple rules), implementation, process, and teamwork. This survey was designed to capture the views of individual team members about how well the team was using the self-organizing school schema. It was distinguished from the individual survey by its focus on the team as the unit of analysis. Where the individual surveys asked raters to evaluate an individual teacher's use of the collaborative process, the development of action plans, or the use of technology, the team form included questions about how well the team was doing with the same items.

In this way, those aspects of the schema, as represented and embedded in the roles of individuals, were scaled up to the expectations and feedback requirements of teams. The team survey included items on instructional decision making, the attainment of team and school goals, the support of team members, and scheduling.

Management Surveys

The school's Level 2 team (teaching and learning team leaders) and Level 3 team (management leaders) gave feedback using a management survey. The questions addressed the following categories: design knowledge and expertise, support, teamwork and supervision, model implementation, and professional growth. Each leader and their selected peers completed the survey, which included a field for a narrative reflection. In sum, 1,346 peer, self, supervisory, and team surveys were completed from September 1997 to December 2001; 213 management surveys were completed during the same period.

Perspectives of Students

Overall, 12,560 student evaluations were gathered over the 5-year period, during which observations and teacher surveys were undertaken.

Students provided feedback for all of their teachers once per semester. Students represent a critical source of feedback related to the implementation of the design. The feedback tool employed for this purpose is described in Figure 4.3, in the example of student self-organization. The items addressed key features of the design from the perspective of students.

Summary

The 15,000-plus pieces of feedback described in this section are comprised of teachers sharing reflections with one another, supervisors and peers observing lessons, and students giving feedback to their teachers on an ongoing basis. All of the tools were a product of the embedded design process described in chapter 6 and together constituted the feedback system described in chapter 8. The connections across the tools made it possible to cross-reference the feedback generated from multiple perspectives and methods.

The body of evidence described here exceeds all benchmarks reflected in the existing comprehensive school reform literature, including the many cases of external evaluation, and it builds a strong case for answering the first question in the affirmative: The emergent feedback approach employed in the self-organizing school project did ultimately produce extensive objective and subjective feedback required to provide adequate evidence of implementation integrity. The scope and volume of that data exceed existing benchmarks described in the comprehensive school reform literature.

It is important to note that this section has addressed only the evidence of the capacity of the self-organizing school design to produce feedback. A discussion of the feedback data produced by those methods follows.

IMPLEMENTATION INTEGRITY

This section focuses on the second question: Did the self-organizing school project produce evidence of sustained implementation? How does this compare with existing evidence from comprehensive school reform?

Findings From the Feedback System

Observations

Table 10.2 describes mean and standard deviation scores for the observation of the teaching approaches described and discussed in the previous section. The results of the classroom observations for cooperative learning and the other teaching approaches show high, sustained implementation. Teachers were able to implement the body of practice with success in the first year of the adoption phase of the design, although, in the case of cooperative learning, at slightly lower-than-acceptable levels for the design (i.e., more than 80%). The use of the body of practice improved year over year to a highly acceptable 90% level in the third year through the fifth.

The decreasing standard deviation scores (a measure of variability from teacher to teacher, in this case) showed that as implementation improved over time, there was less variability in the percentage scores for implementation of the teaching practices from teacher to teacher. These data lend support to the assertion that the challenging pilot phase of the project did ultimately yield high levels of implementation of the teaching approaches included in the design. Further, none of the participating teachers, team leaders, and school leaders had practical knowledge of the teaching approaches described here before the start of the self-organizing school project.

The narrative field that was included in the observation tool provided an opportunity for every observer to describe areas of strength and need in the lesson. The following is an example of a narrative developed during a peer tutoring lesson from a ninth-grade history class conducted in January 1999. A member of the leadership team provided the feedback. Of note is the use of the pattern language in the narrative. The reference to rubrics and products shows that the lesson was embedded in a broader curriculum context and as such represents more than the capacity to implement the basic research-based characteristics of the practice.

> Jane, thank you for allowing me to visit a peer tutoring exercise. In this lesson, students were editing each other's speeches that they had written rough drafts of. There were several strengths of this lesson, which I will list below. The class was quite intentional and your structure of the lesson was made it very clear what students were supposed to do. The overall

Table 10.2. Mean and Standard Deviation Scores of Implementation Integrity for Observations of Teaching Practice

| | | | | | Observation Type | | | | | | | |
| Year | Mastery | | Cooperative | | Math | | Peer | | Engagement | | All | |
	M	SD	M	SD	M	SD	M	SD	M	SD	M	SD
1997	81.54	20.12	73.27	22.04	87.33	7.51	87.00	17.46	88.06	7.97	83.92	16.22
1998	88.31	14.17	86.65	13.72	84.54	10.56	89.12	9.99	89.02	9.77	87.94	12.59
1999	92.74	8.67	91.31	9.90	87.65	9.88	97.00	2.82	88.18	9.12	90.23	9.45
2000	90.44	12.61	89.55	13.15	89.25	10.51	92.04	7.60	88.60	8.90	89.77	11.30
2001	90.48	9.07	90.76	9.07	90.36	9.31	91.85	10.98	91.53	7.19	90.94	8.55

plan allowed you to meet your objectives of the day, which was for each student to have received meaningful feedback from a peer on their speech. The lesson was clearly tied to rubric progress and you made that clear to students at the outset (see comments below for improving this). I noticed your concerted effort to ask students more, checking for understanding questions. During a portion of an engagement measurement during your presentation on how to fill out the feedback form you provided 7 opportunities to respond during 3.25 minutes of observation intervals or roughly 2 per minute. This rate is quite good and should be a goal for you to continue to strive for. You employed the team's behavior management plan (BMP) when students did not have their papers printed with consistency, good humor, and respect. You made excellent use of a proximity control technique by roving around the room, especially when you were presenting information on how to complete the feedback form. The overall engagement was satisfactory at 83%. All of the off-task behaviors observed were during the phase when you were presenting information to students on how to use the feedback form. You were doing the right steps (proximity and asking questions) to address this. Students were completely engaged when working on the editing tasks. I can offer 2 ways to make this lesson even better than it was.

1. It would have been even more effective if you could have referred to a specific visual representation of the rubrics or of portfolio products so that you could illustrate specifically what skills students would be working on with this project. This way the goals of the lesson would have been visually reinforced for the students.

2. The actual feedback form that students used to evaluate their peers could have been modified to provide even better structure to how students provided feedback. The "needs improvement, average, excellent" rating scale may be easy for students to use, but I question how this will help students make changes to their papers. One way to address this would be to have something on the form that caused students to mark or list specific parts of the speech that needed to be improved upon. For example, having something that called on students to underline sentences that are not "clear and easy to understand" would have indicated to their peers what they needed to change.

Also, you asked students to have their speech in a specific format (grabber, etc.), yet there was nothing on the feedback form that called on students to evaluate whether or not that format was being followed. In short, the form should call on evaluators to actually do more to provide specific feedback to their peers.

Finally, this lesson did not call on the peer editors to see if their peer could employ any of the changes they recommended. It would take some additional work on the lesson, but having students see if their peers can make changes to their speech based on the feedback provided would be a nice additional step to consider. This may only be able to be done for more mechanical type errors such as sentence construction, but even that would have helped ensure that the feedback provided would have been utilized effectively.

I hope this feedback is helpful. Thanks for having me!

The following is a second narrative written by a team leader visiting a 10th-grade science lesson conducted in April 2001. Note the reference to facilitator interaction task (FIT) in this narrative. This is the self-monitoring program described in chapter 4 as an example of self-organization.

This is the second day of the Jigsaw II on cancer, and the second day of observation on this lesson. Therefore some of the items checked off above were observed yesterday and not today. You did a good job getting the class started, you had all the students put down their screens and then you asked different students what was happening as the next step in the class. For group one and two they knew they were to prep for a STAD quiz and then take the test, after which they would start the project before the class ended. For group 3 they have completed the STAD test and are now doing the STAD team project. On top of this they completed the student survey.

This did lead to a slower start then they wanted for the STAD work, but you handled it all very well. It isn't easy to keep so many things going at a time but I was pleased with the way you were able to be aware of where different students were and what they needed to do next. It took group 3 a long time to get into the project, but you got them going. Students were interested in getting their STAD improvement points and to get their STAD rewards. It did however take a lot of time to get this information also to the class. Because the different STAD teams did not do well on the quiz passed back, what were the factors which caused this? This Jigsaw II was an activity which I am positive would lead to every team having very good improvement points, therefore I am asking you to look at what happened to this test.

In their STAD teams they were working together, trying hard to help each other, but this was only to get the needed information. This is a good start to students working in teams, but what I didn't hear is members of the teams checking on the teams' total understanding. Some were doing this, but across the class the teams didn't seem willing to do this. This is where the FIT process could give you a way for team members to give others feedback about what it is they are or are not doing. I have a new grade sheet and grading process for FIT which has helped my students in this way. Again I like the way you do a check with the expert team before they actually take the quiz. This should begin to drive home the need for them to do this same thing before they come saying, "We are ready for the test." Keep putting the pressure on them to sit back down and work together if they are not prepared.

Group 3 got started with the STAD team project and each member had a component which they were responsible for which gave them a good focus about what they needed to do. Your grading sheet was not 100% clear as to what their component counted for their individual grade compared to their overall team grade on the components. As we talked together during the class we need to look for an audience for this final project. Maybe web, maybe for the 6th grade, something which lets them know who they are developing this for.

Thanks Justin for setting up the time for us to look at the class design and then making the changes to the lesson. You did a very nice job working on the changes we defined for the lesson, and then you implemented these well. Thanks for having me in.

The third example shows the application of the approaches with advanced curriculum content and at a senior level. The example is drawn from work undertaken by an experienced teacher who was integrating cooperative learning into her classroom practice. Note here the use of the pattern language related to cooperative learning.

Jigsaw II on comparison of Odyssey and Prufrock

Anticipatory set drew from students their speculations about the reasons for comparing these two pieces. You also used this to link previous reading and learning to what students would be doing today. Your questions very skillfully pulled from students significant structures for thinking about what they had read and set the stage for elements to compare and contrast. As I have always observed in your classes, your ability to use questioning is a natural talent that keeps kids engaged and adds energy to the class atmosphere. You do very little talking, managing instead to get kids to supply the ideas by framing questions that make them really think.

You supplied a handout that elaborated the Jigsaw II instructions and grading criteria. Then you reviewed the handouts, having assigned students to groups and recorded these groups on the board. Actual modeling of the steps was not necessary, but you did a very thorough job making clear what the expert questions called for, and how this activity would be assessed as part of a presentation project. Linking the product of this exercise to a presentation with shared grades as well as individual grades was a good way to build in interdependence while making certain the activity also called for individual accountability.

Inclusion of a reward structure could be accomplished by awarding bonus points for groups who achieve a standard you establish. A benefit of using STAD scoring for both STAD and Jigsaw II is that this allows you to award bonus points at the end of the term based on accrued improvement points of the group. It's simple, and it tends to motivate our kids.

The most important past of your lesson was the marvel of the way you structured the expert questions. The questions were both compelling and exciting to think about. You set them up so that the task structure was absolutely clear which helped make sure even the most easily distractible of students would stay engaged. Further, the structure of the materials demanded a product which always increases the sense of importance kids get about an activity. Every student in this very large class jumped to the task and worked energetically for the entire time. Groups shared information, collaborated nicely and were invested in seeing that their finished product was thorough. Your materials reflect your expert knowledge of your subject, your keen understanding of what makes literature come alive, and your intuitive sense of how to inspire students to rise to high expectations.

As I have so often witnessed in your classes, this activity called for analysis and evaluation thinking skills applied to challenging reading material. All your students, regardless of aptitude, demonstrated a thorough understanding of these texts and a mature understanding of the questions they applied. I am eager to see more of this happening throughout the English curriculum, believing that great works of literature can, and should, be offered to all our students. All our students benefit when we expect them to be intelligent and interested in something intellectual, provided we know how to make the challenge interesting and manageable. You are so very talented at doing both!

The three examples described here are representative of the feedback provided to and by teachers, team leaders, and supervisors. The narratives provide strong support for the existence of the pattern language and schema at the level of the school.

When viewed collectively, the observations and accompanying narratives show that it is possible to implement, sustain, and improve the implementation of highly specific features of a comprehensive school reform over time.

Perspectives of Teachers, Supervisors, and Teams

The observational data were supported by the results of the peer, supervisor, and self surveys. Table 10.3 describes the results of those surveys that relate to teachers as well as teaching and learning teams over the 5-year period.

Average ratings in all years on all surveys by all groups exceeded a score of 3.0 and in the latter years were closer to 3.5 (on a 4-point scale). This shows that individual teachers, their peers, and their supervisors all reported that the design and its parts had been implemented most to all of the time. The ratings by supervisors were slightly lower than the peer and self ratings, although not markedly. The teacher views of implementation were consistent with those held by leadership. This finding indicates a commonly held view of the change in practice over time. Further, the overall survey ratings improved year over year for all rating groups with the exception of 1997–1998, when there was a small decline (.028) by peers.

Table 10.3.   Mean and Standard Deviation Scores of Implementation Integrity by Surveys

| | | Scores by Rating Type | | | | | | | |
| | | Self | | Peer | | Supervisor | | Team | |
Year	Total	M	SD	M	SD	M	SD	M	SD
1997	187	3.31	.37	3.50	.28	3.13	.41	3.10	.40
1998	263	3.14	.44	3.47	.37	3.19	.44	3.19	.46
1999	254	3.41	.33	3.68	.27	3.35	.36	3.24	.60
2000	366	3.47	.35	3.66	.30	3.41	.37	3.40	.54
2001	276	3.49	.33	3.66	.29	3.43	.30	3.42	.43

Team Surveys

The average score for teaching and learning team surveys exceeded a score of 3.0 for all years. The overall team ratings improved year over year for all rating groups, although the average difference was small between the first and second year and the last two years of data collection.

Management Surveys

The 213 management surveys generated similar findings to those produced by teachers and teaching teams. Averages across peer, self, and supervisory ratings and across the domains of the survey (i.e., support, knowledge, implementation, and growth) ranged from 3.47 to 3.96. This confirms that the school's leaders believed they were providing effective support to the program. This view was corroborated by the individuals they supervised.

Student Perspectives

Table 10.4 describes data from 12,560 students surveys gathered over the 1997–2001 period. The data described in Table 10.4 were extracted directly from the software tool used in the project and have not been subject to descriptive analysis. As such, the standard deviation was not available to report. The data are broken down, first, by the scheduled teaching block in which the students undertook the evaluation of their teachers and, second, by whether they were members of the lower school (Grades 9–10) or upper school (Grades 11–12) at the time.

Table 10.4.   Student Survey Data

Block	School level	
	Lower	*Upper*
A	3.21	3.42
B	3.33	3.38
C	3.38	3.36
D	3.26	3.28
E	3.26	3.35
F	3.30	3.38
G	3.12	3.61

Students rated items as *never, rarely, sometimes, mostly, always*, using the same (0–4) response format as their teachers. The tool also included a space for providing comments for the teacher. On average, students reported that their teachers were doing the things described on the protocol most of the time. This included the effective use of technology, the use of the body of practice, management of the class, and the differentiation of instruction. This finding was consistent from year to year and across the school's levels. The data also indicate that the student perceptions of teachers were consistent with teacher, peer, and administrator views of their work and the levels of implementation of the body of practice reported by direct observation.

Summary

Overall, the data reported in this section support high levels of implementation integrity that was sustained and improved over time. This includes the 5 years of classroom observation and accompanying narratives; the perceptions of teachers, teams, leaders, students, and managers; and anecdotal information on student conduct, retention, and college participation. The results contrast favorably with the majority of existing comprehensive school reform studies, which predominantly show fading implementation and increased variability form teacher to teacher within schools over time and are based on much smaller data sets (e.g., Cook et al., 1999; Datnow, 2003b; Muncey & McQuillan, 1996). Further, the scope and outcomes described in this section exceed the benchmarks described in the existing comprehensive school reform literature.

These findings indicate that the self-organizing school project produced strong evidence of sustained implementation that exceeds the levels of implementation integrity reported in the existing comprehensive school reform literature.

COLLABORATION AND CULTURE STUDY

This section provides additional evidence of implementation integrity derived from the study of faculty collaboration and culture.

Assumption

The study employed a measure external to the feedback system, to compare the self-organizing school project to other schools. It was expected that the findings regarding collaboration, described in the previous section, should be reflected more broadly in measures of faculty culture and collaboration not directly linked to the self-organizing school design and feedback system. In such a comparison, the self-organizing school project should compare favorably to other schools.

Purpose

The purpose of this study was to find out how faculty members' views of collaboration and school culture compared to a sample of 42 other schools.

Method

The RSM (Research for School Management) Interview Form (Buckalew, 1994) was employed in this study. The RSM form is a 10-item questionnaire that asks faculty members questions about the relationship between their efforts and student outcomes; about feedback from peers, colleagues, and administrators; and about autonomy, collaboration, and the overall supportiveness of the faculty culture. This instrument was also employed as a measure in a 5-year international study of faculty performance and culture in 42 preK–12 private/independent and public school settings in the United States and Canada (Buckalew, 1994).

Faculty members completed the form on three occasions during each phase of the self-organizing school project. The first administration occurred during the pilot phase. The second and third administration occurred 2 and 4 years later, at the beginning the transition phase, and then at the beginning of the continuation phase. Items that relate to faculty collaboration are reported here. For a full description of this study, see Bain and Hess (2000). The selected questions are as follows.

Questions 3 and 4 ask about the relationship between effort and reinforcement from peers and colleagues. Specifically, Question 3 asks for an estimate of days (percentage) when faculty went home feeling a "low degree of reinforcement" from peers, whereas Question 4 pertains to days when faculty went home feeling a "high degree of reinforcement from peers." Respondents selected from a choice of categories (i.e., 0–9% to 90–100%).

Questions 5 and 6 ask about the relationship between effort and reinforcement from administrators. Specifically, Question 5 asks for an estimate of days when faculty went home feeling a "low degree of reinforcement from administration." Question 6 asks for an estimate of days when faculty went home feeling a "high degree of reinforcement from administration." Respondents also selected from a choice of categories (i.e., 0–9% to 90–100%).

Question 8 asks faculty to rate (on a 9-point scale) the time that they spend on "substantive, solution-focused conversation" with colleagues. The scale ranges from *none* (1) to *60+ minutes per week* (9). Question 9 focuses on whether meetings provided opportunities to discuss—in professional, problem-focused, and problem-solving terms—substantive instructional issues at some length (20 minutes or more). Again respondents indicated their opinions on a 9-point scale with 1 being *never* and 9 being *always*.

Question 10, the final question of the survey, asks faculty to rate the overall supportiveness of the faculty culture. The scale is 1 to 9 with 1 being a *low level* and 9 being a *high level*.

Results

Table 10.5 describes the median ratings by item for teachers in the pre-self-organizing-school program and in the pilot, transition, and consultant phases of the project. The last column describes the RSM study findings.

Overall, the results of this study indicate that median scores in each phase of the self-organizing school project were higher than those in pre-self-organizing-school project and the RSM study. There was one exception. Median responses to Question 6, "reinforcement from administration," were reported to be the same as the RSM data.

When asked to interpret Questions 3 and 4, teachers were virtually unanimous in their attribution of higher scores in the self-organizing

Table 10.5.   Median Scores for the Self-Organizing School in All Phases and the RSM Survey for Selected Items

Question No.	Pre-SOS	SOS			RSM
		Pilot	Transition	Consultant	
3	30–39%	10–19%	10–19%	10–19%	20–29%
4	30–39%	60–69%	60–69%	50–59%	40–49%
5	70–79%	30–39%	30–39%	30–39%	20–29%
6	20–29%	50–59%	30–39%	30–39%	30–39%
8	7	8	7	7	5
9	4	6	7	7	5
10	6	7	7	7	6

Note. SOS = self-organizing school; RSM = study findings based on the RSM Interview Form (Buckalew, 1994).

school to team process and the collaborative problem-solving model used in the design. Follow-up responses for Questions 5 and 6 indicated that the shift from an autonomous culture to one based on demonstrable evidence did create perceptions of pressure from administrators that may have accounted for the similarity in ranking between project and RSM scores.

A comparison of median scores for Question 8 indicates that self-organizing school implementation resulted in more frequent solution-focused conversation. Faculty in all phases of the project also reported higher scores for time spent in professional and problem-solving meetings. Again, these data and the responses to follow-up questions attributed the results to the team process.

Summary

When triangulated with the individual and team survey data described previously, the findings from this study lend support to the feedback generated by the project about collaboration and team process. The views of teachers about collaboration, which is essential to the process of self-organization, were positive and existed at higher levels than those reported for comparison schools. The results affirm the findings reported for the observations and surveys and the overall implementation integrity of the design.

TECHNOLOGY STUDIES

It is the position of this work that, when educational in nature, technology is a critical enabler, accelerator, and transformer of a comprehensive school reform design. The reports of teachers and students on the feedback surveys indicate that the community believed that it was making good use of the technology. However, a more objective picture was sought in a study that compared the use of the school's teaching practices under high, moderate, and low levels of technology use. The technology studies contribute evidence in relation to the implementation and achievement effects of the self-organizing school project.

Study 1: Teacher Use of Technology Tools

Assumption

If embedded technology is to play a critical role in comprehensive school reform and, specifically, in the self-organizing school project, high levels of information technology use should make a greater contribution to the implementation of the design in general and to the use of research-based classroom practice in particular.

Purpose

This study was designed to examine the connection between the use of the technology tools employed in the self-organizing school project and the implementation of research-based practice.

Method

The study compared the classroom implementation of teaching practices by high, moderate, and low level users of the curriculum authoring tools described in chapters 7 and 9 and employed to implement the curriculum model. Level of use was used to denote both the sophistication and the frequency of teachers' use of the tools. The tools were designed to assist teachers to design and implement the teaching approaches described earlier in this chapter, and they included the cooperative learning lesson design tool described in Figure 6.4.

The study employed the classroom observation of the teaching practices reported earlier in this chapter as a measure. A total of 30 teachers—10 females and 20 males—participated in the study, conducted over 2 1/2 years from 1998 to 2000 (Bain & Parkes, 2006b). Of these teachers, 12 had 0–3 years of experience, 10 had 4–10 years of experience, and 8 had more than 10 years of experience at the beginning of the study. Notably, the overall experience levels of the teachers did not account for the findings.

Results

Table 10.6 describes the mean observation scores for all teaching practices of teachers according to high, moderate, and low levels of use. In sum, 578 observations were made from September 1998 to December 2000 (Bain & Parkes 2006b).

The implementation of the teaching practices for all groups in all years exceeded 85%, indicating that the approaches were implemented in classrooms with high levels of integrity irrespective of technological condition. A comparison across the three groups indicated that there were statistically significant differences between the levels of implementation, depending on the level of tool use, $F(2, 27) = 4.237, p = .02$. Follow-up comparisons showed statistically significant differences between the means for high and moderate use ($p = .01$) and high and low use ($p = .03$). The difference between the moderate- and low-use groups was not statistically significant.

In short, the data showed that the teachers who made higher-level use of the tools implemented the teaching approaches more successfully than their peers did. The differences across the three conditions were not large, because the design expected high, mastery levels of im-

Table 10.6.   Level of Use of Curriculum Tools

Year	High		Moderate		Low	
	M	SD	M	SD	M	SD
1998	93.94	6.94	85.98	9.80	88.28	7.64
1999	94.07	3.19	87.00	7.05	87.58	6.22
2000	94.53	4.72	89.90	7.23	90.28	6.01

plementation integrity (reported earlier), irrespective of the level of technology used. Nonetheless, the effects size—based on a comparison between the overall scores of the high- and low-use groups—was .83, indicating a profound influence of the tools on the actual practice of teachers. The study supported the position that technology, when embedded in the design, increases the integrity of implementation of research-based practices.

Study 2: Student Use of Technology Tools

Assumption

If technology is critical to the self-organizing school design, then its presence should positively influence student achievement when embedded in the teaching and learning model.

Purpose

This study was designed to examine the effect on student learning of technology embedded in the self-organizing school design.

Method

This study examined the effects of an electronic discussion tool on student achievement,[1] which was a database located on the school network that could be accessed by students outside of school hours. The electronic discussion tool was designed to enable students to answer questions about homework readings and engage in an online dialogue with their peers about their readings. The tool was intended to extend classroom discussion to the homework setting for every student, and it was embedded in the self-organizing school approach to classroom teaching. In this instance, the electronic discussion tool was used predominantly with explicit teaching.

This study sought to establish whether the presence of the electronic discussion tool in the homework setting influenced student achievement. It compared the quiz performances of 39 11th-grade students when they used the tool in the homework setting with those occasions when they did not. All students experienced the same classroom instruction from a module of instruction on American literature. The homework approach alternated between the electronic discussion tool and a standard format for 1-week intervals over a 4-week period. A series of curriculum-based weekly quizzes scored out of 30 points was used as a measure in the study. For a detailed description of the tool, the validation of the measures, and methodology, see Bain, Huss, and Kwong (2000).

Results

Table 10.7 describes the results for student achievement under the traditional homework and the electronic discussion tool technology conditions. The comparison indicated statistically significant differences, $F(3, 27) = 5.00, p = .003$), with higher scores reported for the electronic discussion tool on each occasion it was used (Bain et al., 2000).

As was the case in the previously described technology study, the results were highly statistically significant despite relatively small differences in actual quiz scores. Because the study was conducted within the broader context of the school's mastery-based teaching and learning approach, student scores (under any circumstances) were expected to range between 80% and 100%. Evidence in support of this assertion is reflected in the high, mean, and relatively small standard deviation scores on the quizzes under all conditions. As such, the 4.4% difference in quiz scores between the traditional homework approach and the use of the electronic discussion tool constitutes an actual 20% effect on scores that fall between 80% and 100% and is thus more substantial than the literal differences would indicate.

Table 10.7.   Mean and Standard Deviation Scores for Achievement by Condition

	M	*SD*
Baseline 1	25.60	3.34
Tools	27.03	2.18
Baseline 2	25.57	2.58
Tools	26.78	2.54

Summary

Findings from both technology studies corroborate the perceptions of teachers, supervisors, and students about the importance of technology in the design and provide additional corroboration of implementation integrity. The study of student use in the technology tools also supports the effects of the design on student achievement (third central question noted earlier) and, specifically, the role of technology in generating achievement effects. Both studies support the role of information technology for the purpose of embedding research-based practice in the design and the existence of mastery-based teaching and learning performance in classroom instruction.

ACHIEVEMENT EFFECTS STUDY

This section focuses on the third central question by providing evidence of the longitudinal achievement outcomes of the design and how those findings compared to existing comprehensive school reform and classroom effects overall. Those effects were derived from an 8-year study of student performance on the SAT-I (Bain & Ross, 1999).

Study of Student Performance on the SAT-I

Assumption

Given the high levels of implementation integrity reported in the second section and the claim that the self-organizing school approach scales up research-based classroom practice to the level of the school, it could be expected that the project would produce achievement effects at scale that are consistent with those reported at the classroom level in the broader literature and greater than those reported for comprehensive school reform (e.g., Borman et al., 2003).

Purpose

The study compared the SAT-I performance of students who attended the school from 1992 to 1995 and did not experience the self-organizing school design, with the performance of students who attended from 1996 to 1999 and did experience the self-organizing school design, in order to determine the extent to which the design produced an effect on student performance.

Method

The study involved 160 students who composed all 4-year members of the senior classes at the school. Students who attended Years 10–12 or 11–12 were not included, because their performance could not be attributed to a single secondary school experience. Of the sample, 89 students were in the pre-self-organizing-school project classes 1992–1995, and 71 were in the self-organizing school classes 1996–1999. Thirty-three percent of the total sample (53 students) met the definitional criteria for learning disability (Mercer, 1999), with 26 students in the pre-self-organizing-school classes and 27 in the self-organizing school group.

When comparing students from different cohorts and, in this case, those attending the school before and after the introduction of the self-organizing school project, it is essential to establish any initial differences that may influence a comparison between the groups.

Three recommendations for each student were obtained from English and math teachers as well as the guidance officer at the students' previous schools. These were employed to establish the learning and social characteristics, academic approach, and entry-level performance of the students before their enrollment in the school. No statistically significant differences were found between the cohorts at entry to the school, based on an analysis of the recommendations, $F(1, 148) = 1.08$, $p = .30$.

The SAT-I was used to measure achievement effects in this study. This measure is frequently identified as an outcome measure in secondary school reform initiatives (Tirozzi & Uro, 1997; U.S. Department of Education, 2005; Watt, Powell, & Mendiola, 2004). The SAT-I plays a significant role in the trajectory of college-bound secondary students in all schools.

It is also important to acknowledge that the SAT-I is a highly politicized measure that is frequently misused in comparisons between states, schools, and districts, to sell real estate and justify educational budgets. At the core of the misuse of the SAT-I are the participation rates, which vary from school to school, district to district, and state to state. In situations where the population is self-selected, schools with lower participation rates will usually have higher scores (Fetler, 1991; Montague, 1990). In the present study, participation rates were constant throughout the investigation.

Despite a history of misuse, the SAT-I can be used as an indicator of the educational quality of school programs and curriculum (College Entrance Examination Board, 1999). Average scores analyzed from a number of years to reveal trends in the academic preparation of students who take the test can provide schools with a means of self-evaluation and self-comparison (College Entrance Examination Board, 1988, 1999).

Results: Combined SAT-I

Students who participated in the self-organizing school program scored an average of 92 points higher on their combined SAT-I than students did in the pre-self-organizing-school program. Table 10.8 describes the mean and standard deviation scores for both groups. This proved to be highly statistically significant, $F(1, 158) = 13.57$, $p = .0003$.

Of note is the score of the students who were in the self-organizing school pilot team described in chapters 6 and 7. They were the 4-year subset ($n = 18$) of the first group of students to participate in the self-organizing school project. The students who participated in the project throughout the challenging pilot phase recorded an average combined score of 1057 on the SAT-I. The average score is lower (21 points) than

Table 10.8. Combined SAT-I Scores for Self-Organizing School Project and Pre-Self-Organizing-School Project Classes

	M	SD
Pre-SOS	986	158.5
SOS	1,078	158.3

Note. SOS = self-organizing school.

**Table 10.9.   Combined SAT-I Mean
and Standard Deviation Scores for
Students With Learning Disabilities in
Self-Organizing-School Project and
Pre-Self-Organizing-School Project
Classes**

	M	SD
Pre-SOS	878	125.7
SOS	967	134.5

Note. SOS = self-organizing school.

the overall project average yet 71 points higher than the pre-self-organizing-school project mean. This finding lends support to the assertion that, despite the challenges of the pilot phase, the implementation covaried with improved student performance during those years.

Result: Students With a Learning Disability

Similar results were found for students with a learning disability. A second analysis on the combined SAT-I scores of those students who were classified with a learning disability also proved to be statistically significant, $F(1, 51) = 6.17$, $p = .01$. Students who participated in the self-organizing school program scored 89 points higher than did students in the pre-self-organizing-school program. Table 10.9 describes those findings.

This is an important finding given that a rationale for the self-organizing school project and comprehensive school reform in general is to employ research-based practice to make schools more responsive to learner needs. The consistency of effect for students with learning disabilities indicates that the differentiated curriculum approach and research-based practice employed in the project covaried with improved achievement for a broad range of students.

Results: Verbal and Math

The results showed gains in both verbal and math domains. For the verbal domain, scores improved from 487 ($SD = 88.5$) to 541 ($SD = 85.1$), a gain of 54 points, $F(1, 158) = 15.0$, $p = .0002$. Math scores improved from 499 (SD = 85.3) to 537 (SD = 91.2), a 38-point improvement, $F(1, 158)$ = 7.2, p = .008.

From a practical perspective, a score differential of 92 points in combined SAT-I performance provided students with more choice and alternatives in the college selection process. It also made a student eligible for admission to a college at a selectivity level higher than that which was expected from a school experience that did not provide such a score advantage. This is particularly important to students and parents. The score improvement accelerated the school to a position where its SAT-I scores were above the national and state averages at the time, reversing a decade-long trend of performance below those benchmarks.

The absence of a statistically significant difference between the groups at entry to the school reduces the likelihood that the differences in SAT-I scores between the SOS and pre-SOS groups can be attributed to factors associated with the selection of students, their history, and any changes in the entry characteristics of the student population over the period studied. This is also an important finding given that those qualities evaluated by teachers and the guidance officer on the recommendations are also related to factors that influence performance on the SAT-I.

The improvement is far larger than that expected from SAT-I preparation or coaching programs. Those effects are typically small, between 25 and 32 points on the combined verbal and math sections of the SAT-I, or 15–16 points on each domain (College Entrance Examination Board, 1999).

The SAT-I findings covaried with the high levels of classroom engagement reported in the second section of this chapter and with improved student conduct. Student engagement ranged from 88% to 91% over the 5 years of classroom observation. Over a decade of implementation, the self-organizing school project covaried with significant improvements in conduct, decreasing the ratio of students on an at-risk disciplinary status at the end of the year from 1:3 to 1:10. Further, during the same period, the number of students recognized for outstanding positive behavior and contribution to the school increased from less than 5% to over 60% of the student body (LeBlanc, 2002).

The improved SAT-I results were reflected in high levels of college retention, which consistently exceeded 90% throughout the self-organizing school project (Richardson, 2002). This compares to the national average of approximately 68% for students returning to college for their sophomore year at the time (Collegeways Retention Resources for Individuals and Educational Institutions, n.d.). Over 60% of the students who participated in the self-organizing school project entered colleges in the most competitive, highly competitive, and very competitive categories (Richardson, 2002).

Summary

In summary, the results of the achievement effects study indicate strong positive differences in SAT-I performance that covaried with student participation in the self-organizing school project. Statistically significant improvements were recorded in mathematical and verbal domains of the test and were consistent for students with and without learning disabilities. Such findings are generally elusive in school reform (Scheerens, 1992), especially at the secondary school level and, specifically, when evaluated over time.

The effect size associated with this performance improvement is .58 for the overall combined SAT-I scores and .70 for combined scores of the students with learning disabilities. The average effect sizes for models reported in the comprehensive school reform implementation literature range from .15 to .22 (Borman et al., 2003; Borman et al., 2005).

These findings, albeit from one study, nonetheless support the effect of the self-organizing school project on student achievement and provide an affirmative response to the third central question of the chapter. The self-organizing school project did produce achievement effects that exceeded those associated with the benchmarks in the comprehensive school reform literature. Further, those effects can be related to the strong implementation integrity data generated over the same period of study.

LIMITATIONS

School reform is a messy business where clinical assignment of children to conditions is not possible or desirable, thereby limiting the strength of the conclusions that can be drawn. The limitations of the data and methods employed in the longitudinal study of the project are presented here. Although the cohort design employed in the SAT-I study is recommended in studies of organizations with cyclical turnover, factors related to the selection and history of participants represent threats to the design (Cook & Campbell, 1979).

The longitudinal nature of the study and the use of recommendations to ascertain any differences before attending the school added strength to the design, although selection factors cannot be completely ruled out. Further, although there is a strong precedent for and focus on summative measures of student achievement in the comprehensive school reform literature, the achievement data would be strengthened by the inclusion of more curriculum or criterion-based measures of growth.

The indirect measures described herein comprise a number of point estimates of the perceptions of faculty about the prevailing school culture under different programmatic conditions. Each estimate was taken at a different point in a change process, which itself exerts an influence on the overall culture of the school. The fact that the data were gathered over an 8-year period means that it was subject to the normal faculty turnover and the acceleration effect that comes with a major change initiative. For the faculty who participated in multiple administrations of the survey, a testing effect may represent a threat to the internal validity of the design. These factors should be considered when interpreting the findings of the study.

Borman et al. (2003) found that comprehensive school reform achievement studies conducted in-house tend to generate higher effect sizes. Although numbers of the studies reported in this chapter have been subjected to the scrutiny of the scholarly review process, this is nonetheless a site-based account of a site-based implementation.

Finally, the bulk of the data presented here is from the transition phase of the project. The SAT-I data include results derived from the period when the model was scaling up through the school, as does the comparative collaboration study. This included the original pilot team of students who participated in the full scale-up phase of the project. However, the classroom observation and survey data emerged with the advent of the school's software tools. This occurred at the beginning of the transition phase, meaning that the data, though confirming assertions about the design being in place, do not provide a deep account of the pilot phase of the project. The absence of a deep account of the pilot phase reinforces the significance of information technology in generating the feedback described here. These tools were not available in the pilot phase.

Even with these limitations in mind, there is reason to be optimistic about the findings derived from the self-organizing school project. The design, when implemented at scale across the school, created the conditions for sustained implementation integrity and generated promising achievement effects.

When viewed as a collective body of evidence within the context of existing benchmarks, the data indicate that the three questions that framed this chapter can be answered in the affirmative. The self-organizing school project did generate feedback capable of making a determination of implementation integrity. The actual data generated by those feedback approaches indicated high levels of implementation integrity across methods and sources and over time. The longitudinal study of achievement produced effects consistent with that reported for classroom effects and in advance of the average effects reported in the comprehensive school reform literature.

NEXT-GENERATION IMPLICATIONS

The data presented throughout this chapter lend support to the self-organizing school approach, including its theory, systems, and practices as a strong response to the next-generation design targets presented in chapter 2. This claim is informed by the description of the self-organizing school project from preceding chapters and is made within the context of the benchmarks for implementation represented in the comprehensive school reform literature. This claim is made with full acknowledgment of the limitations identified in the previous section. What follows is a description of the way that the findings relate to each of the nine targets. The targets are represented in italics.

The body of evidence on implementation described in this chapter indicates that the self-organizing school design successfully addressed the high within-school variance, limited implementation data, and fading implementation over time that were described in chapter 2 as issues in comprehensive school reform (Berends et al., 2001; Borman et al., 2003; Desimone, 2002). The data described herein indicate that it is possible to establish comprehensive school reform implementation over time with objective measures of implementation integrity.

The self-organizing school design was also able to exert *schoolwide influence*. Evidence in support of this claim comes from three sources.

First, the *high levels of implementation integrity* found in observations and narratives and by all students, teachers, and administrators indicate that the design had a schoolwide effect. Second, the reports from teams and team members, including the management team, indicate that the team-based organizational design was in active operation at multiple levels across the school. Third, the data generated by those teams at multiple levels indicate that the organizational design was functioning effectively. This was highlighted in individual and team responses to questions about the implementation of the design, the use of research-based practice, the professional support provided by leaders, and overall teamwork and collaboration.

The high-integrity implementation of research-based practices and achievement effects indicate that the design had attained a level of *educational power*, exceeding existing comprehensive school reform benchmarks (e.g., Borman et al., 2003). The effect size (.58), when viewed with the classroom observation data, would indicate that the design was able to magnify the effect of successful teachers and classrooms at the level of the school.

The feedback provided by students, teams, teachers, and school leaders about the design (use of the body of practice; technology; collaborative process and teamwork; and the feedback process, portfolio completion by teachers, and organizational design) supports the view that the model was *comprehensive in its design* and implementation during the adoption phase. This claim rests in part on the descriptions of the design elements, the embedded design process, and the implementation described throughout this book and the evidence presented here in support of the other next-generation design targets.

The results of the two information technology studies indicate the positive influence of *technology* on project implementation and student achievement. These findings are supported by the survey feedback from students, teachers, and school leaders about the use of technology.

The descriptions of the role of information technology throughout the self-organizing school, including its use for curriculum development and to gather and use feedback, indicate that information technology was deployed at scale to gather, manage, and deploy the knowledge of the school.

The bottom-up production of the 15,000 convergent data points over the study period without external evaluation provides evidence of the capacity of self-organizing school project to produce *emergent feedback*. The body of feedback was used to design, monitor, and manage its implementation and effects and to work out its successes and problems as they occurred. The project demonstrated a capacity to deploy these data in ways that supported the growth of teachers and the work of teams and to generate the kind of emergent feedback necessary to work out what to do next instead of reporting about what happened.

Support for the *professional lives* and *effective adoption targets* requires a greater leap of inference from the data, given that they were not subject to specific study. Chapter 2 describes the difficulties that comprehensive school reform has experienced in fully addressing the professional lives of teachers and its reliance on overrationalized adoption processes. The self-organizing school project produced different implementation outcomes, employing different processes of adoption and a comprehensive design (described in chapters 5, 6, and 7). Those outcomes included expressions of satisfaction with role and responsibility and school culture as reported on the individual and team surveys and in the external comparison study relating to collaboration. However, given the absence of specific study, those positive outcomes cannot be directly attributed to the way in which the self-organizing school approach influenced teachers' professional lives or the adoption process overall.

The final next-generation design target, the development of practical theory, is the overarching subject of the book and is addressed in the next section.

SUPPORT FOR THE THEORY

The self-organizing school theory was described as a way of explaining how schools can successfully adopt bodies of research-based practice at scale. At a general level, it is possible to conclude support for the theory based on the successful, sustained adoption of those practices described in the second section of this chapter. Further, the consistency of achievement effects across a range of learners, including those with learning disabilities, indicates that the project, through the application of its underpinning theoretical principles, was capable of providing a more responsive and differentiated experience to the students involved. This is especially important given that a rationale for comprehensive school reform is to employ the kind of research-based practices described in this chapter to create a school experience that is responsive to individual difference in learner needs.

However, given that the genuine value of a theory resides in its structure and the interrelationship between its concepts or beliefs and essential practices, instruments, and systems (Kuhn, 1996), any effort to support the theory of the self-organizing school needs to go further than these summative conclusions. Establishing such a connection requires an interrogation of the relationship between those practices, instruments, and systems and the data they produce. In this section, the data are linked to the design. The principle of embedded design is central to that discussion.

Embedded design means ensuring that the key features and content of the design are embedded in all of its parts. Further, it requires the embedding of those design parts in each other. This principle was employed in the self-organizing school approach and its actively connecting the concepts or beliefs associated with the theory to its essential systems and practices. Establishing such a process involved mapping forward from simple rules to educational practice to roles, trajectories, and technology and, ultimately, to feedback tools in the manner described throughout the book. The purpose of the approach was to minimize the leaps of inference between intention and action to produce a working school schema and design. The schema reflected those consistencies and regularities in the school's design that guided the day-to-day action of agents.

This involved ensuring that the simple rules and the specifics of the teaching and learning approaches of the design were represented in teacher position descriptions and career paths, in technology tools, and in the items on the observation protocols and surveys described in this chapter. It is the intentional nature of these embedded relationships between the theory, the design, and the feedback tools that make possible inferences about the data described in this chapter and more broadly about the systems and practices associated with that theory. The following conclusions rest on the existence of those connections, the data presented in this chapter, and the information described in all of the preceding chapters.

First, the high levels of implementation integrity indicate that a school can articulate a set of beliefs and values as expressed in its *simple rules* of the design and translate them into practice. For example, the classroom implementation of cooperative learning ranged from 73% to 91% during the 5 years studied. This high-integrity implementation maps backward from the tool used to collect that data through lesson design tools, to the roles of teachers and, ultimately, to the simple rules. The observational data can also be triangulated with the evidence from the study of technology reported earlier and the perceptions of agents about their use of research-based practice.

In the same way, the rule "Decision making is collaborative" can be mapped forward to the items on the team and individual survey tools that were used to report collaboration levels in the order of 3.0–3.5 on the 4-point scale for teams at multiple levels in the school. These findings and those for the other simple rules represented in the design and on the scales employed in the project support the existence and effect of embedded design.

Second, the contention about the trajectory from beliefs and values to action can be generalized based on *similar findings* for the other teaching approaches, the role of technology, and the actual use of the feedback tools on a sustained basis over time. For example, the findings for peer mediation, explicit teaching math mastery teaching, and engagement were consistent with those for cooperative learning. These approaches were embedded in the design using the same approach employed for cooperative learning. The volume of feedback, the use of the tools over time, and the results they produced suggest that embedded design existed across multiple research-based practices. Further, both technology studies illustrate the way that information technology became a "pointy end" expression of the embedded design process in tools for teachers and students.

Third, the embedded design principle scaled up to include the roles of students and teams at different levels. This phenomenon was described in the theory as *similarity at scale* (Waldrop, 1993). The responses to items on the feedback tools for students, teachers, leaders, and teams were similar across different levels in the school. The widespread use of the tools and the data they generated indicate that the simple rules and the design scaled up to all levels in the school. The engagement with those tools was widespread. Feedback, as it related to any individual or team, was constituted from diverse sources at multiple levels and over extended periods of time. The perceptions of different agents at different levels and in different groups were highly similar. Irrespective of the source or form of feedback, the perspectives across teams and individuals remained consistent and converged around a common picture of what was occurring in the school. Further, that picture remained generally consistent when different noninstitutional measures were applied (e.g., external collaboration study).

The convergence of feedback from many agents and groups at many levels, as well as the deep embedding of the pattern language in the observation narratives, can be seen as evidence supporting the existence of a school *schema*. The schema is a product of the applying the five principles of self-organization to the school. Evidence of the implementation of those principles indirectly supports the existence of that schema. The consistency and regularity in the 15,000 responses of agents and groups would be highly unlikely in the absence of a common framework for action in the school.

When viewed with an understanding of the manner in which it was collected and deployed, the full compendium of data provides support for the *emergent feedback* principle. The data show that when using the self-organizing school approach, it is possible to gather deeper and more objective evidence of comprehensive school reform implementation over time, in a manner and of a magnitude that stands in contrast to the evidence currently reported in the existing comprehensive school reform literature. For example, the 1,612 classroom observations gathered over 5 years represent a substantive increase over the levels described in the literature (e.g., Datnow et al., 2000; Datnow & Castellano, 2000). Given the absence of external intervention in gathering this data, it would be immensely difficult, if not impossible, to gather this amount of data in a school unless its purpose was deeply embedded in the day-to-day activity of individuals, teams, and the school as a whole.

Further, the survey responses from teams about collaboration, teaching practice, and problem solving indicate that emergent feedback was used to discuss and problem-solve teaching and curriculum implementation at team meetings, to mine data, and to identify strengths and needs in curriculum design and implementation. Feedback was employed in an emergent fashion to determine what to do next and to provide the base of information for the progression of 35 teachers in the school's career path. The collective evidence suggests that the school did get smarter over time in ways that were stimulated by emergent feedback.

The final and most important question about the theory pertains to whether the design produces self-organizing emergent behavior. The way that a self-organizing school implements research-based practice is through *dispersed control* and bottom-up self-organization. This is described as a process of constant adaptation and change that permit a design to evolve away from its developers. Evidence of support for the dispersed control principle focuses on three areas.

First, the feedback from teams and the descriptions of the network design employed in the self-organizing school project suggest that teams were actively engaged, bottom-up, in the work of self-organization, as reflected by the data on team processes and collaborative problem solving.

Second, implementation integrity was sustained and improved over the three phases of the project. During this period, the management approach migrated from a top-down traditional leadership design to the bottom-up team approach described in chapter 7. The survey responses throughout indicate that teams implemented the design for the purposes of effective teaching practice, instructional problem solving, effective use of technology, and faculty growth. During the period when the design strengthened and consolidated, the active engagement of the change agent shifted radically. This shift involved the migration of that role from an active hands-on involvement with the design and implementation of the project to a much more limited consultation role.

Third, over this period the student conduct, teacher transitions in the career path, achievement effects, and college placement all improved.

This substantive evidence of the maturation of the design covaried with numerous anecdotal examples of self-organizing behavior. These included the development of new software and feedback tools by teachers, the delivery of the project's professional development program by master teachers who had progressed to that level in the school's career path, evolution of the design expectations for curriculum and instruction based on the work of Level 2 teams, and faculty management of the portfolio process. Collectively, these efforts produced a range of new design features and an evolution of the school schema.

CONCLUSION

The self-organizing school project was premised on the view that meaningful change arises first from highly focused efforts at small scale. The scope of work and distinctive findings of the self-organizing school project lends support to this "small is big" perspective about school reform as a method to respond to the paradigm crisis discussed in chapter 1. As a site-based effort, the self-organizing school project represents an example of a border effort in response to that paradigm crisis. It is yet to scale beyond the project school. However, the findings demonstrate the value of building a complete foundation for reform based on a deeper articulation of the theory, systems, and practices described throughout the book.

In summary, the results produced by bringing the self-organizing school project to scale in one school support the view that new and more complete ways for improving schools are more likely to emerge from deep efforts that occur on the borders of an existing paradigm, than from within it. Those border efforts start small and, in doing so, have the potential to achieve more robust outcomes. In a field struggling to ground its many contested theories in practice, getting bigger is not synonymous with being more robust or effective.

In looking forward, another round of longitudinal study could strengthen assertions about dispersed control and the long-term sustainability of the self-organizing school project. Such a study would help determine how and whether the self-organizing school approach continues to evolve throughout its second decade.

CHAPTER TAKEAWAYS

1. Evaluating the implementation and effects of comprehensive school reform is a messy business.
2. The data described in this chapter stand in positive contrast to the existing reports of comprehensive school reform implementation and effects.
3. The evidence of implementation integrity in the self-organizing school project shows that research-based practice can be sustained at scale in a school over time.
4. The findings support the contention that a school can build a common schema and pattern language similar to those that exist in other professions.
5. Technology can do much more than automate current practice in comprehensive school reform, and it is critical to making a design sustainable.
6. Emergent feedback is possible when feedback is conceptualized as part of a design and not as an add-on.
7. The data support the contention that school-level influence is possible in comprehensive school reform when a model possesses a school-level design.
8. Theory can make a practical connection between ideas, systems, and practice in a school.

NOTE

1. The electronic discussion tool was developed by English teacher Phil Huss.

CHAPTER 11

Emergence

The significant problems we face cannot be solved at the same level
of thinking we were at when we created them.—Albert Einstein

The self-organizing school project describes a practical theory of comprehensive school reform. This includes examples of the implementation systems, tools, strategy, and longitudinal data that support the theory and that result in the implementation of research-based practice at
scale. The previous chapters describe the way that those features
emerged from a multiphase 11-year reform effort. In this final chapter,
the intent is to present the most important conclusions from the account
of the theory and the self-organizing school project. Each of the preceding chapters concludes with a list of takeaways. This chapter brings
the idea of key takeaways from the end of each chapter into the main
body of the text by describing the nine most important conclusions derived from the 10 chapters.

TAKEAWAY 1: NEXT-GENERATION COMPREHENSIVE
SCHOOL REFORMS WILL REDEFINE WHAT IT
MEANS TO BE COMPLETE

A goal of this book has been to redefine the meaning of the term *complete* as it relates to comprehensive school reform design, implementation, and readiness to scale. The next-generation design targets described in chapter 2 and the theory and practice described throughout

the book focus on the way to make comprehensive school reform more sophisticated in design in order to be complete in practice.

A complete approach requires the application of simple rules, embedded design, similarity at scale, emergent feedback, and dispersed control to create the schema for a self-organizing school. Sustained school-level influence depends on the existence of a school-level schema. Applying the principles of the self-organizing school produces a dynamic and complete framework of practice, curriculum, roles, technology tools, feedback mechanisms, and teamwork that evolve the schema and advance a reform in ways that are realistic for teachers and students. This interdependent framework creates the self-reinforcing relationship across the design, its implementation, and its outcomes that has been so elusive in past efforts.

Being complete also means using the theory and framework of practice to build a plausible base of evidence about the implementation and effects of a reform. The data described in the previous chapter indicate that a more articulated and complete design can link theory to systems and practices, resulting in better implementation, more adaptation, and better outcomes.

> To be sustainable, a reform must be complete. The product of a complete reform is the school-level schema required for school-level influence.

TAKEAWAY 2: IN A SELF-ORGANIZING SCHOOL, THERE IS NO END TO A CHANGE PROCESS

An approach that can connect and sustain a relationship between design, implementation, and outcome generates the system capacity for dynamic and self-organized change. There is no such thing as a sustainable equilibrium condition in school reform. Everything changes. A design that is complete can only be so for a brief time before the conditions change and call for adaptation. This is a phenomenon often misunderstood by reforms that focus on fixed ideas of implementation integrity. The idea of being more complete really means getting to the starting gate in a site-based reform. The gate is the threshold, or the point at which a design possesses the sophistication or complexity to constantly adapt at scale.

Simple sophistication is required to respond to the ever-changing landscape on which schools function. All schools and reforms are surfing the edge of chaos in this regard. For example, a self-organizing school may be more responsive to changing conditions, but because of its simple sophistication, it will also be more sensitive to disturbance (Waldrop, 1993). A disturbance could be caused by such factors as waiting too long to upgrade a critical software system or failing to respond to feedback about curriculum, a teaching practice, or team process. A large or small change in initial conditions can have a significant effect (Gleick, 1987). If a school becomes averse to change or fails to maintain more complex adaptive structures, it can move rapidly toward a far-from-equilibrium condition and the edge of chaos. This perpetual change may seem to be a daunting prospect. However, the fundamental capacity for change is structurally embedded in a self-organizing school, making adaptation part of what the school does to make itself (Urry, 2005). Whether in the process of technology planning, revising a teaching practice, or creating a feedback tool, adaptation is deeply embedded in the way that the school functions day-to-day.

> Self-organization does not make a school immune from equilibrium or chaos. It makes adaptation possible.

TAKEAWAY 3: THEORY DEFINES THE POSSIBILITY OF COMPREHENSIVE SCHOOL REFORM

The starkly contrasting circumstances represented by the precariously incomplete self-organizing school pilot phase and the overall results of the project are uncommon. These circumstances and results were produced in the same project over a span of 7 years. In its early stages, the self-organizing school project managed to generate all of the same issues, problems, and challenges that have become synonymous with site-based school reform. Yet, unlike the predominant findings of the comprehensive school reform literature, the circumstances of the self-organizing school project got much better over time, not worse. The project ultimately generated high levels of implementation integrity, many examples of self-organizing behavior, and substantive gains in student achievement. These outcomes can be attributed in part to the expectations generated by the theory, which helped to define the scope and magnitude of the task and which provided an expectation of what constituted "complete." This helped to explain what was missing and why it could all improve over time.

Theory makes it possible to envision the broader architecture of a reform for stakeholders to see the future possibility and to help analyze what is working or missing. In doing so, theory creates expectancies and predicted relationships that can be tested. A design that is based on a complete theory can ultimately generate the systems, instruments, and practices that make it whole.

> Theory provides a way to see the future possibility in a school reform, including the systems, instruments, and practices required to make it whole.

TAKEAWAY 4: IN A REFORM, PERSISTENCE IS THE QUALITY THAT GUARANTEES ALL OTHERS[1]

Being able to see the possibility of a better school is not necessarily synonymous with realizing that goal. Persistence over time is essential to address the many anticipated and unanticipated challenges associated with comprehensive school reform. This includes the persistence to use theory to craft a better or more complete initial design and to endure a stressful multiyear process of implementing successive approximations.

In the self-organizing school project, the community persisted for over a decade, first in pursuit of the basic implementation of a design and then in pursuit of an ongoing evolution of its simple rules and schema. The period from 1993 to 1997 presented challenges that could have caused any or all of the stakeholders to quit. Yet, they did not. They continued to push on over a period long enough for many reforms to come and go completely or be absorbed by the powerful informal culture of schools. At the time of this writing, both the stakeholders (many of them new) and the school continue working to evolve the design.

Having a theory does not make a project immune from the challenges of site-based school reform, especially if the systems, instruments, and practices that compose that theory are incomplete. Further, although reforms generally need more time than what is normally allotted for successful implementation, a reform can be sustained only if measurable progress is being made toward an anticipated outcome. As with any new endeavor, there is a "burn time," when resources are expended without much apparent return. However, there are also windows of action and opportunity that close if not capitalized on in a timely fashion. Those windows may not reopen.

Time is a friend only if a design is resolving its issues and problems as it proceeds. The failure to address a need over an extended period cannot be ameliorated by a promise to fix it next year if the effect has been to discourage or even disillusion members of the community. It is persistence in the face of challenge that ultimately makes time a friend.

A theory or design does not make a project immune from the challenges of site-based school reform; persistence guarantees the theory.

TAKEAWAY 5: PROFESSIONAL CULTURES OF PRACTICE MAKE IT POSSIBLE TO DISPERSE CONTROL

Complexity researchers are as fascinated by the structure of complex self-organizing systems as they are by the nature and function of the behavior they produce. Order from chaos is a function of design, whether it is a result of natural evolution or a product of human agency. In schools in general the idea of order is frequently evocative of prescriptive programs and repetitive drill-and-kill instruction. This is not what is proposed here. Order here refers to the simple design sophistication required for a school to function as a complex adaptive system.

Innovations in schools that distribute leadership such as communities of practice require a sophisticated organizational capacity to be successful. In a self-organizing school, this order equates to a simple and sophisticated scaled-up capacity with the school's schema. Every agent in the system possesses the pattern language, skill, and understanding of the schema that are necessary to make viable and realistic innovations that disperse control. The order in a self-organizing school is a product of embedded design. When research-based practice is embedded in the roles, trajectories, feedback systems, and technologies associated with a reform, the likelihood of sustainability increases. Embedded design is a benchmark for sustainability over time. The greater the scope and depth of the embedding, the greater the likelihood that a reform can exert a sustainable impact on student learning.

> Self-organizing schools possess the professional order to disperse control. Embedded design predicts the depth of a reform's implementation and its sustainability.

TAKEAWAY 6: IN SCHOOL REFORM, TECHNOLOGY MATTERS WHEN IT BECOMES EDUCATIONAL

Technology appears in nearly every chapter of this book as a critical feature of the self-organizing school design and project. Whether in the form of tools to make differentiation possible in classrooms, for observing the specifics of research-based practice, or for making curriculum available to students, all of the examples show how to make information technology educational.

Educational technology happens when a reform is able to embed its research-based professional knowledge within tools that are used in the school's ongoing practice. This is possible only when a reform has defined what its core activities and transactions mean in the day-to-day lives of teachers, students, and classrooms, to the point that they can be embedded in software tools.

Further, the real power of educational technology is in the management and deployment of this classroom knowledge at the school level. The examples described throughout the book show that with an educational technology, a school can problem-solve curriculum needs, identify patterns of practice at scale, and undertake schoolwide innovation from the bottom up. In practice, this means providing teachers, students, parents, and administrators with the tools that make self-organization possible. When these educational technology tools are available at scale, it becomes possible to exact from information technology the benefits that it has brought to so many other fields and professions.

An educational technology exists when a reform's core professional knowledge and technology are reconciled in tools that are employed in the day-to-day practice of the school.

TAKEAWAY 7: EMERGENT FEEDBACK CAN DEFINE WHAT IT MEANS TO BE A SCHOOL

Chapter 1 flags the importance of feedback in the way that a school learns about what it does. This is based on the idea that a school (or any system) can learn from feedback only if it builds clear and robust self-reinforcing relationships about its beliefs, intentions, actions, and outcomes.

Emergent feedback has enormous practical benefit for schools. It can make students feel good about their growth because the form, quality, and frequency of feedback enable the school to detect their improvement in more sophisticated ways. Teachers can feel better about what they do because their contribution to student learning is clear and profound. When sophisticated emergent feedback happens all the time, schools can become places where the value they add is known and understood in ways that contribute to the growth of every member of the community and the efficacy of the school as a whole.

When feedback is sophisticated and emergent, a school can build a positive organizational sense of self that emerges from the growth of each of its agents.

TAKEAWAY 8: SUSTAINABILITY IS A BASELINE CONDITION FOR COMPREHENSIVE SCHOOL REFORM

The contemporary literature about comprehensive school reform has framed much of what has been shared in the preceding chapters. That literature is dominated by basic concerns related to the sustainability and ultimate viability of those reforms. This book addresses those basic concerns, providing examples and evidence that offer some answers to the visceral issues of comprehensive school reform. The results described in chapter 10 are framed by the big questions of the Comprehensive School Reform literature, yet they represent little more than a baseline for the future possibility of a self-organizing approach.

For example, the book focuses largely on the way that the design influences teachers. What remains to be explored is what happens when a total community of students, teachers, and parents are empowered by a common schema to pool their collective intelligence. In doing so, they can work together in sophisticated ways to make a school a more effective place to learn. Each act of self-organization increases a school's capacity to respond to learner difference by resolving its core activity of teaching and learning.

> The promise of self-organization over time is the emergence of the school at a whole new level of capability, far beyond the current preoccupation with the sustainability of a reform.

TAKEAWAY 9: PARADIGM CRISIS AND THE BORDER

In chapter 1, a case is made for the existence of a paradigm crisis in schools. According to Kuhn (1996), a paradigm crisis characterizes the space between the old and the new. The old no longer adequately explains what is, whereas the new is neither fully articulated nor resolved. Contemporary schooling exists in this space between.

Much is written, most of it pessimistically, about the high levels of resistance to change in schools. However, this resistance is not unlike the way that many systems aggressively seek to retain a state of perceived stability or equilibrium in the face of change. All things ultimately change, although such change is far from uniform, nor does it always occur in the time frame expected by its proponents. This is well evidenced in the case of school reform.

From the perspective of complexity theory, the paradigm crisis in schooling will reach a critical point where chaos or a new order emerges (Prigogene & Stengers, 1984). When such a critical point is reached, it is likely that change will be rapid, not unlike the description in chapter 7 of the way that the self-organizing school project moved from a position of extreme risk to consolidation at a point when the design became genuinely self-reinforcing. At that point, it developed the capacity to make itself (Urry, 2005).

Unfortunately, to date, comprehensive school reform—and school reform efforts, more broadly—has not yet resolved the paradigm crisis in education. The implementation literature and the accounts of the difficulties experienced by comprehensive school reform indicate that it is a large-scale resident of the borderland, the space between the prevailing paradigm and what will or could be. What is needed are complete designs that address the next-generation design targets and are capable of becoming viable and sustainable replacements for the prevailing approach.

The self-organizing school project also lives in the borderland. Although it has produced evidence in support of new theory, systems, and practices, it is yet to scale beyond the level of the school. However, by being theorized in practical ways and by being more complete before being "big" in terms of its instruments, systems, and practices, the self-organizing school project offers the potential for a different understanding of schools and reform that may have more scalable potential. As such, it may be of value to others engaged in similar work.

CONCLUSION

This book began by questioning the modest effects of schools on student achievement. Arguably, those modest effects are inflated by the powerful influence of learner aptitude and history (Bloom, 1976). For example, there will always be a substantive percentage of students who seem to "just get it" even when a school has done little to make itself responsive to research-based practice and individual difference, just as there will always be great teachers who have a powerful impact irrespective of the school's capacity to effect learning overall. These simple observations about schools and learners may explain why, for many, the dominant modern paradigm of schooling is a big problem yet not necessarily a crisis. By way of contrast, imagine schooling and education if learning did not occur at all unless every school and teacher used the research-based professional knowledge of the field to teach well. Crisis would be imminent.

Within this context, the more important questions about schooling should be as follows: Are those students who seem to get it realizing their full potential? What happens to the ones who do not get it, and everyone in between? And, finally, what is a school's practical capacity to do things differently when learning does not happen easily or readily? This book is about what it takes to answer these questions, including the way that all of a school responds to the needs of all of its students.

Responding to these most fundamental questions about schools and, especially, secondary schools requires serious reconsideration of the highly autonomous, one-lesson-plan, one-pedagogy, and extra-help-if-you-don't-get-it model of schooling. Despite thousands of excellent innovations and as many multigenerational reform efforts, this model remains the dominant modern paradigm in secondary education and the prevailing experience of most students. Replacing it is an immensely challenging undertaking. It is clear that more of the same will not successfully answer the aforementioned questions or replace the dominant paradigm. A different type and level of thinking is required.

The fundamental purpose of the self-organizing school project is to provide an alternative to the dominant modern paradigm that would make a school more responsive to individual learner needs. The approach described in the preceding chapters reconciled research-based practice and differentiation with new methods for implementing those practices at scale. This required transforming the school's design, management, and learning process to improve the achievement of all students.

The self-organizing school project has placed a stake in the ground related to what is possible in this regard. In doing so, it has produced some promising findings. They include the possibility that research-based practice can be sustained in schools at scale and over time, the new roles for technology, the new ways to consider and apply feedback, and the levels of achievement schoolwide that are similar in magnitude to those attained in classrooms.

The overall goal of the theory, the next-generation targets, and the self-organizing school design described here is to make schools places where addressing difference is seen less as a problem and much more as the reason why they exist and what they are designed to do (Sarason, 1996). As noted in chapter 1, new theory and practice can produce models of reform that go further, last longer, and possess the sophisticated capacity to respect as well as deeply influence what teachers, students, parents, and schools do. This includes the results they produce. The self-organizing school represents one such model designed to increase educational opportunity by bringing substance, meaning, and results to the widely accepted rhetoric of being a community for learning.

Where to go from here? How can the ideas, systems, and practices described throughout the book be used tomorrow? First, the approach represents a framework for evaluating existing comprehensive school reform. The ways in which this can happen are described at the beginning of each chapter. They include using the principles, design targets, and examples from the self-organizing school project to ask key questions about existing models and as a guide for new site-initiated efforts. Second, the theory and practice of the self-organizing school highlights the need to start small, scale carefully, and, in doing so, enable the many parts and interconnections in a comprehensive reform to work in a self-reinforcing way. This simple admonition can influence basic decisions about the timing and scale of reform that are critical to its ultimate success. Third, the book's redefinition of being complete calls on reformers to ask questions of a different type and level about what constitutes a reform design or model. The answers to those questions can be employed to identify those common points of breakdown in reform processes and change initiatives. Waste no time replicating them.

The evidence derived from the many less-than-comprehensive efforts at school reform is overwhelming. Even when tacitly sanctioned in the guidelines for funding or legitimized by the requirements of agencies and systems, it is irresponsible to reinvent those errors. The cost is immense, including the convulsive disruption to schools and the addition of inordinate stress to the lives of teachers and students. Use the time, energy, and resources that would have been spent on thinly implemented innovation to develop more complete theorized change. The preceding chapters describe an approach that is not easy in this regard. However, it is much better to take on the challenge of complete reform than to engage in an energy-sapping change process that so often ends with a muted claim of victory. Little is gained from reform when the rhetoric of change is its most enduring outcome.

NOTE

1. Winston Churchill first used this expression, although in reference to courage.

References

American Federation of Teachers. (1999). *The importance of staff buy-in in the selection of proven programs*. Retrieved May 25, 2005, from http://www.aft .org/topics/school-improvement/downloads/buy-in.pdf

Appelbaum, D., & Schwartzbeck, T. D. (2002). *Defining, measuring, and supporting success: Meeting the challenges of comprehensive school reform research: CSR connection*. Washington, DC: National Clearinghouse for Comprehensive School Reform. (ERIC Document Reproduction Service No. ED467446)

Aronowitz, S., & Giroux, H. A. (1991). *Postmodern education: Politics, culture, and social criticism*. Minneapolis: University of Minnesota Press.

Artz, A., & Armour-Thomas, E. (1998). Mathematics teaching as problem solving: A framework for studying teacher metacognition underlying instructional practice in mathematics. *Instructional Science, 26*(1–2), 5–25.

Asenio, M. L., & Johnson, J. (2001). *Comprehensive school reform: Perspectives from model developers*. San Francisco: WestEd. (ERIC Document Reproduction Service No. ED473718)

Avgeriou, P., Papasalouros, A., Retalis, S., & Skordalakis, M. (2003). Towards a pattern language for learning management systems. *Educational Technology and Society, 6*(2), 11–24. Retrieved November 12, 2005, from http:// ifets.ieee.org/periodical/6-2/2.html

Bain, A. (1996). *The Future School Institute handbook*. Wolfeboro, NH: Endeavour.

Bain, A. (1997). *Curriculum authoring tools*. Wolfeboro, NH: Endeavour.

Bain, A. (2000). The school design model: Strategy for the design of the 21st-century schools. In C. Dimmock & A. Walker (Eds.), *Future school administration, Western and Asian perspectives* (pp. 131–165). Hong Kong: Chinese University Press and Hong Kong Institute of Educational Research.

Bain, A. (2005). Emergent feedback systems: Lessons learned from a ten-year school reform initiative. *International Journal of Educational Reform, 14*(1), 89–111.

Bain, A., & Hess, P. (2000). *School reform and faculty culture: A longitudinal case study.* Brewster Academy, Wolfeboro, NH. (ERIC Document Reproduction Service No. ED472655)

Bain, A., & Huss, P. (2000). The curriculum authoring tools: Technology enabling school reform. *Learning and Leading With Technology, 28*(4), 14–17.

Bain, A., Huss, P., & Kwong, H. (2000). Evaluation of a hypertext discussion tool for teaching English literature to secondary school students. *Journal of Educational Computing Research, 23*(2), 203–216.

Bain, A., & Parkes, R. J. (2006a). Can schools realize the learning potential of knowledge management? *Canadian Journal of Learning and Technology, 32*(2), 149–162.

Bain, A., & Parkes, R. J. (2006b). Curriculum authoring tools and inclusive classroom teaching practice: A longitudinal study. *British Journal of Educational Technology, 37*(2), 177–190.

Bain, A., & Ross, K. (1999). School re-engineering and SAT-1 performance: A case study. *International Journal of Educational Reform, 9*(2), 148–154.

Barabasi, A. (2002). *Linked: The new science of networks.* New York: Perseus Books.

Barnett, H. (2001, October). *Successful K–12 technology planning: Ten essential elements* (Document No. EDO-IR-2001-06). Retrieved July 10, 2002, from http://www.ericit.org/digests/ERO-IR-2001-06.shtml

Becker, H. J. (2001, April). *How are teachers using computers in instruction?* Paper presented at the annual meeting of the American Educational Research Association. Retrieved January 10, 2003, from http://www.crito.uci.edu/tlc/FINDINGS/Special3/

Bensman, D. (2000). *Central Park East and its graduates: Learning by heart.* New York: Teachers College Press.

Berends, M., Bodilly, S. J., Nataraj Kirby, S., & Hamilton, L. S. (2002). *Facing the challenge of whole school reform: New American Schools after a decade.* Santa Monica, CA: Rand.

Berends, M., Nataraj Kirby, S. N., Naftel, S., & McKelvey, C. (2001). *Implementation and performance in New American Schools: Three years into scale-up.* Santa Monica, CA: Rand.

Berman, P., & McLaughlin, M. W. (1976). Implementation of educational innovation. *Educational Forum, 40,* 345–370.

Bloom, B. S. (1976). *Human characteristics and school learning.* New York: McGraw-Hill.

Bodilly, S. J. (1996). *Lessons from New American Schools Development Corporation's demonstration phase.* Santa Monica, CA: Rand.

Bodilly, S. J. (1998). *Lessons from New American Schools' scale-up phase: Prospects for bringing designs to multiple schools.* Santa Monica, CA: Rand.

Borman, G. D., Hewes, G. M., Overman, L. T., & Brown, S. (2003). *Comprehensive school reform and student achievement: A meta-analysis* (Center for Research on the Education of Students Placed at Risk Report No. R-117-D40005). Baltimore, MD: Johns Hopkins University, Center for Research on the Education of Students Placed at Risk. Retrieved March 20, 2004, from http://www.csos.jhu.edu

Borman, G. D., Slavin, R. E., Cheung, A., Chamberlain, A., Madden, N., & Chambers, B. (2005). Success for All: First-year results from the national randomised field trial. *Educational Evaluation and Policy Analysis, 27*(1), 1–22.

Brophy, J. (1986). Teacher influences on student achievement. *American Psychologist, 41*, 1069–1077.

Brophy, J. E., & Good, T. L. (1986). Teacher behavior and student achievement. In M. C. Wittrock (Ed.), *Handbook of research on teaching.* (3rd ed.) (pp. 328–375). New York: Macmillan.

Buckalew, M. W. (1994). RSM update and overview. *Ideas and Perspectives, 19*, 11–13.

Burns, M. K., & Symington, T. (2002). A meta-analysis of prereferral intervention teams: Student and systemic outcomes. *Journal of School Psychology, 40*, 437–447.

Carlson, R. A. (1975). *The quest for conformity: Americanization through education.* New York: Wiley.

Celio, M., & Harvey, J. (2005). *Buried treasure: Developing a management guide from mountains of school data.* Retrieved December 22, 2006, from the Center for Reinventing Public Education website: http://www.crpe.org/pubs/pdf/BuriedTreasure_celio.pdf

Chrispeels, J. H., Salvador, C., & Brown, J. (2000). School leadership teams: A process model of team development. *School Effectiveness and School Improvement, 11*, 20–56.

Cicchinelli, L. F., & Barley, Z. (1999). *Evaluating for success. Comprehensive school reform: An evaluation guide for districts and schools.* Aurora, CO: Mid-Continent Regional Educational Laboratory.

Cicchinelli, L. F., Dean, C., Galvin, M., Goodwin, B., & Parsley, D. (2006). *Success in sight: A comprehensive approach to school improvement.* Retrieved July 18, 2006, from http://www.mcrel.org/pdf/schoolimprovementreform/5052_ir_success_in_sight.pdf

Coalition of Essential Schools. (2006). [Home page.] Retrieved January 25, 2006, from http://www.essentialschools.org

College Entrance Examination Board. (1988). *Reporting your school's aggregate scores.* Princeton, NJ: College Board.

College Entrance Examination Board. (1999). *Guidelines on the use of College Board test scores and related data.* Princeton, NJ: College Board.

Collegeways Retention Resources for Individuals and Educational Institutions. (n.d.). *College retention rates* [Seidman retention slide]. Retrieved from http://www.college.com.doc/retentionformula2002-A_files/frame.html

Collins, J. (2001). *Good to great: Why some companies make the leap . . . and others don't.* New York: HarperCollins.

Comprehensive School Reform Quality Center. (2006). *Executive summary: CSRQ center report on middle and high school comprehensive school reform models.* Retrieved November 7, 2006, from http://www.csrq.org/documents/executivesummaryMSHSFinal.pdf

Co-nect. (2006). [Home page.] Retrieved December 22, 2006 from http://www.co-nect.com

Cook, T. D., & Campbell, D. T. (1979). *Quasi-experimentation: Design and analysis issues for field settings.* Boston: Houghton Mifflin.

Cook, T. D., Habib, F., Phillips, M., Settersten, R. A., Shagle, S. C., Serdar, M., et al. (1999). Comer's School Development Program in Prince George's County, Maryland: A theory-based evaluation. *American Educational Research Journal, 36,* 543–597.

Core Knowledge. (2006). [Home page.] Retrieved January 25, 2006, from http://www.coreknowledge.org/CK/index.htm

Cuban, L. (1982). Persistent instruction: The high school classroom, 1900–1980. *Phi Delta Kappan, 64*(2), 113–118.

Cuban, L. (2001). *Oversold and underused computers in the classroom.* Cambridge, MA: Harvard University Press.

Datnow, A. (2003a). *Five factors in supporting comprehensive school reform.* Retrieved January 20, 2005, from http://www.usc.edu/dept/education/cegov/publications/5factors.pdf

Datnow, A. (2003b). *The sustainability of comprehensive school reform models in changing district and state contexts.* Retrieved April 15, 2004, from the University of Southern California Education Department website: http://www.usc.edu/dept/education/cegov/publications/sustainability.pdf

Datnow, A., Borman, G., & Stringfield, S. (2000). School reform through a highly specified curriculum: Implementation and effects of the Core Knowledge sequence. *Elementary School Journal, 101*(2), 167–191.

Datnow, A., & Castellano, M. (2000). *An inside look at Success for All: A qualitative study of implementation and teaching and learning* (Center for Research on the Education of Students Placed at Risk Report No. 45). Baltimore, MD: Johns Hopkins University, Center for Research on the Education of Students Placed at Risk. Retrieved July 15, 2005, from http://www.csos.jhu.edu/crespar/techReports/Report45.pdf

Davis, D. R., Ellett, C. D., & Annunziata, J. (2002). Teacher evaluation, leadership, and learning organizations. *Journal of Personnel Evaluation in Education, 16*(4), 287–301.

Davis, B., & Sumara, D. (2006). *Complexity and education: Inquiries into learning, teaching, and research.* Mahwah, NJ: Erlbaum.

Desimone, L. (2002). How can comprehensive school reform models be successfully implemented? *Review of Educational Research, 72*(3), 433–479.

Dieker, L. A. (2001). What are the characteristics of effective middle and high school co-taught teams for students with disabilities? *Preventing School Failure, 46*, 14–23.

Dimmock, C. A. J. (1993). *School-based management and school effectiveness.* London: Routledge.

Dimmock, C. A. J. (2000). *Designing the learning-centered school: A cross cultural perspective.* London: Falmer Press.

Edison Schools. (2005). [Home page.] Retrieved June 10, 2004, from http://www.edisonschools.com/

Edmonds, R. R. (1979). Some schools work and more can. *Social Policy, 9*, 28–32.

Elmore, R. (1996). Getting to scale with good educational practice. *Harvard Educational Review, 66*, 60–78.

Faddis, B. J., Beam, M., Hahn, K. J., Willardson, M., Sipe, D., & Ahrens-Grey, P. (2000). *The implementation of the Comprehensive School Reform Demonstration Program: The work of 40 schools in seven Midwest states.* Naperville, IL: North Central Regional Educational Laboratory. (ERIC Document Reproduction Service No. ED472637)

Fetler, M. E. (1991). Pitfalls of using the SAT to compare schools. *American Educational Research Journal, 28*(2), 481–489.

Fink, D. (2000). *Good schools/real schools: Why school reform does not last.* New York: Teachers College Press.

Fitzpatrick, J. L., Sanders, J. R., & Worthen, B. R. (2003). *Program evaluation: Alternative approaches and practical guidelines* (3rd ed.). Boston: Allyn & Bacon.

Flavell, J. H. (2000). Development of children's knowledge of the mental world. *International Journal of Behavioral Development, 24*(1), 15–23.

Foster, S. L., & Cone, J. D. (1980). Current issues in direct observation. *Behavorial Assessment, 2,* 313–338.

Franceschini, L. (2002, April). *Memphis, what happened? Notes on the decline and fall of comprehensive school reform models in a flagship district.* Paper presented at the annual meeting of the American Educational Research Association, New Orleans, LA. (ERIC Document Reproduction Service No. ED468517)

Frase, L. E., & Streshly, W. (1994). Lack of accuracy, feedback, and commitment in teacher evaluation. *Journal of Personnel Evaluation, 8*(1), 47–57.

Fraser, B., Walberg, H. J., Welch, W., & Hattie, J. (1987). Syntheses of educational productivity research. *International Journal of Educational Research, 11,* 145–252.

Friedman, V. J. (1997). Making schools safe for uncertainty: Teams, teaching, and school reform. *Teachers College Record, 99*(2), 335–370.

Friend, M., & Cook, L. (2003). *Interactions: Collaboration skills for school professionals.* Boston: Allyn & Bacon.

Fullan, M. (1991). *The new meaning of educational change* (2nd ed.). New York: Teachers College Press.

Fullan, M. (2001). *The new meaning of educational change* (3rd ed.). New York: Teachers College Press.

Fullan, M., & Miles, M. (1992). Getting reform right: What works and what doesn't. *Phi Delta Kappan, 73*(10), 744–752.

Furtwengler, C. B. (1995). State actions for personnel evaluation: Analysis of reform policies, 1983–1992. *Educational Policy Analysis Archives, 3,* 1–27. Retrieved October 29, 2002, from http://www.olamed.asu.edu/epaa/v3n4.html

Gell-Mann, M. (1994). *The quark and the jaguar: Adventures in the simple and the complex.* New York: Freeman.

Gipson, S. (2003, Spring). *Issues of ICT, school reform, and learning-centered school design.* Washington, DC: National College for School Leadership. Retrieved February 23, 2004, from http://www.ncsl.org.uk/index.cfm?page ID=edu-publications-index

Gladwell, M. (2002). *The tipping point: How little things can make a big difference.* Boston: Little, Brown.

Glanz, J., & Revkin, A. C. (2003, August 19). Set of rules too complex to be followed properly. *New York Times.* Retrieved August 20, 2005, from http://www.nytimes.com

Gleick, J. (1987). *Chaos: Making a new science.* New York: Penguin.

Goldin, C. (1998). America's graduation from high school: The evolution and spread of secondary schooling in the twentieth century. *Journal of Economic History, 58*(2), 345–374.

Goodlad, J. I. (1984). *A place called school: Prospects for the future*. New York: McGraw-Hill.

Greenwood, C. R., & Delquardi, J. (1995). Peer tutoring and the prevention of school failure. *Preventing School Failure, 39*(4), 21–25.

Gribi, J. (1995, April). Presentation to the Board of Trustees of Brewster Academy. Wolfeboro, NH.

Hansel, L. (2000). *Unlocking the nine components of CSRD*. Washington, DC: National Clearinghouse for Comprehensive School Reform. (ERIC Document Reproduction Service No. ED467034)

Hanushek, E. A., Kain, J. F., & Rivkin, S. G. (1999). *Do higher salaries buy better teachers?* (National Bureau of Economic Research Working Paper No. 7082). Cambridge, MA: National Bureau of Economic Research. Retrieved June 20, 2005, from http://papers.nber.org/papers/w7082

Hargreaves, D. H. (1995). School culture, school effectiveness, and school improvement. *School Effectiveness and School Improvement, 6*(1), 23–46.

Haring, N. G., & McCormick, L. (1990). *Exceptional children and youth* (5th ed.). Columbus, OH: Merrell.

Hasselbring, T. S. (2001). A possible future of special education technology. *Journal of Special Education Technology, 16*(4). Retrieved November 11, 2004, from http://jset.unlv.edu/16.4/hofstetter/first.html

Hattie, J. (2003, October). *Teachers make a difference: What is the research evidence?* Paper presented at the Australian Council for Educational Research Conference on Building Teacher Quality, Melbourne, Australia. Retrieved December 22, 2006, from http://www.acer.edu.au/workshops/documents/Teachers_Make_a_Difference_Hattie.pdf

Herman, R., Aladjem, D., McMahon, P., Masem, E., Mulligan, I., Smith O'Malley, A., et al. (1999). *An educators' guide to schoolwide reform*. Arlington, VA: Educational Research Service.

Hodge, W. (2003). *The role of performance pay systems in comprehensive school reform: Considerations for policy making and planning*. New York: University Press of America.

Hofstetter, F. T. (2001). The future's future: Implications of emerging technology for special education program planning. *Journal of Special Education Technology, 16*(4). Retrieved November 11, 2004, from http://jset.unlv.edu/16.4/hofstetter/first.html

Hoge, R. D., & Coladarci, T. (1989). Teacher-based judgements of academic achievement: A review of literature. *Review of Educational Research, 59*, 297–313.

Houchin, K., & Maclean, D. (2005). Complexity theory and strategic change: An empirically informed critique. *British Journal of Management, 16*, 149–166.

Huberman, A. M., & Miles, M. B. (1984). *Innovation up close.* New York: Plenum.

Huck, R., Meyers, R., & Wilson, J. (1989). *ADAPT: A Developmental Activity Program for Teachers.* Pittsburgh, PA: Allegheny Intermediate Unit.

Jacob, E. (1999). *Cooperative learning in context: An educational innovation in everyday classrooms.* Albany: State University of New York Press.

Johnson, S. (2001). *Emergence: The connected lives of ants, brains, cities, and software.* New York: Simon and Schuster.

Jones, E. M., Gottfredson, G. D., & Gottfredson, D. C. (1997). Success for some: An evaluation of the Success for All program. *Evaluation Review, 21*(6), 643–670.

Kauffman, S. (1995). *At home in the universe: The search for the laws of complexity and self-organization.* New York: Oxford University Press.

Kentta, W. (1996). It takes a team to build a dream. *Journal of Staff Development, 17,* 24–27.

Kowalewski, S. A. (1990). The evolution of complexity in the Valley of Oaxaca. *Annual Review of Anthropology,* 19, 39–58.

Krugman, P. (1996). *The self-organizing economy.* Oxford, England: Blackwell.

Kuhn, T. S. (1996). *The structure of scientific revolutions.* Chicago: University of Chicago Press.

LeBlanc, S. (2002, August). *Dean of students end of year summary 2001–2002.* Paper presented to Brewster Academy Board of Trustees, Wolfeboro, NH.

LeFloch, K. C., Zhang, Y., & Hermann, S. (2005, April). *Adoption: Exploring the initiation of comprehensive school reform models.* Paper presented at the annual meeting of the American Educational Research Association, Montréal, Quebec, Canada.

Leonard, L., & Leonard, P. (2001). Assessing aspects of professional collaboration in schools: Beliefs versus practices. *Alberta Journal of Educational Research, 47,* 4–21.

Lipsky, M. (1980). *Street-level bureaucracy: Dilemmas of the individual in public services.* New York: Russell Sage Foundation.

Little, J. W., & Bartlett, L. (2002). Career and commitment in the context of comprehensive school reform. *Teachers and Teaching: Theory Into Practice, 8*(3), 345–354.

Lortie, D. C. (1975). *Schoolteacher: A sociological study.* Chicago: University of Chicago Press.

Manatt, R. P. (1997). Feedback from 360 degrees: Client-driven evaluation of school personnel. *School Administrator 54,* 8–13.

Marshall, S. P. (1995). *Schemas in problem solving.* New York: Cambridge University Press.

Mastropieri, M. A., & Scruggs, T. E. (2004). *The inclusive classroom: Strategies for effective instruction.* Upper Saddle River, NJ: Pearson/Merrill/Prentice Hall.

McCartney, K., & Rosenthal, R. (2000). Effect size, practical importance, and social policy for children. *Child Development, 71*(1), 173–180.

McLaughlin, M. W., & Talbert, J. E. (2001). *Professional communities and the work of high school teaching.* Chicago: University of Chicago Press.

McQuillan, P. J., & Muncey, D. E. (1994). "Change takes time": A look at the growth and development of the coalition of essential schools. *Journal of Curriculum Studies, 26*(3), 265–79.

Mercer, C. D. (1999). Learning disabilities. In N. Haring & L. McCormick (Eds.), *Exceptional children and youth* (5th ed.) (pp. 109–150). Columbus, OH: Merrill.

Merry, U. (1995). *Coping with uncertainty. Insights from the new sciences of chaos, self-organization, and complexity.* Westport, CT: Praeger.

Mid-Continent Research for Education and Learning. (2006). *Asking the right questions: A school change toolkit.* Denver, CO: Author. Retrieved June 10, 2006, from http://www.mcrel.org/toolkit/process/phasedata.asp

Ministry of Education. (2001). *School administrators guide.* Hong Kong, China: Education Department.

Montague, J. (1990, June). The dangers of using SAT results to compare schools. *American School Board Journal,* pp. 31–33.

Morrison, K. (2002). *School leadership and complexity theory.* London: Routledge Falmer.

Muncey, D. E., & McQuillan, P. J. (1996). *Reforms and resistance in schools and classrooms.* New Haven, CT: Yale University Press.

Murnane, R. J., & Cohen, D. C. (1986). Merit pay and the evaluation problem: Why most merit pay plans fail and a few survive. *Harvard Educational Review, 56,* 1–17.

Nespor, J. (2004). Educational scale-making. *Pedagogy, Culture, and Society, 12*(3), 309–326.

New England Association of Schools and Colleges. (1996). *Self-study report—Brewster Academy for re-accreditation.* Wolfeboro, NH: Brewster Academy.

Newman, M. E. J. (2003). *Properties of highly clustered networks. Physical Review E: Statistical, non-linear, and soft matter physics.* Retrieved January 15, 2005, from http://scitation.aip.org/getabs/servlet/GetabsServlet?prog=normal&id=PLEEE80000680000202612100000 1&idtype=cvips&gifs=yes

North West Regional Education Laboratory. (2004). *The catalog of school reform models: Modern Red School House (K–12).* Retrieved May 12, 2004, from http://www.nwrel.org/scpd/catalog/ModelDetails.asp?ModelID=22

O'Day, J. A. (2002). Complexity, accountability, and school improvement. *Harvard Educational Review, 72*(33), 293–329.

Odell, J. (1998, April). Agents and emergence in complex adaptive systems. *Distributed Computing.* Retrieved October 10, 2002, from http://www .jamesodell.comDC9810JO.pdf

Pascale, R. T., Millemann, M., & Gioja, L. (2000). *The new laws of nature and the new laws of business.* New York: Crown.

Petrides, L. A., & Nodine, T. R. (2003). *Knowledge management in education: Defining the landscape.* Retrieved March 27, 2005, from the Institute for the Study of Knowledge Management website: http://www.iskme.org/kmeducation.pdf

Policy and Program Studies Service. (2003). *Findings from the field-focused study of the Comprehensive School Reform Demonstration Program. Volume I: Final report.* Retrieved April 25, 2005, from http://www.ed.gov/rschstat/eval/other/field-focused-study/ffs-vol1.doc

Prigogine, I., & Stengers, I. (1984). *Order out of chaos: Man's new dialogue with nature.* New York: Bantam Books.

Putnam, J. (1998). The process of cooperative learning. In J. W. Putnam (Ed.), *Cooperative learning and strategies for inclusion: Celebrating diversity in the classroom* (pp. 17–48). Baltimore, MD: Brookes.

Richardson, S. (2002, August). *Dean of college placement May 1994–2001.* Paper presented to the Brewster Academy Board of Trustees Meeting, Wolfeboro, NH.

Riner, P. S. (1992). A comparison of the criterion validity of principals' judgments and teacher self-ratings on a high inference rating scale. *Journal of Curriculum and Supervision, 7*(2), 149–169.

Rosenshine, B. (1986). Synthesis of research on explicit teaching. *Educational Leadership, 43*(7), 60–69.

Rowan, B., Camburn, E., & Barnes, C. (2004). *Benefiting from comprehensive school reform: A review of research on CSR implementation.* Ann Arbor: University of Michigan Consortium for Policy Research in Education. Retrieved January 27, 2006, from http://www.sii.soe.umich.edu/documents/NCCSR%20chapter%20final%20draft%205.24.04.pdf

Rowe, K. (2003, October). *The importance of teacher quality as a key determinant of students' experiences and the outcomes of schooling.* Paper presented at the Australian Council for Educational Research Conference on Building Teacher Quality, Melbourne, Australia. Retrieved November 20, 2005, from http://www.acer.edu.au/research/programs/documents/Rowe_ACER_Research_Conf_2003_Paper.pdf

Rutter, M., Maughan, B., Mortimore, P., & Ouston, J. (1979). *Fifteen thousand hours: Secondary schools and their effects on children.* London: Open Books.

Sallis, E., & Jones, G. (2002). *Knowledge management in education: Enhancing learning and education.* London: Kogan Page.

Sarason, S. B. (1982). *The culture of school and the problem of change.* New York: Teachers College Press.

Sarason, S. B. (1996). *Revisiting the culture of school and the problem of change.* New York: Teachers College Press.

Scheerens, J. (1992). *Effective schooling: Research, theory, and practice.* New York: Cassell.

Scheerens, J., & Creemers, B. P. M. (1989). Conceptualizing school effectiveness. *International Journal of Educational Research, 13*(7), 691–706.

Scott, G. P. (1991). *Time, rhythm, and chaos: In the new dialog with nature.* Ames: Iowa State University Press.

Seel, R. (1999). *Complexity and organizational development: An introduction.* Retrieved October 20, 2005, from http://www.new-paradigm.co.uk/complex-od.htm

Senge, P. (1990). *The fifth discipline: The art and practice of the learning organization.* New York: Doubleday.

Shapiro, E. S. (1987). *Behavioral assessment in school psychology.* Hillsdale, NJ: Erlbaum.

Sizer, T. R. (1984). *Horace's compromise: The dilemma of the American high school.* Boston: Houghton Mifflin.

Skiba, R., & O'Sullivan, P. J. (1987). Implications of the relationship between observational and rating scale data for the assessment of behavioral disorders. In *Programming for adolescents with behavioral disorders* (Vol. 3, pp. 5–15). Reston, VA: Council for Children With Behavior Disorders.

Slavin, R. E. (1991). Synthesis of research of cooperative learning. *Educational Leadership, 48,* 71–82.

Slavin, R. E. (2005). *Evidence-based reform: Advancing the education of students at risk.* Washington, DC: Center for American Progress.

Slavin, R. E., Farnish, A. M., Livingston, M. A., Sauer, D. C., & Colton, B. S. (1994). *Using student team learning* (4th ed). Baltimore, MD: John Hopkins University, John Hopkins Team Learning Project, Center for Social Organization of Schools.

Smethurst, J. B. (1997). Communities of practice and pattern language. *Journal of Transition Management.* Retrieved November 11, 2005, from http://www.mgtaylor.com/mgtaylor/jotm/summer97/community_of_practice.htm

Smith, M., & Fried, C. (1999). *The emergency department as a complex system.* Retrieved November 10, 2005, from New England Complex Systems website: http://nesci.org/projects/yaneer/emergencydeptcx.pdf

Spillane, J. P. (2006). *Distributed leadership.* New York: Jossey-Bass.

Stocker, R., Cornforth, D., & Bossomaier, T. R. J. (2002). Network structures and agreement in social network simulations. *Journal of Artificial Societies and Social Simulation, 5*(4). Retrieved January 20, 2004, from http://cogprints.org/4355/01/3.html

Suarez Orozco, M. M., & Baolian Qin Hillard, D. (2004). *Globalization, culture, and education in the new millennium.* Berkeley, CA: University of California Press.

Success for All Foundation. (2006). [Home page]. Retrieved January 25, 2006, from http://www.successforall.net

Supovitz, J. A., & May, H. (2004). A study of the links between implementation and effectiveness of the America's Choice comprehensive school reform design. *Journal of Education for Children Placed at Risk, 9*(4), 389–419.

Taylor, J. E. (2005, April). *Sustainability: Examining the survival of schools' comprehensive school reform efforts.* Paper presented at the annual meeting of the American Educational Research Association, Montréal, Quebec, Canada.

Thorn, C. A. (2001). Knowledge management for educational information systems: What is the state of the field? *Educational Policy Analysis Archives, 9*(47). Retrieved March 31, 2005, from http://www.epaa.asu.edu/epaa/v9n47/

Tirozzi, G. N., & Uro, G. (1997). Education reform in the United States: National policy in support of local efforts for school improvement. *American Psychologist, 52*(3), 241–250.

Tomlinson, C. A. (2001). *How to differentiate instruction in mixed ability classrooms* (2nd ed.). Upper Saddle River, NJ: Pearson.

Tucker, P. D. (1997). Lake Wobegon: Where all teachers are competent (or, have we come to terms with the problem of incompetent teachers?). *Journal of Personnel Evaluation in Education, 11*, 103–126.

Tunmer, W. E., Herriman, M., & Nesdale, A. R. (1988). Metalinguistic abilities and beginning reading. *Reading Research Quarterly, 23*(2), 134–158.

Tyack, D., & Cuban, L. (1995). *Tinkering toward utopia: A century of public school reform.* Cambridge, MA: Harvard University Press.

Urry, J. (2005). The complexity turn. *Theory, Culture and Society, 22*(5), 1–14.

U.S. Department of Education. (2002). *Guidance on the Comprehensive School Reform Program.* Retrieved July 11, 2005, from http://www.ed.gov/programs/compreform/guidance/index.html

U.S. Department of Education. (2004). *Implementation and early outcomes of the Comprehensive School Reform Demonstration Program*. Retrieved August 21, 2005, from http://www.ed.gov/rschstat/eval/other/csrd-outcomes/index.html

U.S. Department of Education. (2005). *Spellings says SAT results encouraging, more work remains*. Retrieved December 22, 2006, from http://www.ed.gov/news/pressreleases/2005/08/08302005.html

Walberg, H. (1986). Syntheses of research on teaching in teaching. In M. C. Wittrock (Ed.), *Handbook of research on teaching* (3rd ed.) (pp. 754–777). New York: MacMillian.

Waldrop, M. M. (1993). *Complexity: The emerging science at the edge of order and chaos*. New York: Simon and Schuster.

Walker, A., & Dimmock, C. (2000). Developing educational administration. In C. Dimmock & A. Walker (Eds.), *Future school administration, Western and Asian perspectives* (pp. 3–22). Hong Kong: Chinese University Press and Hong Kong Institute of Educational Research.

Watt, K. M., Powell, C. A., & Mendiola, I. (2004). Implications of one comprehensive school reform model for secondary school students underrepresented in higher education. *Journal of Education for Students Placed at Risk, 9*(3), 241–259.

Watts, D. J. (2003). *Small worlds: The dynamics of networks between order and randomness*. Princeton, NJ: Princeton University Press.

Weick, K. E. (1976). Educational organizations as loosely coupled systems. *Administrative Science Quarterly, 21,* 1–21.

Wenger, E. (2006, April). *Organisations and learning in communities of practice*. Professional development seminar, RIPPLE (Research Into Professional Practice, Learning, and Education), Albury, New South Wales.

Wenger, E., McDermott, R. A., & Snyder, W. M. (2002). *Cultivating communities of practice*. Boston: Harvard Business School Press.

West, J. F., Idol, L., & Cannon, G. (1989). *Collaboration in the schools*. Austin, TX: PRO-ED.

Weston, M. E. (2006, July). *Digging in or moving on? Paradigm crisis in public education*. Paper presented at the 25th annual conference of the Georgia Association for Managers of Educational Information Systems, Savannah, GA.

Yamaguchi, R., Harmon, J. A., Darwin, M., Graczewski, C., & Fleischman, S. (2005, April). *A multi-method approach to evaluating elementary school comprehensive school reform models*. Paper presented at the annual meeting of the American Educational Research Association, Montréal, Quebec, Canada.

Zhang, Y., Shkolnik, J., & Fashola, O. (2005, April). *Evaluating the implementation of comprehensive school reform and its impact on growth in student achievement.* Paper presented at the annual meeting of the American Educational Research Association, Montréal, Quebec, Canada.

Index

Note: Page numbers in italic indicate figures.

Kauffman, Stuart, 81n4
knowledge management and
 discovery, 27, 188–91, 196–98.
 See also professional knowledge

language. *See* pattern language
leadership, 30, 31, 35–36
leadership teams, 143, 153–54
learning. *See* student achievement

management of schools. *See* school
 organization and management
matching-steps process, 90–91
math gains. *See* student achievement
Memphis Restructuring Initiative,
 31
metacognitive capability, 76
Moreira, Eladio, 81n2

needs assessment, 30, 31, 83–85,
 89–92, 97, 102–3
network of teams, 140–44; scaling
 up, 152–54, 156–57; scenario,
 145–48; use of technology tools,
 149–50
networks, 55–56, 57, 59, 67–68; and
 design resilience, 150–51, 156,
 166, 170
New American Schools project, 10,
 19, 29; evaluation of, 12, 25,
 32–33, 36–37, 84; expenditure
 on, 20
next-generation design, 240–42,
 249–59
next-generation targets, 22–34,
 38–39, 240–42

organization of schools. *See* school
 organization and management
ownership, 30

paradigm crisis, 3–4, 5, 21, 87, 247,
 256–57
parent portal, 203–4
pattern language, 46–47, 51, 56,
 64–70, 73, 217, 221
permission at scale, 98–100
perpetual change. *See* change
persistence, 252–53
plans. *See* information technology,
 planning
portals, 198–204. *See also*
 information technology
principles (theory of self-organizing
 schools), 41–59, 61–81
professional development, 24,
 35–36, 115–16, 123–25, 128–29
professional knowledge:
 management and deployment,
 194–98; and pattern language,
 46–47. *See also* knowledge
 management and discovery
professional lives, 27–28, 39, 242

reading achievement. *See* student
 achievement
research-based practice, 47, 62, 106;
 adoption at scale, 2, 41–42, 248;
 failure to scale up, 3–4;
 implementation, 229–31, 233,
 236, 241–43; and needs
 assessment, 88–89, 102
resilience of networks, 150–51, 156,
 166, 170
resistance to change, 11, 256
resource issues, 35–36, 121, 133,
 159–60, 168
risk, 34–36, 101, 132–33
role description, 109–10, 121–22,
 140, *141*
rules, 48–49. *See also* simple rules